North Sea cooperation

MANCHESTER
UNIVERSITY PRESS

Issues in Environmental Politics

Series editors Mikael Skou Andersen *and* Duncan Liefferink

As the millennium approaches, the environment has come to stay as a central concern of global politics. This series takes key problems for environmental policy and examines the politics behind their cause and possible resolution. Accessible and eloquent, the books make available for a non-specialist readership some of the best research and most provocative thinking on humanity's relationship with the planet.

already published in the series

Governance by green taxes *Mikael Skou Andersen*

European environmental policy: the pioneers
Mikael Skou Andersen and Duncan Liefferink (eds)

Science in international environmental regimes: between integrity and involvement *Steiner Andresen, Tora Skodvin, Arild Underdal and Jørgen Wettestad*

Congress and air pollution: environmental politics in the US
Christopher J. Bailey

Sustaining Amazonia: grassroots action for productive conservation
Anthony Hall

The protest business? Mobilizing campaign groups
Grant Jordan and William Maloney

Environment and the nation state: the Netherlands, the European Union and acid rain *Duncan Liefferink*

Valuing the environment *Raino Malnes*

Life on a modern planet: a manifesto for progress *Richard North*

Public purpose or private benefit? The politics of energy conservation *Gill Owen*

Environmental pressure groups *Peter Rawcliffe*

The new politics of pollution *Albert Weale*

North Sea cooperation

Linking international and domestic pollution control

Jon Birger Skjærseth

Manchester University Press
Manchester and New York
distributed exclusively in the USA by St. Martin's Press

Published by Manchester University Press
Oxford Road, Manchester M13 9NR, UK
and Room 400, 175 Fifth Avenue, New York, NY 10010, USA
http://www.man.ac.uk/mup

Distributed exclusively in the USA by
St. Martin's Press, Inc., 175 Fifth Avenue, New York, NY 10010, USA

Distributed exclusively in Canada by
UBC Press, University of British Columbia, 6344 Memorial Road,
Vancouver, BC, Canada V6T 1Z2

British Library Cataloguing-in-Publication Data
A catalogue record for this book is available from the British Library.

Library of Congress Cataloging-in-Publication Data applied for

ISBN 0 7190 5809 0 *hardback*

First published in 2000

07 06 05 04 03 02 01 00 10 9 8 7 6 5 4 3 2 1

Typeset in Sabon
by Northern Phototypesetting Co. Ltd, Bolton
Printed in Great Britain
by Bookcraft (Bath) Ltd, Midsomer Norton

Contents

List of tables and figures

Tables

Figures

Preface

In working on this book I have been guided by two – perhaps conflicting – ambitions. The first was a desire to conduct an *in-depth* study of the implementation of international commitments. The actual influence of most international commitments can be determined only by following the long and complex process from international cooperation to the behaviour of those actors actually causing the problems that gave rise to the commitments in the first place. My second ambition was to search for regularities and tendencies in a comparative perspective. The *scope* in terms of empirical cases included is thus quite high, considering the depth of the study.

The background for this tall order is found in the purpose of the study: to examine the functioning and consequences of environmental institutions so as to understand how it is possible to influence the behaviour of polluters. An in-depth analysis implies that actors and institutions are included at both the international and the national level. Both international and domestic institutions are needed to cope with the problems of transnational pollution, since most problems arise as by-products of otherwise legitimate domestic activities, like production of food and goods. A broad empirical scope, rather than a single case study, enables us to reach more solid conclusions on how institutions work, but it also has its costs in terms of the time and energy invested.

If we are to improve the functioning of international and domestic environmental institutions, we will have to learn from previous experience and practice. The North-East Atlantic cooperation, with the North Sea naturally an area on which to focus, has been in place since the early 1970s and provides us with elements of cooperative 'failure', 'success' and, indeed, change. This cooperation has been part of my academic life since I wrote my 1991 Master's thesis at the Fridtjof Nansen Institute on the 'effectiveness' of the Oslo Convention on dumping. I was then puzzled by the fact that states seemed to approach and react quite differently to identical problems. The Unitary Rational Actor perspective proved to be a fruitful tool in identifying varying domestic features and environmental norms as possible explanations of different approaches and reactions. At the same time, however, the perspective constrained my ability to study these phenomena in greater depth.

It was somewhat disturbing for a political scientist trained in international relations to have to recognize the importance of state–society relationships at the national or domestic level. And indeed, the part of the present study dealing with domestic environmental policy necessarily views reality through the spectacles of an international relations scholar. Those preoccupied with studying public administration may find my approach shallow, whereas others trained in international relations will perhaps find it unnecessarily complex and detailed.

With a scholarship from the Norwegian Research Council, I set out to study the missing links of my Master's thesis within a broader empirical and analytical context. I had at that point studied water and marine pollution in other regions and other environmental cooperations and issue-areas such as European Community climate policy and ozone depletion. Most of these studies were conducted as part of an international research project – the Oslo/Seattle project – on the effectiveness of environmental and resource cooperation, led by professors Ed Miles and Arild Underdal. I was also invited to participate in a major international research project on the Implementation and Effectiveness of International Environmental Commitments, at the International Institute for Applied Systems Analysis in Laxenburg, Austria. Through this project – led by Eugene B. Skolnikoff and David Victor – I had the opportunity to work on North Sea cooperation, although from a different angle.

There are many persons who have offered help on my work, and it is impossible to mention them all. In particular I wish to thank three people for their contributions to this study. Arild Underdal has been an indispensable source of inspiration. He has provided valuable suggestions for improvements on most aspects of my work.

Steinar Andresen and Jørgen Wettestad have continued to provide great encouragement and inspiration. When I started my career as a researcher at the Fridtjof Nansen Institute in 1991, they shared with me their expertise on international cooperation in general and the North-East Atlantic cooperation in particular, and taught me the secrets and fun of practical field research.

In addition, I would also like to thank Ann Skarstad and Susan Høivik who have improved the English text considerably. Kari Lorentzen has struggled with my requests for articles and books, as well as with delayed returns. Ivar Liseter has a magic touch with the computer system and has helped me out on many occasions. However, none of the above mentioned persons bear any responsibility for any errors or misjudgements that may be present in the final text. I would also like to thank the Norwegian Research Council and the Fridtjof Nansen Institute for bearing the financial burden of this project, and the Department of Political Science at the University of Oslo for taking me on board the doctor of politics programme.

Finally, I am grateful to Kristin Høgdahl, not so much for her patience with me and my work, but for her substantial suggestions, corrections and never-ending enthusiasm. Eirik and Anne – born at either end of this study – have reminded me of the multi-purpose qualities of a draft manuscript: you can eat it, spill on it, draw on it, make airplanes out of it – and, perhaps, some day read it.

Jon Birger Skjærseth
Lysaker

Acronyms and abbreviations

BAT	Best Available Technology
BEP	Best Environmental Practices
CBI	Confederation of British Industry
CEFIC	European Chemical Industry Council
CIA	Chemical Industries Association
CNIE	Confederation of Netherlands Industry and Employers
CPA	Control of Pollution Act (UK)
CUWVO	Committee on the Implementation of the Pollution Surface Waters Act (Netherlands)
CVC	Group of Chairman and Vice-Chairmen
DoE	Department of the Environment (UK)
EC	European Community
EEC	European Economic Community
EMA	Environmental Management Act
ENDS	Environmental Data Services
ENGO	environmental non-governmental organization
EQO	Environmental Quality Objectives
EQS	Environmental Quality Standards
FNI	Federation of Norwegian Industries
GATT	General Agreement on Tariffs and Trade
HMIP	Her Majesty's Inspectorate of Pollution (UK)
ICES	International Council for the Exploration of the Sea
ICI	Imperial Chemical Industries
IMP	Indicative Multi-Years Programme
INDSEC	Industrial Sectors Working Group

INSC	International North Sea Conference
IPC	Integrated Pollution Control
JMG	Joint Monitoring Group
JMP	Joint Monitoring Programme
MAFF	Ministry of Agriculture, Fisheries and Food (UK)
ME	Ministry of the Environment (Norway)
NCBI	Norwegian Confederation of Business and Industry
NEPP	National Environmental Policy Plan (Netherlands)
NFU	National Farmers' Union (UK)
NGO	non-governmental organization
NRA	National Rivers Authority (UK)
NSCN	Norwegian Society for the Conservation of Nature
NSTF	North Sea Task Force
NUT	Working Group on Nutrients
OECD	Organization for Economic Cooperation and Development
OFWAT	Office of Water Services (UK)
OSCOM	Oslo Commission
OSPARCOM	Oslo and Paris Commissions
PARCOM	Paris Commission
PCA	Pollution Control Act (Norway)
PCB	polychlorinated biphenyl
PCT	polychlorinated triphenyl
PIL	Federation of Norwegian Processing Industries
PJP	Prior Justification Procedure
PRAM	Programmes and Measures Committee
PSWA	Pollution of Surface Water Act (Netherlands)
QSR	Quality Status Report
RWA	regional water authority (UK)
SACSA	Standing Advisory Committee for Scientific Advice
SNM	Society for Nature and Environment (Netherlands)
SPCA	State Pollution Control Agency (Norway)
TWG	Technical Working Group
UES	Uniform Emission Standards
URA	United Rational Actor model

VROM	Ministry of Housing, Physical Planning and Environment (*Volkshuisvesting, Ruimtelijke Ordening en Milieubeheer*, the Netherlands)
WB	water board (the Netherlands)
WTWs	wastewater treatment works

1
Introduction

The international commitments adopted to combat North Sea pollution have been advanced significantly since the late 1980s. The North Sea states have changed their approach, from controlling pollution levels at sea to reducing polluting substances at source. Domestic implementation of measures has necessitated thoroughgoing efforts linked up with significant capital expenditure. Moreover, inputs of regulated substances have been significantly reduced overall, but to varying degrees at the national level. The question is then: to what extent and in what ways have international and national environmental *institutions* affected the changes that have taken place in joint commitments and domestic implementation? Or more specifically, to what extent and in what ways have environmental institutions affected the making of joint commitments of the North Sea cooperation and domestic implementation in three countries: Norway, the Netherlands and the UK?

By asking this question, this book goes beyond the debate on whether institutions matter and focuses on the extent to which and how they matter. International institutions and domestic political and administrative institutions are usually studied separately. Since most pollution problems arise as by-products of domestic activities, which have transnational consequences, both international and domestic institutions are needed to cope with such problems. Accordingly, the first finding presented in this book is that *both* international and national institutions matter in the making and implementation of North Sea pollution commitments. Moreover, institutions affect actors through different behavioural mechanisms. Thus, one must include both cost-benefit rationality based on the logic of consequence and norms based on the logic of appropriateness as fundamental behavioural mechanisms in order to understand the functioning and consequences of institutions.

The second finding is concerned with *how international* institutions matter. A distinction is usually made between hard and soft law institutions. Hard law institutions are based on legally binding treaties, while soft law is based on joint political declarations. The North Sea experience shows that we need both types of institutional arrangements at the same time. These arrangements do not duplicate each other. On the contrary, they actually fulfil different functions that are all needed to make international environmental cooperation effective. The key to understanding the success of the international institutions in the North Sea cooperation lies in the balancing of hard legally binding and soft politically acting institutions in the same issue-area.

The third finding is related to *how national* institutions matter. It draws attention to the observation that the state is not necessarily a victim to globalization of regulation.[1] Globalization is often understood as increased interconnectedness between societies and economies that weakens the states' ability to regulate independently. This book shows that varying institutionalization at domestic level is important to explain differences in implementation of joint international commitments. The strength of states to implement marine pollution control depends largely upon how relevant state institutions are organized to deal with such problems. Distribution of competence between regulatory agencies and policy tools are both important in this respect. In essence, societal demand for environmental quality matters while governmental supply of policies to protect the marine environment decides.

The final finding is concerned with the *vertical links* between international and domestic institutions and the *horizontal links* between international institutions over time. As to the former, international institutions do not only have the capacity to affect governmental priorities and behaviour. In addition, and under certain conditions, international institutions affect implementation through various pathways by determining the 'rules of the game' between governmental agencies and societal actors, i.e. target groups and environmental non-governmental organizations (ENGOs). Such influences are strongest in cases where international institutions are developed prior to national institutions, or where national rules and procedures are but weakly developed. As to horizontal links, this study shows that internal contradictions within the original institution temporarily trapped most of the parties in a situation of inertia. However, the North Sea experience shows how the parties were able to change their path by transforming the institution itself. This led to a 'snowball' effect generating more stringent joint commitments and more effective implementation.

The North Sea/North-East Atlantic cooperation: a snapshot

The North Sea has been the core marine area covered by the North-East Atlantic cooperation since the early 1970s. The quarter-century history of the North Sea/North-East Atlantic cooperation represents a development from water and marine pollution 'anarchy' towards domestic and international regulation and 'governance'. When the coaster *Stella Maris* left the port of Rotterdam in 1971 with 650 tons of toxic waste on board destined to be dumped in the northern part of the North Sea, there were no international guidelines that could give weight to the protests that arose. Today, such dumping is not only prohibited – it has actually been phased out. International and domestic institutions developed relatively simultaneously to combat marine pollution in this area as a reaction to increased attention paid to domestic and transnational pollution problems in the early 1970s. Surrounded by densely populated areas, the North Sea is an area of intense human activity. It has some of the busiest marine traffic in the world, and is home to many of Europe's major ports. Offshore oil and gas exploitation has also made the North Sea one of today's most important bodies of water for petroleum production. Land-based discharges (river input and direct discharge), ocean-based discharges (dumping and incineration at sea) and atmospheric fall-out are among the major sources of contaminant inputs to the North Sea. The intense human activity onshore and offshore is the result of increasing economic activity following the Second World War, which led to a rapid growth in waste production. It was partly in consequence of the *Stella Maris* incident that the Convention for the Prevention of Marine Pollution by Dumping from Ships and Aircraft (Oslo Convention) was established. Signed by all 13 West European maritime states in 1972, the Oslo Convention covers the entire North-East Atlantic up to the North Pole.

In 1972 – the same year as the Oslo Convention was signed – the global UN Conference on the Human Environment took place in Stockholm. This Conference identified land-based sources – such as rivers – as the principal route by which most pollutants reach the sea. In addition, the Conference specifically invited the European Community (EC) to engage itself in the protection of the environment.[2] Two years later, the Convention for the Prevention of Marine Pollution from Land-based Sources – the Paris Convention – was signed in Paris by roughly the same states as the Oslo Convention and allowed the EC to join as a contracting member. The Oslo and Paris Conventions were supported by a joint secretariat, executive commissions and several standing and *ad hoc* scientific/technical bodies. A tiny secretariat was established in London to administer the practical coordinating aspects of the cooperation. Two executive commissions – where the parties met annually – were set up to make joint decisions in order to implement and review the functioning of the Conventions. The Oslo Commission (OSCOM) and the Paris Commission (PARCOM) were assisted by the Standing Advisory Committee for Scientific Advice (SACSA) and the Technical Working Group (TWG) respectively, by *ad hoc* working groups and by the Joint Monitoring Group (JMG).

The development of national-level regulations took place at roughly the same time as international guidelines to control dumping and land-based emissions. In Norway, the 1970 Water Pollution Act was adopted as a basis for regulating municipal sewage, agriculture and industry. The Ministry of the Environment was established two years later. Dumping of hazardous substances at sea has never been viewed as a viable disposal option in Norway. As in Norway, the Dutch Pollution of Surface Water Act entered into force in 1970. This Act, which represented the first truly environmental Act in the Netherlands, introduced a discharge permit and levy system. The Oslo Convention was formally implemented by Dutch authorities by the Pollution of the Sea Act, which came into effect on 1 January 1977. As to the UK, it adopted a Water Act in 1973 and a Pollution of Control Act in 1974, continuing a system of consent established more than two decades earlier. Like the Netherlands, the UK implemented the Oslo Convention by passing its Dumping at Sea Act in 1974.

Despite the international and domestic institutions established in the 1970s, there were growing indications by the early 1980s that specific parts of the North Sea were becoming severely polluted

(Ehlers 1990: 4). Neither national initiatives, nor the work of the Commissions suggested that necessary measures could be initiated without additional political impetus. At the international level, neither the Oslo Commission nor the Paris Commission managed to produce joint commitments with 'teeth'. Most of the decisions and recommendations adopted aimed to control behaviour rather than to change it. European Community water directives also failed to produce widespread improvements in water quality (Haigh *et al.* 1986: 104). Some actions took place at the national level, with mixed results. New legislative measures were adopted in the early 1980s; 'first generation' abatement programmes had some impact, especially on the industrial and municipal sectors of Norway and the Netherlands. However, the agricultural sector, representing a large source of nutrients and pesticides, was largely ignored by the environmental authorities. In England and Wales, the 1985 river quality survey was the first since 1970 to show increased lengths of river degrading in quality rather than improving (Kinnersley 1994: 123).

Spurred by dissatisfaction with existing international institutions, Germany took the initiative to arrange the first International North Sea Conference (INSC) in Bremen in 1984. This was originally conceived of as a one-off event, but these conferences have evolved into a more permanent institution over time. The Bremen Conference was followed by one in London 1987, in The Hague 1990, in Copenhagen 1993 and most recently in Esbjerg (Denmark) 1995. The next conference is scheduled to be held in Norway in 2002. The conference participants have been the eight North Sea coastal states, which represent a sub-set of the original Oslo and Paris Commission (OSPARCOM) parties. The London Declaration represented a turning point by aiming to phase out dumping of industrial waste and incineration at sea, to reduce inputs of nutrients to sensitive areas in the order of 50 per cent between 1985 and 1995, and to reduce total inputs of hazardous substances reaching the aquatic environment in the order of 50 per cent within the same time frame. The 1990 Hague Declaration clarified and strengthened the London Declaration, particularly concerning land-based sources. The Oslo and Paris Commissions as well as the EC took significant steps in the same direction in the wake of the 1987 North Sea conference. In addition, these institutions were appreciably amended in the latter part of the 1980s. The 1987 Single European Act incorporated environmental protection into EC legislation, the 1993 Maastricht Treaty changed EC environmental decision-making, and the Oslo and Paris Conventions were in 1992 negotiated into a single legal instrument for the protection of the North-East Atlantic.

At the national level, there has been a stream of new legislation and administrative directives. Moreover, sub-national target groups have actually changed their behaviour significantly, and emissions of regulated substances have decreased substantially in most of the North Sea states. The result has been significant collective reductions of regulated organic substances, pesticides, heavy metals, nutrients, and dumping and incineration at sea.[3] However, there are also significant differences in the achievements at the national level in general and between Norway, the Netherlands and the UK in particular. In short, the 25-year history of the North Sea/North-East Atlantic cooperation can serve as a fascinating example of development from inertia to action. At the more general level, it also indicates a relationship between institutionalization or institutional change and action. In the following sections and chapters, I will seek to develop and apply some analytical tools for uncovering these general tendencies so that we may identify the causal forces behind this development.

Research strategy

The focus for explanation is joint international commitments and domestic implementation. Studies of international environmental cooperation have evolved rapidly, from focusing predominantly on institutional, or regime, formation and creation to a focus on regime effectiveness. The concept of effectiveness has multiple dimensions, and has been defined and operationalized in a number of ways (Underdal 1992; Young 1994). Based on the reasonable assumption that institutions are effective as long as they are able to solve the problem they were established to solve, some of the early effectiveness projects focused primarily on the link between joint commitments and impact, i.e. the tangible consequences affecting the physical problem at hand. They thus disregarded the importance of domestic implementation efforts.[4] The focus on joint commitments and domestic implementation thus represents one step back in the causal chain – targeting relevant policy (output) and changes in the behaviour of the target groups (outcome) rather than impact. The approach rests on the belief that how to influence collective outcomes and actor behaviour is the most interesting question from the perspective of political science and institutional analysis. Questions not dealt with here are whether behaviour has changed sufficiently to solve a given ecological problem, or the extent to which the required direction of behavioural change is in line with scientific advice. As a political scientist, I will be concerned more with policy-making than with knowledge-making. There are also compelling methodological reasons for choosing outcome as the ending point. Natural variability makes it difficult to identify human-induced changes over time, and attributing causes to observed effects is an even more uncertain process. This approach also implies that we distinguish between domestic implementation and compliance. The former refers to the link between international commitments and efforts to translate international obligations into output and outcome. The latter is a matter of whether and to what extent the actors adhere to joint obligations.

Few have focused in depth on the consequences of international institutions in the North Sea cooperation and virtually no one has dealt with the combined influence of international and domestic institutions.[5] The latter is also the case concerning the study of international environmental regimes in general. As we have seen, both international and domestic institutions are needed to cope with pollution problem since such problems arise as by-products of otherwise legitimate domestic activities, which affect states across borders. Hence, we need to transcend the two traditional institutional strands of political science – the one focusing on domestic political and administrative institutions and the other (frequently labelled regime theory) dealing with international relations – in order to understand the influence of environmental institutions (Powell and DiMaggio 1991: 5).

The hypothesis we wish to refute in this study is that joint commitments and domestic implementation would *not* be different in the absence of institutional change and variance. By focusing on consequences of institutional change we can identify how and the extent to which institutions matter. The alternative hypothesis we wish to support is thus that joint commitments and domestic implementation would be different in the absence of institutional change and variance, due at least in part to the impact of institutions. Other studies strongly indicate that the range and effect of international environmental institutions vary significantly according to types of problems (Wettestad and Andresen 1991; Haas, Keohane and Levy 1993: 409; Miles *et al.* forthcoming). The strategy chosen to test these hypotheses is twofold. First, I will scrutinize the hypothesis we wish to refute by developing and applying a Rational Actor model focusing on problem-related actor interests as core variables. This model is designed to represent a situation 'stripped' of influences from change and variance in institutional factors. Changes in joint commitments and domestic implementation would – according to the Rational Actor model – be attributable to changes in the actors' problem-related interests.

The second strategy aims to show *how* institutions influence joint commitments and behaviour. This is explored by developing what here is referred to as the Institutional model. Traditionally, a dividing line has been drawn between institutionalism in economics and public choice theory, and institutionalism in organization and regime theory. These schools of thought differ on at least two central questions: a) how do institutions affect individual action and collective outcomes? and b) how do institutions originate and change? The principal focus of this book will be on the former question, and institutions will be treated as crucial explanatory factors. However, in order to comprehend the significance of environmental institutions in the North Sea cooperation we need to develop an analytical framework that incorporates some of the insights of different schools, focusing on both *rationality* and *norms* as fundamental behavioural mechanisms. Crudely put, institutionalism in economics and public choice theory emphasize how institutions may affect behaviour through rationality, while organization and regime theory place more emphasis on norms. For the time being, rationality will be understood as intentional and purposive action based on the 'logic of consequence', while norms will be conceived of as not outcome oriented in the sense of being based on the 'logic of appropriateness'.[6]

The Rational Actor model focuses on actor qualities, while the Institutional model emphasizes institutional qualities, here understood as rules and procedures. These perspectives may be considered 'models', not in a formal sense, but as two different and simplified pictures of the real world. Crudely put, these models provide us with two different answers as to why collective outcomes and actor behaviour change and vary. The Rational Actor model would hold that actors agree on joint commitments and implement them as long as it is in their problem-related interests to do so. The Institutional model would say that this is not necessarily so, holding that actors are generally affected by changes in institutions and may, under certain conditions, agree on joint commitments and implement them as a result of norms of collective and individual behaviour.

These models vary in strengths and weaknesses. The Rational Actor model is theoretically strong in the sense that it has a high capacity for generating numerous precise, tenable propositions. On the other hand, it is empirically problematic because it requires input data that are rarely available. Thus, significant modifications are necessary and we easily end up with rather crude assumptions and predicted empirical patterns. The Institutional model is theoretically weaker in the sense that it is more difficult to derive unambiguous assumptions and propositions. However, a central aim here is to make this model theoretically fruitful by deriving implications and propositions beyond statements such as 'factor X is important'. The strength of the Institutional model lies first and foremost in its validity, i.e. its ability to capture the essence of real world phenomena due to its complexity. This also implies that data may be difficult to collect due to time costs rather than lack of availability. Data collection has been based on *multiple sources* available to the author. Interviews, document analysis, archival records, official documents and secondary studies represent the principal sources.

The strengths and weaknesses of the models have some important consequences for the empirical 'tests' we can undertake to evaluate them. There are essentially three kinds of empirical tests we can apply. First, the models can be evaluated in terms of their *heuristic value* emphasizing specific causal or behavioural mechanisms (Allison 1971; Elster 1989a). Mechanisms make no claim to generality, but our knowledge may be increased by understanding why things happen. Second, the models may be judged on the basis of *pattern-matching*, i.e. comparison of specific propositions derived from the models with observed collective or individual behaviour (Yin 1989). The better the match between proposed and actual patterns of behaviour, the more confidence we will have in the model's ability to capture the essence of what it is designed to represent. The third option may be termed *explanation-building*; this strategy may be seen as a 'soft' variant of pattern-matching by way of narratives (Yin

1989). Since narratives as such cannot be precise, precision may be increased by relating narratives to explicit propositions. On the other hand, the final explanation may not have been fully stipulated at the outset of the study, and may therefore differ in this respect from the pattern-matching approach.

The Rational Actor model will frequently be more suitable for pattern-matching since it has a higher capacity to predict precise empirical patterns than the Institutional model. Conversely, the Institutional model will normally be more suitable for explanation-building since propositions derived from this model will be less precise compared to the Rational Actor model. It is important to bear in mind, however, that this difference does not imply that predictions generated by the Rational Actor model are 'better' or more 'correct' than those generated by the Institutional model. Both models are equally suitable to be evaluated in terms of their heuristic value.

Seven specific propositions are derived from the Rational Actor and the Institutional models. In order to minimize the problem of many variables and few cases, two main strategies are applied (King, Keohane and Verba 1994). First, different propositions are related to a wider range of policy than to only one specific dependent variable. For example, domestic implementation processes are analytically split in different relationships at different stages. Second, the number of observations is increased by measuring them at different levels of analysis. Each of the two main models is split into two sub-models designed to match both international and national levels of analysis. This implies that the basic units of analysis in this study are various actors and environmental institutions located at the international and domestic levels.

Among international relations theorists, it is widely recommended to keep to a single level of analysis (Moravcsik 1993:6). Moreover, Waltz (1979) and Keohane (1984:25) have argued that systemic explanations are generally superior to domestic explanations due to their parsimony. While this may be true in the study of international politics in general, I doubt this is the case concerning international environmental cooperation. Owing to the nature of transboundary environmental problems and international environmental implementation processes, it should become clear in the course of this work that more would be lost concerning validity than could be gained in parsimony from this advice.

I commence by applying the Unitary Rational Actor (URA) model. The above discussion should make it clear that the choice of commencing with this model does not represent a 'first-cut' approach rendering alternatives to this perspective to explain any 'residual variance' by opening the 'black box' of domestic politics (Evans, Jacobson and Putnam 1993). Since different models may explain the same patterns by emphasizing different behavioural mechanisms, this choice does not imply any privilege to systemic theory compared to domestic politics, or rationality based on the logic of consequence compared to norms based on the logic of appropriateness. There are essentially two reasons for this choice of research strategy. First, other things being equal, we would prefer a parsimonious model that can explain 'much' with 'little'. Second, it seems sensible from a research-strategic perspective to start with the simplest model. However, we should also note that the URA model may prove more complex than first foreseen. The next step will be to relax the assumption of rationality at international state level and see how international environmental institutions have affected the course of actions. The third step is to look into the interests, preferences and positions of relevant sub-national actors by relaxing the assumption of unity. The last step will take us to the study of domestic institutions by relaxing the assumption of rationality as well as unity.

Delimitations

Research on national-level implementation of the North Sea commitments concerns very complex phenomena and touches upon all levels of society and most aspects of social science theory: from the way states interact and behave on the international arena, to how farmers or corporations actually react to various types of regulations. Hence, some delimitations are necessary.

First, the analysis is focused on Norway, the Netherlands and the UK – three countries among the eight North Sea states. These countries have been actively involved in the North Sea cooperation, and they vary significantly on both achievements and institutional arrangements. Furthermore, they are representative in the sense that any agreement reached between these countries would in many ways represent an agreement for the whole North Sea since they represent the exporters, importers and the 'balanced' in terms of exchange rates of marine pollution. Concerning the UK, most attention will be paid to England and Wales, since the principal polluting sources and the most important environmental regulatory agencies are located here.

Second, the set of rules and procedures operating in the North Sea are also reflected in more general principles operating at the global and regional levels, as well as global treaties covering similar activities such as the 1972 London Convention on dumping. Conversely, some sub-regional agreements on large rivers such as the Rhine are also embedded in the set of rules and procedures operating in the North Sea. The potential consequences of the broader global and narrower sub-regional set of rules and procedures will largely be ignored in this study. Likewise, the North Sea cooperation itself covers a wide range of issues, spanning from oil pollution to atmospheric deposition. Ocean-based activities – dumping and incineration at sea – and land-based discharges of hazardous substances and nutrients have been selected, for different reasons: these commitments cover crucial sources that have been on the agenda since the early 1970s; the most important international commitments adopted were to be implemented by 1995, thus enabling us to assess the extent to which declared goals were achieved.

Third, the EC has played an important role – both as a party to INSC and the Paris Convention, as well as an independent 'supranational' institution with its own water and marine policy potentially affecting especially the UK and the Netherlands, but also Norway as a member of the European Economic Area agreement. The making and implementation of relevant EC directives are not the main focus of this study, although EC developments will be included when such developments appear particularly relevant. Related to this is the possible influence posed by other international institutions. As Hurrell and Kingsbury (1992: 3–4) have reminded us, the international institutions that matter most are not necessarily specifically 'environmental', but rather the core institutions that seek to govern the workings of the world economy such as General Agreement on Tariffs and Trade (GATT) and the Organization for Economic Cooperation and Development (OECD). Such institutions fall outside the narrower focus on environmental institutions.

Outline of this book

The logic developed in the research strategy is reflected in the composition of this book. The combined aim of Chapters 2 and 3 is to develop a fruitful analytical framework for studying the research question. Chapter 4 focuses on developments in international North Sea commitments as well as national-level implementation in Norway, the Netherlands and the UK. This chapter will describe what happened in terms of joint and individual behaviour and analyse the achievements at the international and domestic levels. Chapters 5 and 6 centre on the extent to which and in what ways environmental institutions account for the change and variance identified in Chapter 4. Chapters 5 and 6 are concerned with the international level and focus on the calculus of the core actors, i.e. states, and the significance of international environmental institutions. Chapters 7 and 8 will take us to the national level. Chapter 7 is concerned with the calculus and mobilization of sub-national actors, while Chapter 8 focuses on the functioning and consequences of domestic environmental institutions. In Chapter 9, I will merge the international and domestic levels by focusing on the role of international institutions in shaping state–society relationships as well as the dynamic path-dependent aspects of institutions. Do international institutional arrangements established in the early phases of the cooperation shape opportunities and constrain challenges faced at a later stage? Concluding remarks are presented in Chapter 10.

Notes

1 For a general introduction to globalization and world politics, see Baylis and Smith (1997). See Vogel (1995) for an excellent discussion of globalization and environmental regulation.

2 The term 'European Community' will be used throughout this book also when referring to the European Economic Community. The Treaty of Maastricht also created the European Union, of which one of the three pillars was the EC.

3 See *Progress Report* (1995).

4 This follows largely from the assumption that states are unitary actors, an assumption common in the study of international regimes. See e.g. Andresen and Wettestad (1995) for a description of an 'effectiveness' project that focuses on the link between joint commitments and impact.

5 Most studies have focused on the international level. For some central contributions, see Sætevik (1988), Skjærseth (1991; 1992), Wettestad (1992), Haas (1993), Pallemaerts (1992), and Nollkaemper (1993). To my knowledge, the only piece explicitly dealing with domestic implementation in any depth is a study conducted by Gibson and Churchill (1990) on problems of implementation of the North Sea Declarations in the UK.

6 See Elster (1989a: 113; 1989b: 98) for a distinction between rationality and social norms. For a discussion of Elster's conception of norms, see various critical reviews in *Agora*, 1–2. 1990. See March and Olsen (1989; 1994; 1996) for the distinction between the 'logic of consequence' and the 'logic of appropriateness'.

2

Anatomy of environmental institutions

Under the rubric of 'new institutionalism', the study of institutions has developed within various social science disciplines, including economics, sociology and political science, and various relatively distinct schools of thought have developed under this heading (Hall and Taylor 1994). No wonder, then, that using the term 'institutional' today is to evoke a host of competing conceptions about what institutions are and how they function (Caporaso 1992: 620). The main purpose of this chapter is not to discuss the differences and similarities between the various schools of thought, but rather to utilize some of their contributions to clarify the meaning of environmental institutions in this study and the extent to which, and how, they may affect collective outcomes and actor behaviour.

Since the term 'institution' has different meanings we need an explicit definition as a point of departure. In order to incorporate insights from various schools that may be applied empirically, I will argue that we need a narrow definition with a 'thin' substantive core that can leave the way open for broad consequences. The next topic focuses on how institutions matter. One core question here is whether different perspectives on institutions necessarily render them incompatible. The answer suggested is largely negative in this respect. Different institutional perspectives are integrated to sketch out how environmental institutions may affect collective outcomes and actor behaviour.

What are environmental institutions?

A definition of environmental institutions suitable for our purposes here should conform with three criteria. First, it should be narrow enough to allow for as concrete empirical scrutiny as possible. Second, it should be sufficiently broad to incorporate some insights from different perspectives on the consequences of institutions – here labelled the rationalistic and institutionalistic approaches. Third, the definition should enable a study of both international and domestic environmental institutions. In essence, we need a definition with a 'thin' substantive core that can leave the way open for broad consequences. Against this backdrop, environmental institutions will be understood as *politically or legally binding sets of explicit procedures and rules established by actors in order to regulate directly or indirectly anhtropogenic sources of environmental problems.*[1]

This definition is both narrow and broad, but with regard to different aspects. It is narrow in the sense that its initial focus is on *explicit* rules and procedures. I believe that the criterion of explicitness will enhance our ability to conduct empirical studies of the functioning and consequences of institutions. One major difference between rationalistic and institutionalistic perspectives on institutions is that the former focuses on how institutions may affect rational choices in certain situations *given* the interests and preferences of the actors. The latter perspective emphasizes how institutions may affect the identities and interests of actors in which the development of norms plays an important role (March and Olsen 1989: 160–1). Hence, excluding norms from the definition of institutions does not imply that rules and procedures may not lead to co-operative and/or individual norms of behaviour. The point is merely that this should be open to empirical scrutiny based on the assumption that rules and procedures do not necessarily lead to such norms.

This point of departure raises two questions of main importance and empirical relevance. Can norms exist and change without being institutionalized? If so, how can we then trace the impact of subsequently established institutions? The answer to the first question depends on the range of the definition applied. A broad definition including implicit and informal features would comprise a norm to an institution in itself and hence render the first question meaningless. On the other hand, the narrow definition applied here permits both the existence of norms in the absence of institutions and the existence of institutions in the absence of norm-guided behaviour. Accordingly, we have to take seriously the problem indicated in the second question. However, the problem is minimized since the principal focus here is placed on the consequences of institutional *change*. It is not very likely that changes in norms will occur at the same time as changes in institutions unless they are linked to these changes.

Excluding norms from the definition itself and including explicit rules and procedures is also a reaction to criticism of vagueness and the problem of distinguishing between the various components of the classical definition of international regimes.[2] One counterargument has been that the exclusion of norms risks the charge of formalism paralleling the study of international law and making the definition of institutions equal to formal agreements. This argument has again been met by the demand for adding an element of observable behaviour to the definition (Haggard and Simmons 1987: 494). However, this solution has been regarded as both theoretically and methodologically problematic (Keohane 1993: 27). I seek to resolve the problem by retaining the focus on explicit legally and *politically* binding rules and procedures that may, or may not, lead to (implicit) norms. However, resolving this problem concerning international institutions may create another problem related to domestic institutions, which I elaborate below. The definition is also narrow for a second reason: it limits the focus to environmental, or pollution-related, institutions and, consequently, to interests and norms relevant for environmental problems.

The definition of environmental institutions suggested here is broad in the sense that it is compatible with both rationalistic and institutionalistic perspectives on how institutions matter. It also leaves open the question of how institutions come into existence, since this is not under scrutiny here.[3] The only restriction in this respect introduced by the 'established by actors' criterion is that institutions are conceived of not as 'God-given', but as a result of actor interaction (Skjærseth 1995).

Institutions can be termed environmental when they directly or indirectly aim at dealing with environmental problems. There would appear to be no theoretical reasons for considering environmental institutions as systematically and significantly different from institutions established in other substantive issue-areas, such as trade and human rights. Empirically, however, there is much to suggest that most transnational pollution problems share some common basic characteristics: a) they directly affect segments of society; b) they cut through various governmental sectors and levels; c) they are closely related to the natural sciences; d) a considerable time span is normally involved concerning causes and effects (Weale 1992b). This would mean that identifying transboundary environmental problems and their solutions typically takes a long time and involves scientific uncertainty as well as a multitude of actors operating within different sectors at different levels. This is why such problems and environmental institutions may be described as *complex*. Hence, given that environmental institutions exist to cope with anthropogenic sources of pollution, they are likely to reflect such characteristics. Thus, instead of arguing that environmental institutions share unique qualities, we may argue that institutions dealing with the core elements that characterize transboundary environmental problems share some common features. On the other hand, environmental institutions can and frequently do vary along many dimensions.

Rules and procedures constitute the core components of environmental institutions and they may operate at two levels, respectively. At 'micro' level, institutional rules should be understood as prescriptive statements that forbid, permit or require some action or outcome (Ostrom 1990: 139). Procedures operate at 'macro' level as 'rules of the game' aimed at handling collective choice situations. Organizations, by contrast, are material entities possessing physical locations, offices, personnel, equipment, budgets and frequently legal personality (Young 1994: 4). Organizations are conceived of as actors within broader institutional structures or networks. In political terms, the Secretariat for the Oslo and Paris Commissions is an organization within a broader 'institution' made up by the Oslo and Paris Conventions and the rules and procedures adopted within the relevant Commissions. Likewise, the State Pollution Control Agency in Norway is a governmental organization within a broader institution made up of legal and political rules and procedures.

International versus domestic environmental institutions

As we have seen, the rationalistic and institutionalistic perspectives have developed within two strands of political science: one focusing on domestic political and administrative institutions, the other deals with international relations. While the above definition is aimed at both domestic and international institutions, international systems will be assumed to deviate from domestic systems in at least three ways, though not necessarily dramatically.

First, the international system lacks a common government in world politics, including environmental politics. On the other hand, the degree to which interactions are structured by institutions and the means by which they are structured will vary (Axelrod and Keohane 1986). The existence of a government at the domestic level has at least two important implications with particular relevance for our topic. First, there is a government that has the authority to solve disputes among affected actors. Second, there is a government that has the authority to enforce regulations. However, while the assumption of the existence of governments remains constant, the degree to which national systems depart from international systems is likely to vary. There may be 'governance without government' (Rosenau and Czempiel 1992), and poor governance with government. The notion of 'supra-national' institutions, such as the EC, would seem to bridge the gap between pure international and national systems, indicating a sliding scale between national and international institutions (Skjærseth 1994).

A second difference between international and domestic institutions is that general efforts at environmental and pollution control date back over a century in some industrial nations, while international environmental institutions are a comparatively recent phenomenon. For example, water pollution control in the UK dates back to the Rivers Pollution Act of 1876. Hence, national approaches to regulation need to be understood within the political and social context in which they evolved (Vogel 1986: 26). This phenomenon is captured by the concept of regulatory *styles* referring to presumably distinct national approaches to regulation. Hence, tracing the roots of the effects of domestic institutions may be quite problematic, ideally it would require an in-depth study of the history of pollution control in each country. There are no simple and parsimonious solutions available to this analytical problem, but there is an important implication: any conclusions concerning the effect of domestic institutions should be drawn with caution in this particular respect.

Third, although international institutions may be embedded, or nested, into broader institutional frameworks, the international environmental institutions under scrutiny here have been established specifically to cope with water and marine pollution. At the domestic level, different sectors and functions are woven tightly together. Marine and water pollution is normally one aspect of pollution policy, which in turn is one aspect of environmental policy. Environmental policy is then one aspect of governmental activities, and increasingly an aspect of other sector policies such as agriculture and industry policy. This implies that also domestic institutions not specifically established to deal with marine and water pollution may have significant influence on the implementation of the international commitments. This is the reason why 'indirect' regulations have been included in our definition of environmental institutions.

How do environmental institutions matter?

Young (1986: 116) argues that almost everyone believes that domestic institutions are of importance. Conversely, the potential impact of international institutions has been a contested issue within the grand theoretical international relations debates (Grieco 1988; Mearsheimers 1995). The most severe criticism has perhaps been offered by Susan Strange (1983), who has argued that the analysis of international regimes is a passing fad, since regimes are merely reflections of the distribution of power and interests. Different views on this issue are also mirrored in the study of international environmental institutions (Mitchell 1994a: 4–10). As pointed out by Young (1994: 2), many formal instruments purporting to establish institutional arrangements are dead letters.

There is one particularly interesting proposition compatible with the 'dead letter' observation: rules and procedures may simply reflect the lowest common denominator of the interests and preferences of the actors, known as the 'law of the least ambitious program' (Underdal 1980a: 36: Sand 1991).[4] Hence, institutions in a narrow sense may merely codify the behaviour of the most 'reluctant' actor. That could mean that the general relationship identified in the introduction concerning institutionalization and actual outcomes in the North Sea cooperation may be spurious. Even among those who claim that international institutions matter it is frequently argued that the significance of institutions is relegated to the realm of assumptions rather than brought to the forefront of empirical scrutiny (Young 1989a: 206; Keohane 1993: 30). Thus, empirical testability will serve as a basic premise for studying the extent to which and how institutions matter.

The rationalistic and institutionalistic perspectives on institutions differ not so much on whether institutions matter, but rather the extent to which and how they matter. One of the major differences would appear related to what we may refer to as different scopes of validity, i.e. that they pretend to say something about different phenomena. This is clearly illustrated by Ostrom's (1986; 1990; 1991) work on what she terms 'institutional choice'. In her framework for analysing institutional choice, expected costs and benefits as well as shared norms which individuals frequently internalize are central elements. Ostrom characterizes this perspective as:

> A major contribution of scholars working in the Public Choice tradition has been the serious effort to examine the combined effect of preferences and rules to explain actions and outcomes. Substantial progress has been achieved by assuming that individuals select from within a set of rule-constrained alternatives using their own preferences (*which may be derived from social norms and culture*) to evaluate the benefits and costs of various actions and likely outcomes. (Ostrom 1991: 96, emphasis added)

In short, focusing on given interests and preferences does not logically imply denying that also other factors may have shaped those identities and interests (Wendt 1992: 423).

A second, although closely related, difference is that rationalistic approaches emphasize *one* behavioural mechanism through which institutions may affect behaviour, while institutionalistic approaches frequently presume that actors have a mixture of behavioural mechanisms that may be affected under different conditions. According to March and Olsen (1996: 251–2): 'Within an institutional framework, "choice", if it can be called that, is based more on logic of appropriateness than on the logic of consequence that underlies conceptions of rational action. Institutionalised rules, duties, rights, and roles define acts as appropriate (normal, natural, right, good) or inappropriate (uncharacteristic, unnatural, wrong, bad).' Thus, institutionalistic approaches open the way for a wider range of institutional consequences than the rationalistic perspective. The institutional 'micro level' within the rationalistic tradition may provide some sort of incentive 'correction' or supply of information. At 'macro level', institutions may reduce transaction costs and integrate or aggregate interests and preferences. From the institutionalistic perspective, it does not follow that institutions may not have such effects. However, it does follow that these effects represent only a subset of possible effects. At 'micro level', institutions may affect identities and interests. At 'macro level', institutions may lead to, for instance, the development of cooperative norms.

The growing recognition that differences do not necessarily equal incompatibility is probably an important reason behind a recent tendency in the literature on institutions, a tendency towards convergence between different approaches (Hall and Taylor 1994; Ostrom 1995).

Towards an integrated approach

Environmental institutions affect collective outcomes and actor behaviour through various institutional factors and behavioural mechanisms conditioned by problem characteristics. A theory of how environmental institutions matter would require precise assumptions concerning how institutional factors and behavioural mechanisms interact in different problem situations. My ambition here is merely to take one step in that direction by seeking to disentangle the content of these concepts and relationships between them.

Behavioural mechanisms The basic idea is that actors have *dual utility functions* (Levi 1991; Lewin 1991; Rothstein 1994). Generally, the point is that actors seek to balance 'self-interest' and 'the common good' by so-called contingent consent. This means that actors under certain conditions may be more preoccupied with doing the 'right thing' than with calculating costs and benefits. Actors may do what seem 'appropriate' according to March and Olsen (1989: 161). This may actually reduce transaction costs due to minimization of requirements to monitoring and enforcement. Contingent consent is based on the assumption that one actor expects that most other actors will contribute towards providing the common good as well. The use of voluntary agreements – if they are truly voluntary – in environmental policy may serve as an example of willingness to do the right thing.

In order to make this general idea applicable to the study of environmental behaviour, we need a more precise conception of the *content* of the two utility functions that are analytically distinct.

Rationality does not necessarily equal self-interest, but this assumption is normally included in practice by those working within the rational choice tradition and game theory (Lewin 1991: 3). The precise meaning of rationality varies within the literature: the rationality assumption has been variously regarded as necessary, empirical, superfluous or false; and more than 20 senses of rationality have been distinguished (Føllesdal 1982). Without delving into these controversies, we may offer a lenient interpretation of rationality: 'When faced with several courses of action, people usually do what they believe is likely to have the best overall outcome' (Elster 1989a: 22). This definition merely stresses that you should consciously search for the best means to achieve whatever aims you have. The emphasis on outcomes places the assumption of rationality within the explanatory framework of *intentionality*. Outcomes in this particular meaning and within the context of this study are related to environmental decision-making. More specifically, I assume that relevant actors evaluate options in terms of environmental problem-related costs and benefits, and only in those terms, and choose whichever option they believe will maximize net gains. In environmental politics, this means that actors will favour environmental regulations and choose alternatives on the basis of marginal abatement costs and damage costs (up to the point where marginal costs equal damage costs).

Unlike rationality, *norms* are at the extreme conceived of as not outcome oriented at all (Elster 1989a; 1989b). According to March and Olsen (1994: 251), institutional theories subordinate the logic of consequence to the logic of appropriateness. Likewise, the sociological approach applied to international institutions conceives of norms as not derived from the calculation of interests (Keohane 1988: 381). Like rationality, norms are understood in many different ways and various norms as behavioural mechanisms have been identified (Elster 1989b). Here I will focus on norms related to environmental decision-making and behaviour. Within this specific context, actors may very well evaluate options in terms of environmental costs and benefits – but not only in those terms, nor will they necessarily choose whichever option is believed to maximize net gains. This immediately raises the question of whether such behaviour is necessarily guided by norms. The answer is clearly 'no' since actors may have *mixed motives* related to concerns other than environmental ones. The existence of non-environmental motivations is a well-known element in environmental cooperative efforts (Skjærseth 1993). Thus, we need a positive conception of norms emphasizing that actors do not evaluate any options at all, but behave in accordance with what they think is right. This assumption appears just as empirically false as the strictest requirements of rationality found within the rational choice tradition (Tsebelis 1990). However, combining the two – rationality and norms – may provide us with analytical distinct assumptions whose validity lies precisely in their combination, i.e. that actors have dual utility functions.

In their simplest form, norms take the form of imperatives guiding individual behaviour: 'do X' or 'don't do X'. 'Do not use the sea as a trash can, dispose of your waste onshore.' As this example shows, norms may, or may not, have useful consequences, depending on whether dumping at sea represents a better environmental solution than land-based alternatives. More complex norms are cooperative, like the norm of *pacta sunt servanda* (treaties are to be obeyed) in international cooperation (Franck 1990). One implication of this norm is that one should not free-ride. Norms are frequently guided by the threat of sanctions in some version: actors may obey norms in order to avoid social or material sanctions. In such cases, norms may be entirely cost/benefit oriented and vulnerable to the view that apparently norm-based behaviour is essentially intentional and based on the logic of consequence. To paraphrase Elster's (1989a: 119) response to this argument, norms may be internalized in the sense that they do not need external sanctions to be effective. Norms may be followed even when violations would pass unobserved and would not expose the violation to sanctions.

In short, by assuming that actors have dual utility functions consisting of norms and rationality we open the way for a wider range of institutional consequences than by relying on only one behavioural mechanism.

Institutional factors Different institutional factors affect and trigger different behavioural mechanisms. As we have seen, institutions may operate at both 'micro' and 'macro' levels, affecting both collective outcomes and individual behaviour. Rationality and norms may also operate at these levels. Actors may adopt joint commitments and implement their commitments because it is in their own material interest to do so. Conversely, actors may adopt joint commitments due to norms of cooperative behaviour and implement their commitments due to some norm of obligation. Hence, institutions may affect individual behaviour and collective outcomes through both rationality and norms. The basic pathways are crudely sketched out below.

Levy, Young and Zürn (1995) have proposed six behavioural 'models' through which institutions may have an impact. Four of these seem particularly relevant here. First, institutions may serve as utility modifiers. The behavioural mechanism underlying this model equals rationality as defined above. Actor's behaviour can be influenced by institutional arrangements to the extent that they alter the costs and benefits attached to different options. Utility calculations may be modified through the production of new information or by some sort of incentive 'correction'. The second model views institutions as enhancers of cooperation and this model is based on the same behavioural mechanism, but directs attention to problems of cooperation and collective action. The essential point is that there are circumstances under which rational actors engaged in the making of joint commitments fail to reap joint gains due to the consequences of strategic behaviour. Since collective action problems may take different forms, institutions may affect cooperation in various ways, including reducing incentives for defection, mitigating fears of cheating or simply reducing transaction costs by eliminating the necessity to cope with the consequences of strategic behaviour again and again.

The third and fourth models will take us from the rationality assumption towards norms. The third model is concerned with institutions as bestowers of authority. This model is based on the premise that actors may be more preoccupied with doing the 'right thing' than with calculating the costs and benefits involved in doing so. At micro level, institutions may stimulate such mechanisms through socialization and routinization. It is the authoritativeness of institutional rules that trigger the behavioural response, rather than calculations of anticipated costs and benefits associated with different options. At macro level, routinization of iterative collective decision-making may lead to various norms of reciprocity. The last model views institutions as role definers and emphasizes that institutions may operate at the constitutive level by affecting the identity and interests of the actors. The core of this perspective is that institutions may define and assign new *roles*. This perspective is nicely captured by Allison's (1971: 176) aphorism 'where you stand depends on where you sit': different actors will emphasize different decision criteria when confronted by similar problems. Such criteria may to a large extent be traced back to formal roles.

Problem-characteristics Linkages between institutional factors and behavioural mechanisms are conditioned by problem-characteristics. As we have seen, other studies strongly indicate that the range and effect of international environmental institutions vary significantly according to types of problems. Different problems may lead to more or less favourable conditions with regard to the potential impact of environmental institutions.

Differences in political characteristics may make some pollution problems more difficult than others. Political characteristics may influence the actors' willingness to reach and implement given solutions. By political characteristics, we mean mainly the various types of *collective good* and the type of *interdependence mechanisms* at work. A clean North Sea may generally be described as a *public good*, even though the quality of the sea varies between different regions. An actor who cannot be excluded from the benefits of a collective good once the good is produced will have scant incentive to contribute voluntarily to the provision of that good (Olson 1965). The characteristic of non-exclusiveness creates incentives to free-riding – i.e. incentives where actors can benefit from the good without contributing to its production. The dilemma of collective action may apply to all levels of society. The government of Norway may have incentives to free-ride in relation to other states, one regional administration may have incentives to free-ride in relation to other regions and a farmer may decide to continue to use nitrogenous fertilizers, assuming that a sufficient number of others will refrain from doing so.

Cooperation in order to provide a clean sea is based on *interdependence*, since it is only under such conditions environmental cooperation makes sense. Even though no one is interested in a grossly polluted sea as such, environmental cooperation is difficult because some actors are frequently more dependent than others; in other words, interdependence between actors is rarely symmetrical. Underdal (1987) has distinguished between two main mechanisms of interdependence: 'hard' problems of incongruity, and 'easy' problems of cost-efficiency. Hard problems may be caused both by externalities and by competition. Such problems can be particularly hard to solve if they are characterized by asymmetry and/or cumulative cleavages (Underdal 1997). A problem is asymmetrical to the extent that parties are affected differently by the problem, so that interests are correlated negatively, as in a typical upstream–downstream relationship. In cases where problems are multi-dimensional, cumulative cleavages may make the situation even worse, i.e. more difficult to cope with through voluntary cooperation. Cleavages are cumulative to the extent that parties find themselves in the same situation on all sub-problems or issues.

Easy cost-efficiency problems parallel coordination 'games' where none of the options are preferable as such to one of the actors, but where harmonization is necessary. The essence of a hard problem is incentive 'distortion', while easy problems are related to imperfect information and communication failure. The point is that the integrative potential is more easily tapped when actors are faced with easy problems of cost-efficiency. Hence, the more widespread the hard problem, the more asymmetrical the configuration of interests and incompatible preferences. Conversely, a perfectly easy problem is here conceived of as one characterized by identical interests and preferences. Empirically, many pollution problems will have both hard and easy elements. Moreover, problems may change over time, e.g. due to new information and changing perceptions.

Conclusion

What are environmental institutions and how do they matter? I proposed a nominal definition of environmental institutions with a thin 'core' that leaves the way open for broad consequences. This core consists of explicit rules and procedures aimed at affecting collective outcomes and actor behaviour. I argued further that this definition is applicable to both international and domestic institutions, provided that some specified restrictions were kept in mind. Instead of arguing that institutions may be labelled 'environmental' because they share some unique qualities, I indicated that institutions dealing with the core elements of transboundary environmental problems share some common features. On the basis of some central insights from both rationalistic and institutionalistic perspectives on *how* institutions matter, I presented the view that these traditions are clearly different but not incompatible. Their differences lie partly in differing scopes of validity, and partly in their emphasis on one or more behavioural mechanisms. This point of departure was used to design an integrated approach based on the idea that environmental institutions affect collective outcomes and actor behaviour through various institutional factors and behavioural mechanisms conditioned by problem-characteristics.

Concerning behavioural mechanisms the basic idea is that actors have dual utility functions consisting of rationality based on the logic of consequence and norms based on the logic of appropriateness. This means that actors may sometimes be more preoccupied with doing the 'right thing' than with calculating costs and benefits. Different institutional factors affect and trigger different behavioural mechanisms. For example, actors may adopt joint commitments because it is in their own material interest to do so, or they may adopt joint commitments due to some norm of obligation. In turn, linkages between institutional factors and behavioural mechanisms are conditioned by the nature of the problem at hand in the sense that the range and effect of institutions will vary according to the malignancy of the problem.

These conceptual clarifications and theoretical ideas will serve as building blocks for the design of the analytical framework to be presented in the next chapter.

Notes

1 For broader definitions, see Puchala and Hopkins (1983: 63), Krasner (183: 2) and Kratochwil (1993). For example, Puchala and Hopkins argue that a regime exists in every substantive issue-area in international relations where there is discernibly patterned behaviour. For more narrow defintions, see Mitchell (1994a; 1994b) and Keohane (1993: 28). For example, Mitchell focuses on explicit treaty rules intended to contribute to the larger debate on international regimes. The definition used in this study comes close to the definition of environmental institutions developed by Bernauer (1995: 352). Note that Bernauer's definition applies only to the international level.

2 The classic definition of international regimes is quite broad: 'sets of implicit or explicit principles, norms, rules and decision-making procedures around which actors' expectations converge in a given area of international relations' (Krasner 1983: 2).

3 According to Young (1989a: 84–9), international regimes may come into existence by three different processes. First, they may be self-gen-

erating or *spontaneous,* i.e. the product of the action of many, but not the result of human design. Second, they may be classified as *negotiated* and characterized by conscious efforts to agree on their major provisions. Third, they may be *imposed* by dominant actors in a process typically not involving consent on the part of subordinate actors.

4 Another proposition states that a 'coercive' hegemon may establish coordinated arrangements that reflects the interests of the hegemon and compel other to comply (Snidal 1985). In particular, the 'hegemonic stability' hypothesis predicts that international regimes will tend to decline where there is no 'hegemon' to provide incentives for compliance. However, unlike France in the Mediterranean cooperation (Haas 1990: 42) none of the North Sea states may be classified as a hegemon in terms of control over events important to oneself and to others. In addition, the super-power(s) have not invested any strong interest in this issue-area. Accordingly, there will not be a systematic focus on 'power-based' explanations.

3
Towards an analytical framework

In recent years, many large-scale research projects have been initiated on international environmental politics, with a focus on the consequences of international environmental institutions (Young and von Moltke 1994). Very few of these projects have dealt systematically with international environmental policy-making and domestic implementation. However, research on international (environmental) cooperation and domestic (environmental) policy can offer bits and pieces of insight relevant for most aspects under scrutiny here. Against this backdrop, the main purpose of this chapter is to design an analytical framework for studying the role of international and domestic environmental institutions in the making and implementation of North Sea pollution control.

The first section will take us to two crucial questions largely neglected so far: what is the precise meaning of joint commitments and domestic implementation, and how can we analyse the dependent variables that represent the focus for explanation. The next two sections are based on the theory discussion in Chapter 2 and aims at transforming these general ideas into models and testable propositions. The overall purpose of these sections is to help us understand the extent to which, and how, change and variance in joint commitments and domestic implementation may be accounted for by environmental institutions. In the last section, the focus is in the dynamic role of international institutions and their impact on state–society relationships.

Focus for explanation: implementation of international commitments

Implementation means 'to carry something into effect' (Weale 1992a: 43). This straightforward definition raises several questions. What is this 'something' to be carried into effect? What do we mean by 'effect' in this respect? How and when can we compare and evaluate implementation 'effects'?

The implementation of an object negotiated at the international level may be seen as the process of converting *formal* commitments reflecting an agreement of governments.[1] This approach distinguishes problem-solving 'effectiveness' studies from implementation studies, since the former requires that we take the ecological problem at hand as our starting point. This delimitation is important since it excludes failure and success in recognizing a problem. Formal commitments refer to clusters of joint decisions, or bargaining outputs. International commitments may vary, or change in stringency. Stringency refers first and foremost to the 'amount' of behavioural change required, here measured in terms of advocated reductions in emissions of relevant substances according to a deadline and a baseline. In addition, there may be considerable variation concerning specificity and legal status of commitments. The requirement of formality is included to minimize the risk of studying statements or policy intentions that were never seriously intended. The world is full of political statements and propositions at all levels that are never formally adopted and never realized – a well-known phenomenon from election campaigns and international diplomatic conferences.[2] Formal adoption at the international level, then, refers to commitments that have been decided upon by governmental representatives authorized to make decisions on behalf of their governments. The next question is, what are such commitments converted into?

By domestic implementation of international commitments I mean the process of converting international commitments reflecting a formal agreement of governments into domestic policy and behavioural change of *target groups*. Target groups represent those actors who cause pollution and consequently those actors who are required to change their behaviour in order to fulfill joint commitments and domestic policy goals. Such an approach further distinguishes problem-solving 'effectiveness' studies from implementation studies, since the former requires that we take ecological impact as our ending point.

The process of domestic implementation of international commitments may follow various pathways. A distinct implementation process may take place at the international level, here referred to as *international implementation*. International implementation means the extent to which international commitments adopted within one environmental institution are actually changed according to stringency by another institution covering the same issue-area. At the domestic level, we may apply Easton's (1965) distinction between *output* and *outcome* as a starting point. Output is here conceived of as domestic policy, i.e. initiatives undertaken by governments and subordinated agencies in response to domestic challenges and joint commitments. Outcome is related to the consequences of environmental policy, i.e. relevant behaviour by target groups. The link between output and outcome may encompass at least two stages: first, ratification or acceptance of international commitments; second the exercise of national measures and policy tools through the administrative system, and the target groups' response to regulation. The link between international commitments and domestic ratification or acceptance will be referred to as *Level I* implementation. The remaining stage will be referred to as *Level II* implementation (see Figure 3.1). Hence, Level I implementation centres on the *formal* aspects of implementation, while Level II implementation concerns *substance*, i.e. actual implementation efforts at the

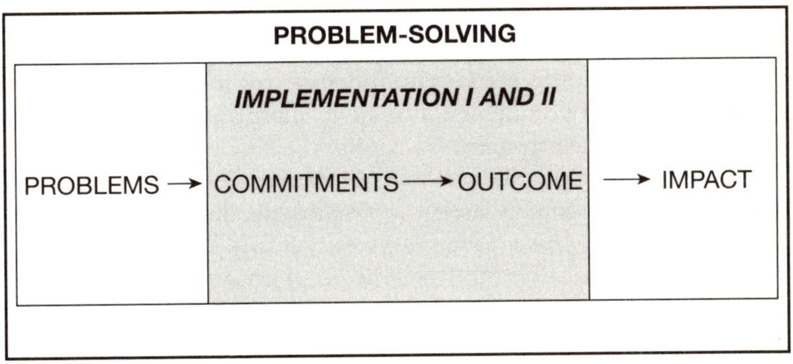

Figure 3.1 *Differentiating implementation and problem-solving perspectives*

level of regulatory agencies and target groups. Note that I do not assume any necessary causal relationship between international commitments, domestic output and outcome. Target groups may very well change their behaviour in the required direction, without this having anything to do with joint commitments; it may be due to, e.g. technological development or economic fluctuations (see Chapter 4).

Implementation effects and evaluation criteria

Since domestic implementation of international commitments may have a wide range of 'effects' or consequences, I will narrow in on what we may term 'direct internal' effects. We may distinguish between two distinct dimensions or effects (Levy, Young and Zürn 1995). The question of whether effects are direct or indirect is a matter of the 'length' of the causal chain from commitments to the behaviour in question. Indirect effects cover unintentional, or 'second-order', consequences. For example, sewage treatment leads to contaminated sewage sludge that may be incinerated onshore or used as fertilizer. In this case, a cause of marine pollution may easily end up as a cause of air or soil pollution. The distinction between internal and external effects refers to scope of membership. Internal effects mean consequences for those parties adopting a specific commitment, while external effects also include consequences for other actors. The latter phenomenon has been described as 'diffusion' of commitments and regulations, meaning that actors outside the cooperation may informally 'borrow' commitments and regulations (Sand 1991: 254–66).

In order to compare some level of implementation across countries and over time within countries, we need to relate what has been accomplished to some criterion that can serve as a baseline. Concerning Level I implementation, this should be a fairly manageable task. The strategy will be to undertake a qualitative evaluation of the extent to which the content of international commitments is explicitly included in domestic policy goals. However, Level II implementation is the more important concern. Baseline year may serve as a minimum criterion of behavioural change aimed at identifying the extent to which behavioural change is going in the right *direction*. Formal and explicit goals may serve as a criterion of goal achievement. Since the ultimate goal of implementing international environmental commitments is to improve the quality of the environment, I assume that providing more behavioural change than strictly required deserves a higher relative score on goal achievement than would providing less. Thus, the assumption is that emission reductions in general will lead to reduced stress on ecosystems in the long run.

The most important analytical requirement in any evaluation is to make the evaluation criteria explicit. Goal attainment has one important methodological advantage and one important normative advantage compared to other evaluation criteria.[3] Different national priorities and goals are seen as a major obstacle in comparative studies of the 'effectiveness' of national environmental regulations (Vogel 1986). Internationally agreed goals will give us an opportunity to compare goal attainment across countries within the same international institution. Focusing on explicit goals will also minimize the subjective element in empirical analysis compared with more diffuse criteria such as 'the spirit' of an agreement (Mitchell 1994a: 30–1) – minimized, but not necessarily eliminated, because joint commitments are sometimes hard to operationalize.

Different analytical Level I and II implementation categories may now be proposed on the basis of goals and baseline years. Level I implementation categories:

- Ambitious: domestic goals more ambitious than international requirements.
- Intermediate: domestic goals in line with international requirements.
- Reluctant: domestic goals less ambitious than international requirements.
- Indifferent: domestic goals unrelated to international requirements.

Level II implementation categories:

- Ambitious: more behavioural change provided than internationally required.
- Intermediate: match between behavioural change and international goals.
- Reluctant: less behavioural change provided than required.
- Indifferent: behavioural change unrelated to international commitments and possibly going in the wrong direction.

By ambitious domestic implementation of international commitments, I mean a close relationship between ambitious Level I and Level II implementation within time frames or a fairly long time span. When time frames are part of commitments, it makes sense to use these time frames as benchmarks. In other cases, major criticism has been raised against the studies of public policy implementation conducted in the 1970s, because large programmes were evaluated after only a few years. Changing the behaviour of a large number of actors takes many years, and implementation is a matter of incremental change. Approximately 10–15 years from the adoption of commitments to evaluation is recommended in pure public policy studies (Sabatier 1986a).

In conclusion, domestic implementation of international commitments should here be understood as the long-term process of converting international commitments reflecting formal agreement of governments into domestic policy goals and behavioural change of target groups.

Explaining commitments and implementation: the Rational Actor model

Before I specify the Rational Actor model, we should briefly recapitulate the status of the Rational Actor model within the general framework. The hypothesis we wish to refute claims that international commitments and domestic outputs and outcomes would not be different in the absence of change and variance in institutional rules and principles. Hence, in a 'no-institutional change and variance' condition, states would develop the same commitments as well as the same set of outputs and outcomes. The Rational Actor model is designed to represent this condition. The alternative hypothesis is that commitments as well as outputs and outcomes would be different in the absence of institutional change at international level and variance between states at domestic level. The Institutional model is designed to show how and why. Hence, a first step towards understanding the extent to which institutional factors have influenced the adoption and implementation of relevant international obligations is to imagine commitments, outputs and outcomes, given that the hypothesis we wish to refute is true. This is a counter-factual way of reasoning, which represents a special way of comparison since it makes claims about events that did not occur.[4] In order to 'test' this hypothesis we should control for interest-based explanations. We should try to identify situations where the parties have adopted joint commitments significantly different from those they would have adopted on the basis of *unilateral action*. Second, we should try to identify situations where compliance with joint commitments seems *inconvenient* with regard to the parties' interests.

Now, let us turn to the content and implications of the Rational Actor model. Within this perspective, I assume that actions of actors will be motivated by costs and benefits, and that actors will choose those options that are believed to maximize net gains. This approach is generally referred to as the 'interest-based explanation' of international environmental cooperation (Sprinz and Vaahtoranta 1994). I intend to proceed in two steps. First, I will assume unitary rational actors. Second, the assumption of unity will be relaxed and the interests of sub-national actors included.

The calculus of unitary states

This perspective seeks to capture the incentives of a rational decision-maker representing a given state. Such incentives are assumed to influence unilateral national positions, joint action and incentives to comply with international commitments. According to Underdal (1995), the unitary rational actor perspective builds upon three basic assumptions: a) states are unitary, rational actors; b) decision-makers evaluate options in terms of costs and benefits to their nation, and only in those terms, and choose whichever option (is believed to) maximize net national gain; c) states are in full control over 'their' societies. Unfortunately, these assumptions cannot serve as adequate descriptions of the making and implementation of international commitments, and this perspective scores low on validity. On the other hand, this perspective is regarded as parsimonious and highly conducive to theory development and deductive reasoning for the purposes of empirical studies.

The assumption that unitary states act rationally is part of a systemic approach which seeks to explain the behaviour of states in terms of the context or circumstances in which they operate, rather than structures and processes internal to the parties. States are assumed to be the most important actors in international environmental politics; they are further assumed to operate in an environment characterized by anarchy. The requirements of unity and control over society imply an automatic relationship between domestic output and outcome. Hence, the distinction between Level I and Level II implementation becomes irrelevant in the sense that the possibility of domestic implementation 'failure' is ruled out by the assumptions. States actually do as they wish in this respect. The notion of an implementation process is replaced by the notion of *compliance*, which is a question of deliberate decisions. Such decisions are related to instrumental objectives concerning some notion of optimizing national welfare. In environmental politics, this means that states will favour environmental regulations and choose alternatives on the basis of marginal *abatement* costs (AC) and *damage* costs (DC) (up to the point where marginal costs equal damage costs). In the case of *transfrontier pollution*, the relationship between own damage and abatement costs will also be affected by the 'balance of pollution exchange' in relation to other states.[5]

Expected national positions and joint commitments National positions are conceived of as a function of three determinants. First, abatement costs represent a motivation for avoiding stringent regulation. However, abatement efforts may have positive side-effects that are hard to predict, such as in the form of new technology that may prove commercially profitable. Ecological 'modernists' even argue that instead of seeing environmental protection as a burden upon the economy it should be generally viewed as a potential for future economic growth (Weale 1992b). The assumed validity of this premise is closely related to the time dimension. Abatement costs tend to be certain and immediate, while benefits are uncertain and distant. Thus, a central question related to the heuristic value of this model is whether decision-makers have actually approached the problem in terms of abatement costs and damage costs.

Second, damage costs are seen as the most important motivation to adopt stringent regulations. It seems quite reasonable that environmental regulations will normally be implemented to avoid, or as a response to, some perceived environmental threat. Third, marine pollution is also a *transfrontier* pollution problem, which implies that the AC–DC relationship will be determined not only by own emissions and abatement, but also by the 'balance of pollution exchange' in relation to other states. This (im)balance is likely to determine the extent to which *joint action* is advocated, thus linking national positions to international cooperation and Level I implementation. If a country is mainly affected by own emissions, joint action will not necessarily be important for coping with the problem. If a country is an exporter of pollution, it may have incentives to avoid joint action, since cooperation could imply a risk that others would try to persuade or force the net exporter to internalize externalities. If a country is mainly affected by others' emissions, i.e. is an importer, then joint action becomes crucial since own efforts will be insufficient to reduce damage costs significantly (see Table 3.1).

Table 3.1 *Positions predicted by the Unitary Rational Actor model*

Export/import	*Damage costs*	*Abatement costs*	*Position*
Importer	High	Low	Ambitious
Exporter	Low	High	Reluctant
Balanced	High	High	Intermediate
Balanced	Low	Low	Indifferent

Source: Based on Andresen *et al.* (1996: 123).

The most ambitious will be the highly affected net-importers facing low abatement costs. They will push for stringent commitments. The least ambitious, or the reluctant, will be net-exporters facing low damage costs and high abatement costs. They have incentives to advocate lenient commitments. The intermediates are characterized by a balanced exchange rate of pollution combined with high damage costs and abatement costs. The intermediates have incentives to support joint commitments in between the reluctant and ambitious. Actors with low abatement costs and damage costs will, under conditions of balanced exchange of pollution, tend to pay minor attention to joint obligations. These actors may be expected to take an indifferent position.

The stringency of joint commitments will be determined by the interests and preferences of the least ambitious, or reluctant, party, given that agreement is required and issue-linkages are absent (Sebenius 1983). Against this backdrop, the following proposition related to the stringency of joint commitments has been suggested by Underdal (1980a: 36):

P_1 Where international commitments can be established only through agreement among all significant parties involved, and where such a regulation is considered only on its own merits, collective action will be limited to those measures acceptable to the least enthusiastic party.

When joint commitments have to be made through agreement, the appropriate notion of collective optimum is the Pareto frontier: this frontier is reached when no further increase in benefits to one party can be obtained without thereby leaving one or more prospective partner(s) worse off. If we consider the various positions together, the ambitious and reluctant represent the two opposite poles assumed to have strong interests and preferences in opposite directions. The ambitious may go too far, thus leaving others worse off. The reluctant may not go far enough also leaving others worse off. The position of the intermediates may be close to a collective optimum, while the indifferent are not interested in joint commitments and might well block an agreement whenever unanimity is required. In this situation, the intermediates may be particularly important. When the intermediates follow their self-interest, they represent a compromise position between the ambitious and the reluctant. It is not unlikely that a compromise position may be utilized to forge solutions acceptable to all parties and/or activate the indifferent in support for joint commitments. The notion of instrumental or entrepreneurial leadership may be one possible mechanism linking a compromise position to actual innovative behaviour (Underdal 1991; Young 1991; Malnes 1995).

Expected incentives to comply If the parties succeed in adopting joint commitments, the next question is whether they have incentives to comply. The will to advocate joint action does not necessarily imply high incentives to comply with own commitments. An agreement *links* the behaviour of one actor to the behaviour of other actors. By definition, an agreement is an exchange of conditional promises whereby one actor commits itself to a certain course of action in exchange for certain contributions from its partners (Underdal 1995: 5). There are essentially two reasons why actors choose to comply with their commitments, given that no 'external' benefits or costs are provided (Hovi 1992).[6] First, there may be situations where none of the parties have any incentives to defect regardless of what others may do. Compliance would then be a dominant strategy for all parties. The second possibility occurs when compliance is not the dominant strategy for each and every party, but is still the best option for each as long as all others comply. Thus, there may be a temptation to free-ride, but this temptation can be cured by a fear that the agreement may collapse. Hence, no actor has any incentive to defect unilaterally. However, governments are sometimes highly reluctant to embark upon policies concerning international environmental obligations. Since transnational pollution problems are frequently asymmetrical in the sense that actors are affected differently by the actions of others, a given commitment may be less favourable than what an actor would have chosen by itself. For example, a net importer of pollution would probably prefer that others contribute more in reducing discharges (notably the exporters), while the actor itself contributes less.

Potential benefits stemming from compliance with joint commitments will be determined by a combination of change in own behaviour and change in the behaviour of the other partners. Hence, damage-cost reductions depend partly upon what others do whenever relationships may be characterized by interdependence. The more important the compliance of others is for oneself, the more will incentives to comply depend on the effect of own contribution upon the behaviour of others. Under conditions of net import or net export of pollution, the link between own damage costs and abatement costs following from compliance is weak. In such cases, there may be weak incentives to comply. The compliance of others is not important for an exporter and incentives to comply will depend less on own contributions in relation to others. Conversely, for the importer, the compliance of others is crucial, but its own behaviour is not likely significantly to affect the behaviour of its partners. In both these cases, the causal link between an actor's own compliance and that actor's own benefits from the project is weak. If compliance implies a strong link between own abatement costs and damage costs, there will be strong incentives to comply. Under conditions of balanced export and import of pollution, the benefits to accrue from the compliance of others may equal the benefits that others enjoy from own compliance. Hence, there will be a strong causal link between an actor's own compliance and that actor's own benefits from the project. Thus, we may deduce the following proposition:

P_2 There will be strong incentives to comply when the relationship between own AC and DC is strong. There will be strong incentives to defect when the link between own AC and DC is weak.

The link between the behaviour of different partners is also sensitive to the size of contributions in terms of pollution load. The more one party contributes, the more sensitive will its partners be to its level of compliance. However, if the link between own abatement costs and damage costs is strong, i.e. when abatement efforts needed to fulfil joint commitments also curb own damage, the size of contribution seems of little relevance. In cases where actors are large exporters we would expect that they were especially sensitive to the 'victims' of their export. Conversely, when actors represent small importers (victims) incentives to defect may be reinforced.

The calculus of sub-national actors

This perspective seeks to capture the interests of affected and interested domestic sub-national actors by taking us over to the state-society dimension and Level II implementation. Just like states, sub-national actors may be affected by both the consequences of the problem in question (DC) and by the costs needed to change current behaviour (AC). The general assumption is that the interests of affected domestic actors may deviate (more or less systematically) from state interests and possibly influence the implementation of international commitments. Hence, this perspective is based on the premise that governments defect not so much by deliberate choice but rather owing to lack of implementation *ability* due to resistance at sub-national level. Thus, in the absence of a perfect hierarchy, states are only in partial control over 'their' societies. Consequently, there is no automatic relationship between Level I and Level II implementation. One core assumption is relaxed compared to the URA perspective. States are conceived of not as unitary actors, but as complex units consisting of sub-national actors.

The core of the question here is the extent to which sub-national actors have incentives to defect from, or comply with, higher-order domestic goals following from international commitments. Since target groups frequently 'control' the behaviour that has to be modified, governments depend upon their reluctant or active cooperation. In order to understand the incentives of target groups to comply with higher-order policy goals, the most important question is how these actors are affected, including the extent to which they are affected in the same way. I will here focus on two determinants: the extent to which costs and benefits are widely distributed or concentrated (Wilson 1973; Underdal 1995).

First, regulatory policy tends to impose costs upon target groups. When such costs are concentrated on specific subgroups of society while the benefits are widely distributed, there is reason to assume high incentives to oppose national policies. Commitments are most difficult to implement under such circumstances, owing to the risk of vertical disintegration in pollution policies – meaning that the aggregate of 'micro decisions' among target groups may deviate more or less systematically, or substantially, from higher-order policy goals (Underdal 1979). If costs are distributed, and benefits concentrated few would gain, and many pay. This situation may be rare, but it is perfectly possible that an industrial sector can improve its competitive edge or achieve direct profit from environmental regulation. For example, those producing sewage treatment facilities may profit directly from a stringent North Sea policy. In such cases, we assume strong incentives to support national commitments, and implementation is assumed to be relatively easy under such conditions. If both costs and benefits are widely distributed, mobilization is likely to be low, and target groups are unlikely to have any strong incentives either in support for, or in opposition to higher order commitments. In cases where both costs and benefits are concentrated, incentives are likely to depend on whether costs and benefits are equally certain and immediate. The above assumptions can be translated into the following proposition:

> P_3 When benefits are concentrated and costs widely distributed, target groups are likely to support stringent national goals. In cases where both costs and benefits are widely distributed throughout society, there will not be strong support for, or opposition to, higher-order goals. When costs are concentrated and benefits widely distributed, resistance is likely to arise. Accordingly, implementation will be difficult.

While the distribution of costs and benefits is assumed to be fundamental for target groups' incentives, the 'size' of costs involved may be important as well. It is reasonable to assume that target groups facing high abatement costs tend to be more reluctant than those facing low abatement costs, under conditions of equal distribution of costs and benefits.

When costs and benefits are highly asymmetrically distributed, conflict tends to increase. This is likely to be reinforced if the problem or activity in question stem from point sources that are easy to identify and are highly visible to the public at large. Such situations are likely to trigger mobilization of environmental non-governmental organizations (ENGOs). Since ENGOs do not have to bear the burden of regulation, I will assume that they have general incentives to support national policies or to press for over-achievement. The proposed relationship to be empirically studied will here be formulated as a general assumption rather than as a specific proposition, due to relatively limited *foreknowledge* (Eckstein 1975).

If we consider these groups together, it is reasonable to assume that ENGOs may represent a counterbalancing force to reluctant target groups. According to this perspective, we may perhaps say that environmental policy is formed and implemented in the area of tension between ENGO mobilization and distribution of costs and benefits among target groups. Accordingly, the key to explaining implementation may in some cases lie in the relative support and strength among ENGOs and target groups.

According to Milner (1991) societal actors can limit the strategies available to a state; policy-makers depend on these groups when international commitments are negotiated because they will be the key to ratification. A more 'state-centred' variant of this perspective has been suggested by Putnam (1988), who focuses on domestic and international politics as two-level games. At the national level, affected groups will promote their own interests by seeking to induce their government to adopt 'their' policy, and politicians will seek to acquire power through the formation of coalitions between the groups. At the international level, the government will seek to maximize its possibilities of satisfying the same groups, while simultaneously minimizing national costs of international commitments. While these perspectives suggest some mechanisms linking subnational constellations to domestic and international policy-making, they differ in at least one important way from the perspective suggested here. Implementation is conceived of as a matter of ratification only and limits the focus to joint commitments legally binding within international law. Thus, these perspectives largely exclude politically binding commitments and what I have referred to as the domestic implementation process linking output to outcome.

Explaining commitments and implementation: the Institutional model

How may institutions affect states' willingness and ability to make and implement international environmental commitments? Even though we are able to identify joint commitments and compliance levels that are unlikely to be explained by actor interests, we cannot conclude that institutions have caused any mismatch between expectations and observations. Thus, the main argument advocated here is that the propositions derived from the Rational Actor model will not necessarily be verified due to the effect of international and domestic institutions. The first part of this section centres on international environmental institutions and relaxes – but does not remove – the assumption of rationality based on the logic of consequence. The second part focuses on domestic institutions and relaxes both the assumptions of both rationality and unity.

Institutionalisation of international pollution cooperation

The argument here is that international environmental institutions may: a) influence international commitments beyond the interests and preferences of 'the least ambitious actor'; b) stimulate compliance even though (short-term) costs may be higher than benefits. A basic premise for this argument is that the rationality assumptions underlying the unitary rational actor model are relaxed in the following ways. First, the actors do not necessarily know what they want when they participate in international pollution cooperation. Typically, they enter into an international process of discovering, inventing and exploring both own interests and possible solutions (Walton and McKersie 1965; Underdal 1990). Second, they do not want only to maximize own interests in terms of costs and benefits: They are also sensitive to norms of cooperative and individual behaviour. Actors are sometimes guided by what seems 'appropriate' rather than calculation of costs and benefits.

Students of international institutions or regimes have focused on a broad set of phenomena, only some of which are included here. According to Krasner (1988: 67), institutions serve as the building blocks of social and political life by forming and conditioning preferences, capabilities and basic self-identities. At a more specific level, Zürn (1991) distinguishes among 15 groups of variables that international institutions may affect. Many consequences may be extremely hard to observe and measure empirically; here I shall focus on a more limited set of institutional factors. The study of international institutions is also distinguished according to phases in which a dividing line is drawn between regime formation and regime functioning and consequences. However, according to Young (1989a: 102), there is no necessary relationship between how regimes are established and how they develop. We may also differentiate between different (sub-)phases of regime functioning and consequences. This is the logic behind having joint commitments as a dependent variable. International institutions may first affect the stringency of joint commitments due to changes in the institutional procedures. In turn, joint commitments can affect actor behaviour and domestic implementation.

With the above considerations and delimitations in mind, we may say that international environmental institutions may serve at least three different functions: a) promote cooperative environments; b) integrate and aggregate actor interests and preferences; c) constrain actors' behaviour. The main argument here is that these functions are taken care of by different hard and soft law institutions operating in the same issue-area. The following discussion concerns collective problems that have an element of asymmetrical interests and preferences. The challenge of developing joint commitments that are implemented is greatest concerning such problems.

Cooperative environments: specific and diffuse reciprocity Various authors have emphasized the importance of cooperative environments in handling collective choice situations. (Underdal 1990; Haas, Keohane and Levy 1993; Levy, Young and Zürn 1995.) Cooperative environments provide the actors with opportunities to adopt and pursue a constructive approach to the making and implementation of joint commitments, for instance through sharing information and hampering cheating. We will now try to go one step further and examine the consequences of different institutional factors for the evolvement of cooperative environments, and the consequences of different types of cooperative environments for collective action and individual behaviour. Hence, the specific questions here are how institutions can affect the evolvement of cooperative environments, and what consequences are likely to result from different cooperative environments. What, then, is meant by 'cooperative environments'? In international environmental politics characterized by absence of a common government, *reciprocity* emerges as an effective strategy for maintaining cooperation among states. Reciprocity may be defined as: 'Exchanges of roughly equivalent values in which the actions of each party are contingent on the prior actions of the others in such a way that good is returned for good, and bad for bad' (Keohane 1986: 8).

Such reciprocity may be *specific* or *diffuse*. Specific reciprocity is based on rational self-interest. Diffuse reciprocity is in addition based on common norms of cooperative behaviour. Such norms may express the actors' conceptions of their self-interest, but their conceptions of self-interest must be broad and their confidence in the good faith of others fairly great (Keohane 1986: 25). Accordingly, diffuse reciprocity is related to the existence of some cooperative norms of obligation. Specific reciprocity may lead to diffuse reciprocity, and vice versa. For example, if the same representatives meet year after year in the same forum, confidence may increase. Conversely, if some exploit this confidence, the process may be reversed. The general assumption is that the larger the element of diffuse reciprocity, the more cooperative will the environments be. However, this does not necessarily imply that diffuse reciprocity is more 'effective' in the sense of producing more stringent commitments and more compliance. On the contrary, specific and diffuse reciprocity may serve different functions that may be equally important.

The likelihood of developing specific reciprocity is closely related to actor qualities, while the evolvement of diffuse reciprocity is closely related to institutional factors. Specific reciprocity depends on: a) whether the actors have interests in common; b) the 'shadow of the future'; c) the number of actors (Axelrod and Keohane 1986). According to Keohane (1986: 25), diffuse reciprocity depends on the 'strength' of institutions. However, we do not know exactly which institutional factors may foster diffuse reciprocity, or how they may do so. Against this backdrop, I will indicate some institutional factors that may increase the likelihood of developing diffuse reciprocity. These factors can in principle be manipulated by decision-makers and serve as tools in the design of international institutions. However, other factors that are not easily manipulated may also be important. For example, building confidence takes time, and diffuse reciprocity is more likely to evolve in an 'old' institution than in a new one.

Formal cooperative fora and frequent meetings among the parties where actors meet face to face tend to promote strong interpersonal relationships based on mutual understanding and confidence among decision-makers. The level of cooperation may also be important. Civil servants may have better opportunities to develop close personal ties than ministers and heads of state, since politically appointed representatives come and go as governments change. The presence of 'systemic actors' tends to increase stability. By systemic actors we mean permanent administrative or scientific bodies with an explicit mandate to focus continuously on common challenges. Such bodies may increase stability by stimulating cooperative continuity in between the meetings of the parties. Decision rules requiring unanimity and wider decision-making procedures that stimulate incremental change are also likely to stimulate stability and reduce the likelihood of severe conflict. We would assume that continuity in the sense that yesterday's experience affects today's decisions would point in the direction of incrementality. Conversely, *ad hoc* 'across the table' negotiations will tend to reduce stability and increase conflict. Restrictive procedures for access to 'outsiders' may stimulate both stability and mutual confidence. Low and stable number of state actors and restricted access for non-governmental organizations (NGOs) appear as particularly important in this respect. And finally, the bindingness of rules and procedures may increase mutual expectations of joint conformity with generally accepted standards of behaviour. Moreover, legally binding rules and procedures are more difficult to change, as compared to soft law, and may thus encourage stability in the institutional framework.

This list is by no means exhaustive; some of these factors may be more important than others. However, it does not seem feasible to weight their relative importance at this stage. Instead, I shall suggest an additive index (Table 3.2) where each factor is ascribed equal weight. On the basis of this index, we may assume that the higher the additive score the more likely is the development of cooperative environments. Conversely, the lower the score the less likely is the development of cooperative environments.

The distinction between specific and diffuse reciprocity is a

Table 3.2 *Additive index for cooperative environments*

Institutional factors	*High (1)*	*Low (0)*
Formal fora	Yes	No
Frequency of meetings	Frequent	Less frequent
Systemic actors	Present	Absent
Access	Closed	Open
Bindingness	Binding	Not-binding
Level of cooperation	Low level	Minister/head
Decision-making procedures and rules	Incremental/ unanimity	'Across the table'/ majority

This index has eight values (0–7). Maximum score is seven points and minimum score is zero points.

matter of degree and type, and degree of reciprocity is hard to observe directly. However, one indicator of cooperation 'climate' may at least indicate the extent to which diffuse or specific reciprocity has developed. Cooperation based on specific reciprocity will probably channel the actors' attention towards establishing comprehensive arrangements to monitor compliance, since mutual expectations of identifying any defectors serve as a crucial premise for such reciprocity. If the cooperation is based on good faith there will probably be less need for checking compliance.

The cooperative environment index points towards cooperative behaviour rather than outcomes. However, we may at least indicate some likely consequences of different types of reciprocity, even though it does not seem feasible at this stage to suggest any specific propositions. The main argument to be explored is that these types of reciprocity may actually serve different functions. Accordingly, an 'optimal' way of institutionalization would perhaps involve different (in terms of the index factors) institutions operating in the same issue-area. Cooperation based on specific reciprocity is likely to be unstable, malleable and flexible. Such interaction has the capacity to react swiftly to new challenges, e.g. to new information. Accordingly, there may be a positive relationship between the stringency of joint commitments and specific reciprocity. Its weakness lies first and foremost in securing compliance since flexibility also works the other way around. If there are incentives to defect when joint commitments are to be implemented, there would be good opportunities to do so at low cost. Diffuse reciprocity points in the opposite direction. Stability, persistence and mutual confidence may provide stimuli to restrict defection in situations where such incentives exist due to the existence of common norms. On the other hand, the incremental nature of such cooperation may impede swift collective action.

Institutional aggregation and integration capacity Crucial to joint decision-making is also the extent to which international institutions may aggregate and integrate actor interests and preferences, as is how they do this (Underdal 1990). However, less attention has been paid to the combined effect of integration and aggregation capacity, not only for the adoption of joint commitments, but also for the likelihood of that such commitments will be implemented. Let us examine how institutional factors may influence aggregation and integration capacity as well as the combined effect of these functions on joint commitments and Level I implementation. The underlying assumption in this section is that how we institutionalize our problem-solving efforts in this respect will make a significant difference to the ability to reach stringent commitments likely to be implemented, regardless of whether diffuse or specific reciprocity has developed.

Institutional factors stimulating *integration* capacity seek primarily to: a) influence the interests and preferences of the parties; b) design politically feasible agreements given the interests of the parties. Hence, the first type seeks primarily to encourage less enthusiastic parties to be more enthusiastic, while the latter type seeks to bypass, or overcome, potentially blocking parties. The first type may be split into two main categories of institutional factors. First, interests may be influenced by the establishment of selective incentives that serve as one motive for collective action (Olson 1965). Certain fringe benefits may persuade a party to support joint commitments that it would otherwise not do. In environmental politics, such benefits may be provided by specific institutional arrangements that increase access to funding, resources, markets and technology (Sand 1991: 221). Second, international environmental cooperation is normally closely related to some form of scientific uncertainty concerning the causes of specific problems, their effects and possible solutions. Accordingly, actors typically enter into a cooperative process without a clear and precise perception of their interests concerning specific proposals for joint action. This is why so much importance has been accorded to the role of knowledge-production processes and the science–politics relationship in international environmental institutions (Skodvin and Underdal 1994). Hence, the basic premise is that science, in some sense, does matter to environmental policy-making and implementation.

As a point of departure, we may distinguish between what we may term 'damage science' and 'abatement science'. Damage science is concerned with diagnosing problems – identifying causes and effects of pollution problems. Abatement science is concerned with identifying possible solutions to such problems. The basic assumption combines the two: it is reasonable to assume that integration capacity will increase when both damage and abatement scientific bodies are established. Any change in the degree of uncertainty and/or consensual knowledge along these dimensions may affect not only the stringency, but also the robustness of joint commitments. It is reasonable to assume that joint commitments based on a sound scientific basis will increase the willingness of the parties to follow through and implement their obligations. The work of Haas (1989; 1990; 1992) on transnational 'epistemic community' networks has been particularly influential within the knowledge-based perspective. A more substantial reason for not including this particular approach is that Haas's study of the Baltic and North Sea cooperation concludes that epistemic communities were all absent (Haas 1993: 178–9).

The second type, i.e. design of politically feasible agreements, is essentially adaptive including various 'fast track' options such as the principle of *differential* obligations and *regionalization* (Sand 1991). By differential obligations we mean simply that there are institutional procedures to treat actors differently according to special circumstances. Regionalization is related to what Sebenius (1983) has termed the adding and subtraction of issues and parties, and can be used to restrict membership and lift the common denominator. Moreover, secretariats may be important for developing integrative solutions (Sandford 1992).

Aggregation capacity is determined largely by *decision rules* and procedures, although the level of negotiations can also be important

(Underdal 1990). Aggregation capacity reaches its maximum in purely hierarchical systems and its minimum in systems requiring unanimity. *Majority procedures* are likely to increase aggregation capacity either through voting or as means of political pressure to ensure agreement. Either way, such procedures are likely to produce 'losers' with minor interests, if any, in following up the commitments. Hence, there is no necessary relationship between high aggregation capacity and incentives to follow through. Summits are sometimes used to forge trade-offs that reach far beyond the authority of low-level officials. Summits are by the nature of their participants (normally ministerial or head of state) more likely to open for high-level politics. High-level representation may magnify pressure at the high governmental level where major policy decisions can be made. Hence, summits may stimulate the use of external political pressure, which in turn may lead to strong free-riding incentives for those who are being pushed.

Table 3.3 *Institutional aggregation and integration capacity: predicted outcomes*[7]

Integration capacity	*Aggregation capacity*	*Stringency of commitments*	*Implementation incentives*
H	H	H	H
H	L	L(+)	H
L	H	H(–)	L
L	L	L	L

The combination of integration and aggregation capacity is likely to affect both the probabilities of reaching joint commitments as well as the incentives to implement such commitments (Table 3.3). The central assumption here is that having relative *balance* between integration and aggregation capacity is crucial to ensure the adoption of joint commitments, as well as of incentives to implement them. High aggregation capacity may stimulate the adoption of stringent commitments, but incentives to implement them are likely to be determined by the corresponding integration capacity. Conversely, high integration capacity may affect incentives to implement joint commitments, while aggregation capacity is crucial for reaching common goals. In situations where a majority is willing to go further in terms of stringent commitments than the minority, these considerations point toward the following proposition:

> P_4 High integration and aggregation capacity will lead to stringent commitments and high implementation incentives. Conversely, low integration and aggregation capacity will lead to lenient commitments and low implementation incentives. Imbalance between aggregation and integration capacity will lead to imbalance between the stringency of joint commitments and implementation.

International commitments: affecting the behaviour of states Several scholars have emphasized that international institutions have the potential to constrain activities and limit discretion (Ruggie 1983; Nollkaemper 1993). However, different views exist as to whether behaviour is influenced by the authoritativeness of the rules, or by the anticipated costs and benefits associated with options available to decision-makers, i.e. that actors defect whenever it is in their interest to do so (Chayes and Chayes 1993). Here, we need to examine the behavioural consequences of changing discretion and constraint, and identify the specific behavioural mechanisms at work.

Given the existence of cooperative environments and some combination of aggregation and integration capacity, collective outcomes in the form of international commitments are likely to be produced. Such commitments may be characterized along a continuum from *discretion* to *constraint*. Discretion is defined as the degree of freedom an actor has to judge independently whether certain activities are permissible. Constraint is located at the opposite pole. Actors are constrained if the institutional programme does not leave room for actors to decide for themselves whether an activity is permissible (Nollkaemper 1993: 3).

Discretion and constraint may be seen as a function of *strength* and *compliance* control. Strength is determined by legal status and specificity. Legal status centers on whether the commitments are binding within the framework of international law. The fundamental norm of international law is referred to as *pacta sunt servada* (treaties are to be obeyed). Chayes and Chayes (1993: 85–6) argue that such norms exist in international affairs and that a growing body of empirical study and academic analysis supports this view. According to Stokke and Vidas (1996: 23), legitimacy of an international regime can be defined as the persuasive force of its norms. Hence, we assume that legally binding commitments – within the framework of international law – may increase willingness towards implementation simply because they are binding. Specificity determines the extent to which the actors know precisely what to do. Young (1979: 99) refers lack of specificity, i.e. vagueness, as the problem of 'operationality'. Specificity is linked to, but not necessarily determined by, the level of consensus. Due to the technical and scientific complexity of marine pollution and solutions, high specificity does not follow automatically from a high level of agreement.

Compliance control is regarded as a function of verification and enforcement. Verification centres on monitoring of actor performance, while enforcement refers to measures aimed at promoting compliance with international commitments. Verification systems to check that other actors comply with their obligations will make it easier to identify defectors. Credible verification systems increase *transparency* and are likely to stimulate mutual expectations that cheating will be detected and, hence, remove incentives for free-riding. Procedures for dispute settlement may check whether states remain within the intended scope of discretion. Enforcement systems may provide additional incentives for states to comply with their obligations. Such systems may be of two kinds. First, they may make desired behaviour less costly when obligations are to be implemented. The other possibility is negative, aiming at making undesirable behaviour more costly. As we have seen, such systems are normally, but not necessarily, linked to centralized domestic systems, in contrast to decentralized international systems.

Any propositions concerning the consequences of discretion are sensitive to how implementation is defined. On the one hand, increase in the precision of obligations may increase the probability of defection when goal achievement serves as the point of departure. On the other hand, it is reasonable to assume that increased preciseness will increase the likelihood that corresponding behaviour will go in the right direction according to baseline years. Since I have assumed that providing more behavioural change than strictly required deserves a higher relative score on goal achievement than does providing less, we may suggest the following proposition:

P_5 Reduced discretion will increase the probabilities of implementation, here understood as behavioural change going in the right direction according to baseline years. Moreover, change in behaviour will be due partly to the authoritativeness of commitments.

It is extremely hard to settle empirically the question of which behavioural mechanism that trigger action due to change in discretion since both rational calculations and norms of obligation may be at work simultaneously. The following considerations may at least provide us with some rules of the thumb. As we saw in Chapter 1, norms do not need external sanctions to have an impact on behaviour. If there is a tendency to couple stringent commitments in terms of behavioural change required to non-binding obligations and lenient commitments to binding obligations, this may at least indicate that actors perceive the binding–non-binding dimension as important in itself, given that no real sanctions exist in either case. If it is perceived as less acceptable to breach binding rules than non-binding rules, we would also assume that increased transparency will tend to produce less legally binding commitments, given that incentives to defect exist.

Institutionalization of domestic pollution control

Unlike the case of international institutions, with domestic institutions we will have to change the assumption of lack of a common government. The presence of governments implies authority to solve disputes among affected actors and to enforce regulations. Previous research strongly indicates that governmental regulation represents a crucial factor in changing the behaviour of target groups.[8] Second, the assumption of unity is relaxed in the sense that states are seen as complex organizations. Governments are not in full control over either societies or regulating agencies. Level II implementation depends not only on the configuration of subnational actors' interests, but also on the qualities of relevant domestic institutions.

Analytically, pollution policies can be conceived of as functions of societal demand for environmental quality and governmental supply of policies to protect the environment (Underdal 1995: 12). One advantage of this point of departure is its capacity to transcend the 'top-down' and 'bottom-up' discourse in implementation research by combining the two (Sabatier 1986b).[9] Although different types of numerical-democratic electoral systems and corporate political institutions may affect how social demands are channelled, this will not be pursued here.[10] Accordingly, I will focus on the 'strength' in social demands in general. More specifically, the values and attitudes of public opinion toward environmental protection and the role of 'their' agents (like green parties and ENGOs) form the basis of this analysis. We may generally assume that when international commitments are initially incorporated when environmental concerns are 'down' and the implementation process takes place when environmental concerns are on their way 'up', the probabilities for successful implementation are bright.[11] With the opposite situation, we might expect domestic implementation failure due to reduced governmental ambitiousness.

Governmental supply of environmental policy, i.e. ability to affect target-group behaviour, is likely to depend upon the following two factors: a) distribution of competence between regulatory agencies; b) type of policy tools applied. Given that change in outcome is due to governmental intervention, then the adoption of measures and policy tools becomes a necessary condition for behavioural change at the target- group level. In line with the work of Jänicke (1992; 1997), this approach challenges the *convergence* hypothesis that suggests significant differences in environmental policy achievements across countries can no longer be found despite widely varying regulatory arrangements (Knoepfel *et al.* 1987). The convergence hypothesis is based on several comparative environmental policy studies concluding that, although differences in institutional arrangements are more striking than the similarities, institutional arrangements tend to work in the same direction (Lundqvist 1980; Vogel 1986). This observation is traced back to the interplay between different institutional arrangements working in different political, historical and cultural contexts.

Regulatory agencies: distribution of competence The disjunction between the 'holism' of the natural world and the fragmentation of the administrative and organizational relationships for developing and implementing pollution control policy has often been criticized (Weale 1992b: 94). The 'cure' suggested is some version of integrated policy, or pollution control that can penetrate all policy levels and all government agencies involved in its execution (Underdal 1980b; Jänicke 1992). Here we need to look at the consequences of distribution of competence among relevant ministries and agencies.

The basic assumption is that different regulatory actors will tend to perceive pollution problems differently and to apply different decision criteria on such problems. Perceptions and criteria are in turn largely shaped by formal roles for governmental agencies. This assumption is captured by Allison's (1971: 176) aphorism, 'where you stand depends on where you sit'. Thus, if you sit in the Ministry of Agriculture, you will typically emphasize the interests of farmers. Conversely, representatives of the Ministry of Environment will typically put more emphasis on the environmental damage done by agriculture and the long-term costs of no regulatory action. The essence of fragmentation is the distribution of competence between ministries and subordinated regulatory agencies involved in regulating target groups within environmental policy (internally) and across other relevant public policy sectors (externally).

Fragmentation has both a horizontal and a vertical dimension. Horizontal fragmentation centres on the number of governmental agencies involved at each level of government. Vertical fragmentation centres on the number of levels involved, i.e. the distribution of competence among the state, provinces and municipalities. At the municipal level, problems may look very different compared to state level. In particular, what is perceived of as national 'interests' at state level will not necessarily match preferences at regional and municipal level. Likewise, authorities at these levels will not necessarily feel obliged to comply with international commitments in the same way as the government. The potential dilemma between regulatory effectiveness and local democratic accountability may be particularly evident concerning the implementation of national goals linked to international commitments due to the distance between international negotiations and local politics and priorities. Whenever local perceptions of interests deviate from what the government has defined as the 'national interest', local opposition to national goals can be expected. If local opposition goes hand in hand with decentralization of competence in the relevant sector, there is a risk of defection from national goals. In short, the risk of vertical and horizontal disintegration of policies between competent authorities tends to increase with increasing fragmentation of competence.

Note that disintegration takes on a different meaning related to governmental agencies compared to target groups. Vertical disintegration means that the aggregate of lower-level administrative decisions tends to deviate from higher-order policy goals. Horizontal disintegration means that the aggregate of decisions at the same level, but in other affected sectors, tends to deviate more or less systematically from pollution policy goals. Accordingly, we might expect that the adoption of *measures* necessary to implement national goals would become increasingly problematic when horizontal and vertical fragmentation of pollution control increases. Thus, we may assume that:

> P_6 Horizontal and vertical fragmentation within the state apparatus itself or within various levels of government tend to increase disintegration between national goals and the adoption of measures needed to implement relevant goals.

Measures are here defined as the specific activities to be undertaken at target-group level, such as the introduction of Best Environmental Technology in industry sectors, or change in cultivation techniques in the agricultural sector. Measures should not be confused with policy tools, which are means by which measures are implemented.[12]

Policy tools: affecting the behaviour of target groups The next institutional factor to be considered is policy tools. While claiming that: 'instruments embodied in policy and the ideas upon which they rest are as important as the exercise of power and influence that produces policy', Schneider and Ingram (1990: 510) hold that we know little about the choice of policy instruments and their effect. Here we wish not to challenge or refine the extensive literature on policy tools, but rather to see whether and how change and variance in policy tools may shed additional light on change and variance in domestic implementation.

In contrast to international commitments, domestic efforts to affect target groups may be characterized by the set of specific *policy tools* introduced by domestic decision-makers to achieve domestic goals linked to international commitments. The main difference is that international commitments normally seek to establish common or differentiated goals – and sometimes measures – for more than one state, while domestic measures are implemented by policy tools at target-group level. It seems reasonable to assume that some types of policy tools will be more effective than others in changing target-group behaviour. Of particular interest here is the match between tools and the behavioural mechanisms that promote action among target groups. A major finding that has survived the past 20 years of implementation research is that erroneous causal assumptions are often among the most important factors explaining performance gaps in governmental policies (Pressman and Wildavsky 1973). Thus, implementing agencies may behave completely in accordance with the intentions of higher-order policy goals, and adequate measures may be adopted – and yet measures may still fail to secure behavioural change if they are implemented by tools based on an inadequate model of the critical factors that affect behaviour.

Policy tools are here categorized according to behavioural mechanisms. First, we have tools that seek to make desired behaviour less costly, or undesired behaviour more costly, by influencing incentives. Command and control and a wide range of economic tools belong to this category, which is essentially based on the logic of 'sticks' and 'carrots'. Second, we have an increasingly popular set of tools aimed at influencing or stimulating norms of environmental behaviour, based on the principle of shared responsibility. Voluntary agreements and information/advice belong to this category. At the extreme, one may argue that the same measure cannot logically be implemented by coercion and voluntary tools simultaneously. In practice, however, different target-group sectors are made subject to a wide range of different measures that may be, and actually are, implemented by different tools. Hence, since we assume that actors have dual utility functions, including both cost/benefit rationality and norms, we may propose the following:

P_7 A combination of policy tools affecting both cost/benefit incentives and norms of environmentally friendly behaviour for each target-group sector is likely to be most effective in changing target-group behaviour in line with national goals.

Institutional relationship between levels and phases

This section seeks first to combine the analysis of international institutions with domestic politics. Previously, we have focused on the effects of international institutions on states conceived of as unitary actors. In contrast, this perspective is concerned with effects of international institutions on state–society relationships. The underlying assumption is that international institutions have the capacity to affect implementation by affecting the 'rules of the game' between governmental agencies and societal actors. As such, this perspective parallels the 'second image reversed' approach focusing on the international sources of domestic politics, in contrast to the focus on the effects of domestic structures on international relations (Gourevitch 1978; Zürn 1993).

Second, we will focus on the dynamic nature of international institutional influences which has largely been ignored so far. The way in which institutions are designed in an early phase of the co-operation process may be important for later stages. The dynamic element of institutions may lead to path-dependent processes affecting joint commitments and may necessitate, as well as influence, the parties' ability to transform institutions.

International institutions and domestic politics

As Putnam (1988: 427) has noted, it is fruitless to debate whether domestic politics really determines international relations, or the reverse, since the answer is clearly 'both, sometimes'. According to Moravcsik (1993: 9), the challenge is not whether to combine domestic and international explanations, but how. I will focus on how international institutions may affect domestic politics. This will mean relaxing the assumption of states as unitary actors and combining it with the focus on international institutions.

Over the past decade, systematic changes have taken place within the area of marine pollution control, due to the growing importance of transnational marine pollution problems and international institutions. This has increased the relevance of studying the impact of international institutions on domestic relationships. The relevant literature indicates at least three main pathways through which international institutions may affect domestic politics (Cortell and Davis 1996). These pathways are by no means mutually exclusive and may very well coexist. First, international rules and procedures may become institutionalized into the domestic political process by being incorporated in national law. The *legal pathway* has the capacity to affect not only the ambition level of domestic policy, but also the interactions between governmental and societal actors. Second, government officials and societal actors can invoke international political declarations to further their own specific interests in domestic policy debates. The *political pathway* may empower sub-national actors in domestic policy debates. Hence, international institutions or regimes may serve as 'agents of internal realignments' (Levy, Young and Zürn 1995: 307). For example, Haas (1989) concludes that the Mediterranean Action Plan empowered new domestic groups of marine scientists that, in effect, led governments to comply more firmly with international obligations. A third pathway suggested in the literature is that international institutional procedures may become enmeshed domestically through the standard operating procedures of bureaucratic agencies (Young 1989a: 78–9). The *administrative pathway* leads our attention to how international institutional procedures may affect national institutional procedures.

The conditions under which international institutions may affect domestic politics are more difficult to pinpoint at the outset. However, it is reasonable to assume that the likelihood of such influences is strongest in cases where international rules and procedures have been developed prior to domestic rules and procedures or, alternatively, in cases where national rules and procedures are weakly developed. This point of departure can provide us with some ideas as to *how*, *when* and with which *consequences* international institutions may affect domestic politics.

Path dependency and dynamic development

Institutional dynamics – i.e. the development and transformation of international institutions or regimes – is an important topic within the study of international institutions. This strand of analysis focuses on the broad questions concerning why and how institutions are established, how they change, and with which consequences. A dynamic perspective will take us from the narrow institutional 'factor approach' to the broad and comprehensive study of 'The Rise and Fall of International Regimes' (Young 1989a: 81). The question in focus in this section is more narrow, but it belongs to this general approach of institutional dynamics: To what extent and how did the international institutional arrangements originally established in this issue-area change and affect what happened later in the cooperative process? In other words, did the institutions governing the North Sea cooperation constrain or promote subsequent actions due to their initial qualities?

First, we have the notion that institutionalized cooperation gathers momentum through a 'snowball' effect generating positive feedback and facilitating further steps (Andresen *et al.* 1996). According to Young (1989a: 95), international regimes evolve continuously in response to their own inner dynamics. Levy (1993) has labelled such dynamics of international environmental institutions as 'tote-board diplomacy'. According to this perspective, we can expect that, over time joint commitments will become more stringent and governments more ambitious in implementing them. An alternative perspective is based on the economists' 'law of diminishing returns' (Andresen *et al.* 1996). According to this perspective, the first steps are likely to be the 'easy ones' in which marginal benefits clearly exceed marginal costs. Then, when attempts are made to extend the scope of the institution or to tighten up joint commitments, marginal abatement costs will tend to increase and benefits in the form of environmental quality will tend to decrease. For example, according to a rule of thumb applied by industry, costs will remain constant for each 50 per cent cut in discharges. This perspective would suggest that it will become increasingly difficult to step-up joint commitments, and governments will become more reluctant in implementing them over time. A third perspective focuses on the persistence and stability of institutions (Young 1989a; Powell and DiMaggio 1991). According to this perspective, institutionalized cooperation is hard to change especially when collective norms, behavioural regularities and convergent expectations have developed. This perspective would suggest that both joint commitments and governmental responses remain roughly constant and stable over time.

Conclusion

This chapter has sought to design an analytical framework for studying the functioning and consequences of institutions in making and implementing North Sea pollution control. The focus for explanation is joint commitments and domestic implementation – the latter defined as the process of converting international commitments reflecting a formal consensus of governments into domestic goals and behavioural change of target groups over a fairly long time span.

In order to explain change and variance in commitments and implementation, a Rational Actor model was developed and specified in order to capture the interests and preferences of unitary states as well as sub-national actors. The main purpose of this model lies primarily in its ability to serve as a hypothesis we wish to refute concerning what would have happened in the absence of institutional change and variance. This may help us to identify situations where joint and individual behaviour do not match the expectations derived from this model. However, identification of such situations is clearly insufficient for us to conclude that institutions have caused any mismatch. In order to show how institutions matter, we also developed an Institutional model. The basic idea underlying this model is that environmental institutions may serve different functions through specific institutional factors that may affect both rationality and norms as basic behavioural mechanisms. In short, the key to understand institutional impact lies in the functioning of different institutions in the same issue-area. In the last section of this chapter, I brought the Institutional model further by introducing the dynamic element of institutional 'path dependency' and by briefly indicating how international institutions may affect domestic environmental politics.

We can now progress to Chapter 4, where we seek to uncover change and variance in joint commitments and domestic implementation.

Notes

1 The requirement of agreement does not necessarily imply agreement between all relevant parties on all relevant issues. Thus, it makes perfectly sense to study implementation of joint commitments agreed upon by a sub-set of the parties. Conversely, it does not make much sense to study domestic implementation in country X if that country has explicitly reserved its position.

2 The famous report of the UN-established World Commission on Environment and Development (1987), *Our Common Future*, both diagnosed global threats and proposed various 'cures'. However, despite the Commission's broad global representation at high political level, its conclusions failed to represent any intergovernmental consensus because the members served on the Commission in their individual capacities.

3 First, we have the notion of the Pareto frontier that is reached when no further benefits to one party can be obtained without thereby leaving other prospective partners(s) worse off. According to Underdal (1992),

this option is less attractive for purposes of empirical research than in abstract reasoning. Second, the match between consensual and independent scientific advice and achievements can be assessed. The main problem here is that scientific advice rarely stands up to these requirements. The third alternative is based on criteria taken from the researcher's own value preferences, such as fairness. This approach could easily lead to a conclusion of implementation failure despite perfect goal achievement.

4 See Elster (1978), Fearon (1991), Dessler (1992) and Biersteker (1993) for various discussions of advantages and disadvantages with counterfactual hypothesis.

5 High uncertainty exists concerning marginal costs and benefits, so we will have to undertake the following modifications to develop empirical testable propositions: first, the ambition concerning level of measurement is reduced from cardinal to ordinal level; second, damage costs are operationalized as affectedness of pollution; third, data will be used reflecting the state of knowledge at the time decisions were made; fourth, data will be preferred related to both the 'objective' and the 'subjective' (i.e. how the situation is perceived) decision situation.

6 External in this respect means external to the issue-area covered by the agreement and/or parties that are not members to an agreement. It is problematic to include this dimension in empirical studies since one would have to include a potentially infinite number of other issue-areas and actors.

7 The (+) and (-) signs are added to Table 3.3 to indicate that integration capacity is assumed to have a certain influence on stringency of commitments.

8 See Jänicke (1997) for a review of previous studies emphasizing the importance of governmental regulation.

9 See Andresen, Skjærseth and Wettestad (1995) for a review of implementation research with particular relevance for environmental policy. Despite some lessons to be drawn from over 20 years of public policy research, the authors conclude that the field is diverse and characterized by conflicting approaches and lack of cumulative knowledge.

10 For an account of how different electoral and corporate institutions have affected the channelling of social demands in Norway, the Netherlands and the UK, see Skjærseth (1999).

11 See Inglehart (1971) and Downs (1972) for two different views on fluctuations in environmental values and attitudes.

12 In practice, however, the distinction between measures and tools is not always clear-cut. Sometimes policy tools are applied to reach a specific goal, leaving the choice of measures to the target groups themselves.

4

Linking joint commitments and domestic implementation

The world is full of political statements that are never realized – a phenomenon well known from international diplomatic conferences. To what extent and how have the international commitments covering the North Sea developed in terms of stringency? And, have the North Sea commitments generated any substance at the national level? These questions form the core of this chapter, which will focus on the development and implementation of international commitments from the mid-1970s and up to 1995.

Development of international commitments

Two phases may be distinguished in the development of international commitments within the North Sea cooperation. From the mid-1970s to the mid-1980s, international commitments were developed within the framework of the Oslo and Paris Commissions as well as the EC. With some exceptions, the parties did not succeed in adopting prescriptions for action aimed at significant behavioural change in this period. In the second decade, the International North Sea Conferences took over as the goal-producing engine. This led to a fundamental change in international commitments in terms of stringency. Moreover, an increase in the depth of the commitments can also be witnessed. The 1984 Bremen Declaration was directed at international implementation. The 1987 London Declaration was mainly directed at domestic implementation, while the 1990 Hague Declaration and relevant EC Directives included commitments directed at specific domestic sectors.

The first decade: low activity and lenient commitments

The Oslo Dumping Convention was signed by all 13 West European maritime states in 1972. The main objective of the Oslo Convention is to take all possible steps to prevent pollution of the sea by substances liable to create hazards to human health, harm living resources and marine life, damage amenities or interfere with other legitimate users of the sea. Membership is restricted to European states, but others may be invited to participate. As of 1995, 13 Parties are members; there are no signatories without ratification or accession. Geographically, the Convention covers the North-East Atlantic and the North Sea including the high seas, territorial seas and internal coastal waters. The Convention is structured around a black–grey annex system. Dumping of substances listed in Annex I (black list) is entirely prohibited; dumping of substances in Annex II (grey list) requires a specific permit, whereas other substances (Annex III) require approval from national authorities. Annex IV deals with incineration at sea.

The executive body of the Convention is the Oslo Commission where the parties meet annually. The Commission exercises overall supervision and generally reviews the condition of the sea and the effectiveness of control measures, and decides on other necessary measures. The Oslo Commission has dealt with a wide range of waste problems, the most important being dumping of industrial waste, contaminated sewage sludge and dredge spoil. In 1983, the Oslo Convention was amended to cover incineration of hazardous wastes at sea as well. The Commission may adopt decisions, recommendations and other 'agreements' to draw up programmes and measures for the prevention of pollution. Decisions are regarded as binding within the framework of international law, i.e. they oblige the parties to implement and act in accordance with the decision. Recommendations are prescriptions concerning how the parties should act in certain situations. Other 'agreements' relate mainly to methods and procedures on classification of substances, selection of monitoring areas as well as codes of practices concerning various activities. The Commission agreed at their joint meeting in 1984 that, as a general rule, binding legal decisions were to be preferred to recommendations.

The Oslo Commission held its first meeting in October 1974. The collective result of the ten subsequent years of work does not appear very impressive. Only one decision and two recommendations were adopted. The only commitment made with direct relevance for inputs of Annex I substances was the 1980 recommendation to take all possible steps to reduce at source the contamination of sewage sludge by heavy metals.[1]

The Convention for the Prevention of Marine Pollution from Land-Based Sources was signed in Paris in 1974, and allowed the EC to join as a contracting party. The main objective of the Paris Convention is to take all possible steps to prevent pollution of the sea by adopting, individually and jointly, measures to combat marine pollution, and by harmonizing the parties' policies in this regard. As with the Oslo Convention, membership is restricted; 12 parties including the EC have ratified the Convention. Moreover, also the Paris Convention is structured around a 'black–grey' list system. The Parties are required to implement measures to eliminate pollution by substances in the 'black list', and to reduce or eliminate pollution by substances in the 'grey' list. The Convention originally applied to watercourses from the coast, but was in 1986, amended to include atmospheric sources as well. The Paris Commission shall exercise overall supervision of implementation of the Convention. In addition to the separate annual meetings of the Oslo and Paris Commissions, joint meetings of the two commissions have focused mainly on procedural matters relevant to both commissions.

The Paris Commission held its first official meeting in November 1978, although an interim Paris Commission had been in place since 1974.[2] Compared to the Oslo Commission, a somewhat higher level of activity can be observed within the Paris Commission. The Parties took action of some kind or other at all meetings. Two recommendations were adopted aimed at phasing out aldrin, dieldrin, endrin (drins) and polychlorinated biphenyls (PCBs) and polychlorinated triphenyls (PCTs), all of which are Annex 1 substances. Many of the remaining decisions and recommendations were aimed at two other Annex 1 substances: mercury and cadmium. However, the recommendations and decisions must be characterized as vague, since they were not linked to any timetable or baseline. For example, the drins were to be phased out as soon as substitutes were available, while PCBs and PCTs should be phased out in new equipment as soon as possible. Cadmium discharges were not made subject to any specific goals, while legally binding limit values were adopted for mercury.

The EC Commission is a member of the Paris Commission together with a number of individual EC member-states. Overlapping membership created problems of competence in the Paris Commission, especially in the early 1980s. The Paris Commission tried in 1985 to clarify the extent of Community competence, to which the EC responded by a general and not very helpful declaration stating that the distribution of competence between the EC and its member-states was an internal Community matter (Prat 1990: 107).

Water policy was the first sub-sector developed under EC environmental policy. Up to 1990, 27 items of EC water legislation had been passed; it has even been argued that EC water legislation today constitutes a more comprehensive framework than national systems of water regulation (Richardson 1994: 145). However, the EC did not succeed in adopting a dumping directive, even though the first proposal had been submitted to the Council as early as in 1976 (Suman 1991). The 1957 Treaty of Rome, which established the European Economic Community (EEC), did not include any explicit reference to environmental protection. However, a generous reading of Article 2 and 36 made it possible for the EEC to base their environment policy on Articles 100 and 235 of the Treaty of Rome.

The most significant directive concerned with water and marine pollution was the 1976 Directive on Pollution Caused by the Emission of Certain Dangerous Substances into the Aquatic Environment of the Community, the so-called *Dangerous Substance* Directive, which covers inland, coastal, and territorial waters. Like the Oslo and Paris Conventions, the Directive is structured around two lists, with List I substances generally more dangerous than List II substances. In 1982, a list of 129 candidate substances for inclusion in List I was adopted. The specific substances are to be controlled by subsidiary Directives. The first subsidiary Directive, adopted in 1982, concerned mercury from the chlor-alkali industry and covered roughly the same activities as various Decisions adopted in the Paris Commission in 1980, 1981 and 1982. Up until 1985, two other hazardous substances had been addressed, including cadmium.

In addition, the 1979 Directive for the Protection of Shellfish Waters and the 1976 Directive for Bathing Waters were of some significance for marine pollution. Still, the environmental policy of the EC did not gain a firm legal basis until the Single European Act was adopted in 1986. Another initiative taken through the EC in the early 1980s was perhaps to become more important for North Sea pollution than the specific Directives adopted. The German initiative to convene a North Sea conference was prepared through the EC system.

The second decade: towards stringent commitments
By the early 1980s there were growing indications that specific regions in the North Sea were becoming severely polluted. At international level, neither the work of the OSPARCOM or the EC suggested that stringent commitments could be initiated without additional political impetus. As we have seen, the Oslo Commission went at idling speed and the Paris Commission had addressed only a few hazardous substances. Of the 129 candidate substances for inclusion in List I of the EC Dangerous Substance Directive, three substances were made subject to specific Directives. Against this backdrop of inertia, Germany took the initiative to arrange the first INSC at ministerial level in Bremen in 1984. This conference was followed up in London 1987, The Hague 1990, in Copenhagen 1993 and in Esbjerg (Denmark) 1995.

The 1984 Bremen Declaration The first International North Sea Conference (INSC) took place in Bremen, 31 October–1 November 1984.[2] The aim of the Conference was not to create a new set of international agreements, but to provide political impetus for intensifying the work of the existing international bodies. References to OSPARCOM and the EC are sprinkled throughout the Declaration, which was not perceived as a binding international agreement. Moreover, the Bremen Conference was to examine *all* polluting sources. Ministers of the eight North Sea Coastal States – Belgium, Germany, France, the Netherlands, Norway, Sweden, Denmark and the UK – met, as did representatives from the EC Commission. However, the Bremen Declaration did not significantly strengthen international commitments. The elasticity of such concepts as 'as far as possible', 'practicable' and 'economically feasible' meant that the Declaration contained hardly any substantive commitments (Pallemaerts 1992: 6). On the other hand, the Bremen Declaration was probably the first international text to hint at the *precautionary principle by* stressing that the coastal states must not wait for proof of harmful effects before taking action. The Bremen Conference had initially been envisaged as a unique event, but the Ministers welcomed an invitation of the UK to host a second INSC to review implementation and adopt further measures.

The 1987 London Declaration Particularly with respect to dumping at sea, the London Declaration represented a turning point in stringency compared to the Bremen Declaration as well as OSCOM and the EC. For the first time, it was decided to impose significant targets on dumping and incineration at sea within fixed time-limits. Commitments covering land-based sources were made subject to similar targets. Eutrophication was included for the first time, and ambitious goals were agreed upon concerning phosphorus and nitrogen substances. In effect, the agricultural sector was affected by joint commitments. The commitments made with regard to hazardous substances also appear quite specific at first glance. However, the Ministers failed to agree on specific substances beyond those already covered by international commitments. In contrast to the Bremen Declaration, the London Declaration focused directly at domestic implementation by requiring the preparation of national action plans on implementation.

The key elements of the 16 sections of the London Declaration related to dumping, incineration and land-based sources were as follows: a) a substantial reduction (of the order of 50 per cent) between 1985 and 1995 in the total inputs to the North Sea via rivers and estuaries of substances that are persistent, toxic and liable to bioaccumulate (hazardous substances); b) a substantial reduction (of the order of 50 per cent) between 1985 and 1995 in inputs of phosphorus and nitrogen to those areas of the North Sea where such inputs are likely, directly or indirectly, to cause pollution (sensitive areas); c) to phase out the dumping of industrial wastes in the North Sea by 31 December 1989 and to reduce the use of marine incineration by not less than 65 per cent by 1 January 1991 and to phase out practice totally by 31 December 1994.

The 1987 London Declaration was also the first international environmental text ever to incorporate explicitly the principle of precautionary action (Cameron 1994: 267), a principle which was to become very important for the North Sea cooperation. In addition, the Declaration included an obligation to establish a North Sea Task Force (NSTF) to enhance scientific knowledge and understanding of the North Sea.

The 1990 Hague Declaration The Hague Conference clarified and strengthened the London Declaration particularly concerning land-based sources. With regard to hazardous substances, the aim of reducing discharges before the year 2000 of such substances to levels not *harmful to man or nature* was adopted for the first time, as a principle in Article 1. Against this backdrop, a list of 36 hazardous substances was adopted and directly linked to the 50 per cent reduction target concerning hazardous substances. With regard to nutrients, measures in the municipal, industrial and agricultural sectors were agreed upon, the most specific covering the municipal sector. Targets aimed at 70 per cent reduction of land-based and atmospheric inputs were adopted for the most dangerous substances – dioxines, cadmium, mercury and lead. The termination date for marine incineration was also brought forward to 31 December 1991. Some new obligations were also adopted at the Hague Conference. Agreement was reached on phasing out and destroying PCBs and hazardous PCB substitutes by 1999 at the latest.

From The Hague via Copenhagen to Esbjerg At The Hague Conference, it became clear that most countries would face problems in achieving the targets set for nutrients and pesticides. These concerns, among other things, led to an intermediate ministerial meeting (IMM-93) as a preparatory conference to the 1995 Esbjerg Conference. For the first time, Ministers of Agriculture were invited to discuss common measures on nutrients and pesticides. The 1995 Esbjerg Conference identified previously adopted EC Directives and regulations as the principal measures for attaining certain goals of the various Declarations. While this indicates important changes in EC marine and water policy, it also reflects the fact that Norway and Switzerland were the only non-EC countries of the North Sea conference parties in 1995. The commitments adopted on hazardous substances in 1995 may stand as a symbol of the significant change in the 'amount' of behavioural change required from the 1970s to the present. In the mid-1980s, only a few substances were under international regulation and even fewer were made subject to elimination. Only, ten years later, the Ministers were agreeing to prevent the pollution of the North Sea by phasing out all hazardous substances: 'by continuously reducing discharges, emissions and losses of hazardous substances thereby moving towards the target of their cessation within one generation (25 years) with the ultimate aim of concentrations in the environment near background values for naturally occurring substances and close to zero concentrations for man-made synthetic substances'.[3]

As we have seen, the 1984 Bremen Conference had initially been intended to be a unique event. In this context, we should also note that the 1995 Conference decided to make its *ad hoc* institutional structure more permanent by establishing a permanent Committee of North Sea Senior Officials. The next North Sea Conference is scheduled to be held in Norway in 2002.

International implementation

The INSC process also systematically introduced 'soft law' that was not legally binding for the parties. Since ministers come and go as governments change, the Declarations clearly carried the potential risk of ending up as 'paper tigers'. Below, we shall see how this was avoided. The direct consequences of international implementation of the North Sea Declarations would be twofold. First, the North Sea Declarations would be transformed into legally binding commitments within the framework of international law in the form of OSPARCOM Decisions and EC Directives or Decisions. Second, the geographical coverage of the Declarations would be extended to the EC area and/or the North-East Atlantic area. The specific pathways through which international implementation occurred can be understood in the light of a deliberate effort to link the activities of different institutions. As we have seen, the INSC addressed issues and adopted commitments explicitly aimed at subsequent action within – to paraphrase the Declarations – 'other competent bodies'. The key to understanding how this worked lies in (partly) overlapping participation. The OSPARCOM were not invited to participate in the preparatory work of the INSCs, although they participated as observers. The Secretariat, acting on behalf of OSPARCOM, responded to the Declarations by preparing documents on the implications of the Declarations for OSPARCOM jointly, as well as the Oslo and Paris Commissions separately. The link between the EC and INSC was even closer in the sense that the EC Commission was a party to the INSC.

The Bremen Declaration aimed specifically at international implementation. However, it did not succeed in speeding up the work of OSPARCOM. The main official conclusion on the implementation of the Bremen Declaration presented at the 1987 Conference was: 'In broad terms it is clear that there has been some action at both national and international level on all these fronts since autumn of 1984, but progress has been uneven, and implementation of the Declaration remains incomplete.'[4] However, the Secretariat prepared documents on the implications of the Bremen Declarations in 1985 as well as progress reports on the implementation of the requirements in 1986. These documents support the official evaluation since implications were vague and action was accordingly minor (Skjærseth 1999).

The cooperative process within OSPARCOM in the wake of the 1987 Conference followed the same path as after the Bremen Conference. However, the second INSC was given higher priority than the first. The London Declaration made its strongest impact on the Oslo Commission. The Oslo Commission achieved significantly more from 1987 to 1990 than it had from 1974 to 1987. The first decision adopted by OSCOM in 1988 stated that the riparian states of the North Sea would apply the principles on the reduction and cessation of dumping of polluting materials as set out in the North Sea Conference Declaration. The aim of previously regulations adopted by the Commission was changed from control to termination of dumping and incineration operations. This represented a fundamental change in dumping policies. The precautionary principle turned the burden of proof upside down through a new Prior Justification Procedure, as potential dumpers were now obliged to prove that substances could not harm the environment.

There was also a closer match between the London Declaration and PARCOM decisions and recommendations than before. The parties adopted several 'new' commitments including a recommendation on the reduction of inputs of nutrients in 1988 and a coordinated programme for the reduction of nutrients in 1989. Moreover, three recommendations on Best Available Technology (BAT) were adopted, as well as one recommendation on the principle of precautionary action. EC responses to the 1987 conference related mainly to inputs of nutrients. In 1988, the Council adopted a resolution specifically related to the protection of the North Sea, requesting the Commission to take two specific actions. First, the Commission was requested to combat nutrients from different sources, particularly agriculture. Second, the Commission was requested to present proposals on urban waste water treatment. The

Nitrates and the Urban Waste Water Directives were adopted in 1991 and they were to become the major means of combating eutrophication.

The Hague Declaration made its strongest impact on the Paris Commission. A total of 23 recommendations and five decisions were adopted during 1991–93, as compared to 12 recommendations and eight decisions from 1974 to 1984. On the basis of the list of hazardous substances adopted at The Hague Conference, the Paris Commission started systematically addressing discharges from specific industrial sectors. Many of the decisions and recommendations were adopted during the 1992 ministerial meeting of the Oslo and Paris Commissions. In September 1992, the Ministers representing the parties to the Oslo and Paris Conventions, as well as Luxembourg and Switzerland, met in Paris to sign a new convention for the protection of the marine environment of the North-East Atlantic. This new Convention mainly codified achievements of the Oslo and Paris Conventions and to a more limited extent the Declarations of the INSCs. The main achievements were the prohibition of dumping of industrial waste, sewage sludge and incineration at sea. With regard to land-based sources, the precautionary principle and BAT have been included. Other new principles included were sustainable management and the polluter-pays principle. The new Paris Convention known as OSPAR, (but here referred to as the new Paris Convention) has been ratified by all of the signatories to the Oslo and Paris Conventions and entered into force in March 1998. However, the new Convention took effect immediately in the sense that the Oslo and Paris Commissions were merged in practice. One important reason for this change was the fact that the Oslo Dumping Convention had in many ways rendered itself superfluous by ceasing the activities it had been established to control.

Two important EC Directives were adopted in 1991 based on the initiatives in the late 1980s. Besides being important for the North Sea, the Nitrates and the Urban Waste Water Directives reflected a slightly different approach as compared to previous directives. Like the North Sea commitments, the new directives attack the sources of pollution and describe clear goals within time frames, while relying less on quality objectives (Richardson 1994: 150). The Urban Waste Water Directive sets specific requirements on waste-water collecting systems to be implemented by the year 2000 or 2005 concerning nutrient discharges. This Directive also introduces a ban on the dumping of sewage sludge from the end of 1998. The Nitrate Directive aims at supplementing the above directive by specifically addressing nutrient emissions from the agricultural sector. The agricultural sector was also made subject to a regulation on environmental friendly production methods in 1992. These commitments overlap both the INSC Declarations as well as OSPARCOM commitments.

Joint commitments: concluding remarks

Commitments of the North Sea regime have grown in stringency especially during the last decade. The amount of behavioural change required has increased significantly, from rather general prescription covering only a few substances towards joint obligations on significant reductions of a wide range of hazardous substances and nutrients. Joint commitments have also become more specific, with baseline years and time frames. Moreover, the legal nature of many commitments has changed through the process of international implementation. Today, commitments adopted affect a wide range of sectors of the participating states. With regard to domestic implementation, we will further examine the following joint obligations covered by clusters of different commitments:

- to phase out dumping and incineration at sea;
- to reduce emissions of nutrients to sensitive areas in the order of 50 per cent between 1985 and 1995;
- to reduce emissions of 36 specified land-based hazardous substances to water by 50 per cent between 1985 and 1995.

The change in commitments took place via different pathways. Of major importance was the North Sea Conference process that speeded up work and strengthened commitments within the framework of existing Conventions through a process of international implementation. Even though the 1984 Bremen Conference had this as its primary goal, the breakthrough on dumping came with the 1987 Conference, while the 1990 Conference made its strongest impact on land-based sources. The EC followed up in 1991 with two new Directives. Hence, the North Sea Conferences and the political Declarations triggered a process which significantly strengthened the joint commitments on water and marine pollution. The next section aims at assessing to what extent these commitments have been implemented at the domestic level.

Domestic implementation

It has been suggested that the vertical pathway, in which action is initiated at the international level and implemented downwards, hardly works, easily ending up as verbal declarations (Jänicke 1992: 88). In this section we shall see that the North Sea commitments have generated significant, although varying, substance at national level in Norway, the Netherlands and the UK. First, the international commitments have generally been incorporated into national water and marine pollution policy plans (Level I). Second, there is a general match between actual behavioural change and the national goals following from international commitments (Level II). Together, Level I and II implementation constitute the core elements of the implementation of international commitments, which we have previously defined as the process of converting international commitments reflecting a formal agreement of governments into domestic goals and behavioural change in target groups.

Norway: high ambitions, significant achievements

Norwegian legislation on water pollution may be traced back to an Act of 1970. This was the Water Pollution Act, which formed the basis for various regulations and guidelines directed towards municipal sewage, agriculture and industry. The Water Pollution Act was later replaced by the Pollution Control Act of 1981, covering pollution of air, water and ground. In Norway, sea-dumping of industrial waste and sewage sludge has never been viewed as a viable disposal option. However, Norway did deliver waste for incineration at sea up to 1989.

Up until the second half of the 1980s, Norway did not consider the Paris Commission as particularly important, and international commitments did not significantly affect Norway's water and marine pollution policy. Domestic vulnerability due to national causes and sources was the major motivating factor behind the comprehensive first-generation action programme launched by the government in the mid-1970s.[5] Ten years later, the government produced a White Paper on water pollution in which only one page was devoted to international cooperation.[6] The measures adopted between 1975 and 1985 were described as 'partly successful'. Industry seems to have been most successful in reducing inputs of hazardous substances. For example, inputs of heavy metals were reduced by 70-90 per cent. Moreover, local eutrophication problems were reduced due to investments in municipal treatment plants. Measures in the agricultural sector had been taken on point sources only (silos, spreading and storage of manure). This was perceived as quite unsatisfactory, and the government went on to state that agriculture stands out more and more as a significant source of water pollution. Additional measures were proposed for all three sectors. From this White Paper we can see that Norwegian efforts to combat land-based sources of water and marine pollution were mainly motivated by domestic concerns; international obligations affected these efforts only to a minor extent.

The turning point in the link between international commitments and national policy came shortly after the 1987 London Conference. In the wake of the 1987 and 1990 Conferences, international commitments on land-based sources began to have an influence on national policy programmes and goals. After the 1987 Conference, international obligations were included at the Nordic level as well as in domestic policies. In the 1988-89 White Paper prepared by the Ministry of the Environment, the international commitments on nutrients and hazardous substances were adopted.[7] After the 1990 Conference, specific measures were incorporated in domestic programmes in order to enable Norway to reach both national goals and international commitments. In a 1991-92 White Paper, the government focused exclusively on the implementation of The Hague Declaration.[8] With regard to hazardous substances, the chief effect has been the inclusion of additional substances in domestic plans. In the municipal sector, international obligations have speeded up existing national plans. Measures in the agricultural sector have to a significant extent been motivated by international commitments.[9] According to the OECD (1993: 49), water pollution control in Norway is: 'dominated by the requirements of the North Sea Declarations agreed by all North Sea countries'. In essence, Norway has increasingly incorporated international commitments into national policy. The major turning point came in the wake of the 1987 Declaration.

Concerning Level II implementation, Norway stands out as the only country to have achieved the targets for all heavy metal and organic hazardous substances. There has actually been a high degree of over-achievement in relation to the 50 per cent targets. Concerning the eight heavy metals included in the 1990 Hague List, the average reduction from point sources has been 87 per cent between 1985 and 1995.[10] Most of these discharges are caused by the industrial sector. Data on pesticide *use* show that reductions have been below 50 per cent for two substances, while the use of four substances has been reduced by 100 per cent between 1985 and 1995.[11] The OECD concluded that good progress had been made in reducing discharges of hazardous substances (OECD 1993: 54). Quantities of waste delivered in port of loading for incineration at sea increased between 1986 and 1988, before this practice was finally terminated in 1989.[12]

The latest comparable data on nutrients are from 1992. These data include reductions between 1985 and 1990 and expected reductions up to 1995. The most important sectors causing nutrient discharges are agriculture and municipal waste water. Between 1985 and 1995, estimated reductions amount to 50 per cent for phosphorus substances and 40 per cent for nitrogenous substances.[13] While estimates as to reductions in phosphorus substances proved roughly correct, expectations as to decreases in nitrogen were too optimistic. Actual reductions of nitrogen have lagged far behind the 1992 estimates and the 50 per cent reduction target. Between 1985 and 1994, only about 20 per cent reduction in discharges to sensitive areas was achieved.[14] There are two main reasons for this situation. First, reductions in the agricultural sector lag far behind both national goals and international obligations. According to the government, 44 per cent reductions were to be achieved by 1995, while actual achievements were 19 per cent in 1994–95. Second, nitrogen removal facilities were not installed as planned in the municipal sector. Still, the North Sea commitments had significant impact on both municipal and agricultural sectors.

The government had launched comprehensive programmes in the municipal sector before 1987; the official position has been that measures in the municipal sector would have been introduced in any case in order to realize national goals, although measures would have to be speeded up to some extent in the sensitive are. However, a recurrent problem in Norway has been that action taken by municipalities lags far behind requirements. Thus, the North Sea commitments appear to have had significant impact, as echoed by the OECD (1993: 123): 'While the Government says these investments [in the municipal sector] would have been made even without the North Sea Declarations, the Declarations have had a very positive effect in inducing and accelerating stronger action.'

The link between international commitments and Norway's actions in the agricultural sector appears as strong and direct. Prior to 1987, most measures had been directed towards technical facilities at point sources. According to the government: 'A large proportion of the efforts needed [in the agricultural sector] in the next few years will be linked to the fulfilment of the North Sea agreement by which Norway is committed to reduce discharges of nutrients to sensitive areas with 50 per cent by 1995.'[15] Thus, while actual reductions have been insufficient in the agricultural sector the initiatives taken after 1987 were directly linked to the North Sea commitments. On the one hand, we may conclude that Norway has performed well overall in terms of national goals derived from international commitments. On the other, there are variations across sectors and substances. Norway's industrial sector has been very successful in reducing inputs of hazardous substances as well as in phasing out incineration at sea. By contrast, particularly the agricultural sector, but also in the municipal sector, there have been problems concerning nutrient emissions.

The Netherlands: even more ambitious, varying achievements

As in Norway, the Netherlands' Pollution of Surface Waters Act (PSWA), the first true environmental Act in the country, came into force in 1970. Prior to 1987, Dutch water policy was influenced by international commitments to a greater extent than was the case in Norway. The EC especially was important for the Netherlands concerning water pollution. The Netherlands also dumped industrial waste and incinerated waste at sea within the framework of the Oslo Convention. The 1972 Oslo Dumping Convention was implemented by the Pollution of the Sea Act, which came into force on 1 January 1977. However, most actions taken in the Netherlands were based on domestic concerns and causes.

The Netherlands is renowned for its national planning system, in which the environment has been subject to comprehensive planning. The broad policy lines for water management in general are established in various national policy documents on water management. Policies for the control of surface water quality have been set out in a series of five-year action programmes by the Minister of Transport and Public Works, commencing in 1975. In the first Water

Action programme (1975–79), minimum objectives were set for water quality and emissions.[16] Deadlines for some objectives were imposed by EC Directives, especially related to the quality of bathing water. Even though various EC directives were formally implemented by means of national legislation in this period, they failed to affect Dutch behaviour significantly (Haigh *et al.* 1986). The case of heavy metals illustrates that the Netherlands has also been ahead of PARCOM regulations in this period. Mercury and cadmium were, among other heavy metals, selected as priority substances already in the 1975 plan. In the Paris Commission, the first Decision on limit values for mercury emissions was adopted in 1980 while the first recommendation on cadmium was not adopted until the sixth meeting of the Paris Commission in 1984.

National vulnerability due to domestic discharges prevailed as the principal motivating factor behind the second Water Action programme (1980-84). As in the Norwegian 1984–85 White Paper, only one perfunctory page is devoted to international cooperation and consultation. Notwithstanding the relatively weak relationship between Dutch water policy and international commitments, significant results were achieved in this period. The Dutch action plans focused on industrial discharges and municipal waste water as the prime sources of water pollution, whereas agriculture was completely left out of domestic action programmes. Oxygen-consuming substances in specific industrial sectors were reduced by about two-thirds between 1969 and 1980. According to Andersen (1994: 161), this experience must: 'astonish most implementation researchers, since this ambitious aim was in fact attained'. In addition, many heavy metals were significantly reduced. Discharges of mercury and cadmium were for example reduced from 4.8 and 30 tons per annum in 1975 to 0.41 and 14 in 1980, respectively. However, some industrial sectors made slow progress on lead and zinc as well as some organic substances.[17] In the period from 1975 to 1979, the Dutch government carried out 117 sewage treatment projects. However, this represented only 65 per cent of the public sewage plants foreseen in 1975.

As in Norway, this general picture changed after the 1987 North Sea Declarations as well as the Rhine Action programme, and international commitments were increasingly incorporated into national programmes. The 1987 commitments were included in the 1988–89 Dutch National Environmental Policy Plan (NEPP) presented to the Second Chamber of the Parliament. The 50 per cent target on hazardous substances was adopted, and larger (50–70 per cent) reductions were aimed at by the year 2000 for some of the substances.[18] Moreover, the Netherlands went beyond the requirement of reducing 36 hazardous substances by adopting a national list including 46 priority substances. With regard to nutrients, the 50 per cent target was adopted for the year 1995, and a balance between input and output of nutrients was aimed at by 2000. In sum, the nutrient goals would require a 70–90 per cent reduction in emissions of eutrophying substances. In the wake of the 1990 Declaration, the Dutch North Sea Action Plan was presented. All important goals were adopted and a detailed list was included, designating the regulatory bodies in charge of implementing the various obligations. All relevant sectors in the Netherlands have been affected by international commitments. According to the OECD (1995: 52) the target of the NEPP eutrophication and hazardous substances is derived directly from the North Sea Action Plan's international commitments. In addition to the ambitious percentage reduction goals, the Netherlands has also adopted quite demanding water quality objectives. Moreover, the Netherlands decided to phase out dumping of industrial waste in 1986 before any joint commitments were adopted, and issued its last permit for such dumping in 1987. Thus, the Netherlands rapidly and ambitiously adopted international obligations and generally aimed at national targets that were even more stringent.

With regard to Level II implementation, the results are mixed. Concerning the 50 per cent target on heavy metals to water, the Netherlands failed to reach the target for four out of eight heavy metals. The average aquatic reduction from point sources between 1985 and 1995 has been 51 per cent as compared to Norways' 87 per cent.[19] The OECD (1995) reports that annual average concentration of heavy metals in surface waters has decreased sharply over the past 20 years, but to varying degrees still exceeds water quality objectives at most sampling sites. Of the 12 organic substances included in The Hague list, the Netherlands falls short of the 50 per cent target with regard to five substances. In addition, some pesticides have actually increased in use. Point discharges of organic substances are diminishing, but levels still only partly meet basic water quality standards. However, the Netherlands has phased out the practice of dumping and incinerating industrial waste at sea.

With regard to nutrients, Dutch aggregate achievements roughly parallel those of Norway. Agriculture and municipal waste water represent the main sources of phosphorus and nitrogen inputs. In addition, in the Netherlands industry represents a major source of phosphorus substances. As to the similarities, the problem experienced with the nitrogen target is related to both the municipal and the agricultural sectors. In contrast to Norway, no reductions whatsoever were achieved within the Dutch agricultural sector for both phosphorus and nitrogenous substances between 1985 and 1995.[20] Total phosphate concentrations in surface waters have declined since 1985, but they still exceed Dutch water quality objectives in more than three-quarters of all samples. Nitrogen concentrations have shown less improvement; they exceed limit values at 145 out of 163 measuring points (OECD 1995: 39).

The preceding patterns of outcomes lead us to the following main conclusion: The Netherlands has performed fairly well overall in the sense that inputs of all regulated substances have been reduced, as measured against baseline years. However, there is clearly a mismatch between Level I and Level II implementation, and the Netherlands has – in relative terms – achieved less than Norway although ambitions have been higher. Dumping and incineration at sea have been phased out, but achievements concerning hazardous substances lag somewhat behind international obligations. The Netherlands has experienced significant difficulties in reducing nutrients; here the agricultural sector clearly stand out as least successful, since actual reductions between 1985 and 1995 were nil.

The UK: rising ambitions, rising achievements

In contrast to both Norway and the Netherlands, legislation and policy programmes in the UK lagged behind international obligations until the late 1980s. Unlike Norway and the Netherlands, the UK had no centrally coordinated and national coherent policy on water and marine pollution. In 1973, the UK adopted a Water Act continuing the system of consents established more than two decades earlier. In 1974, ten river-based regional water authorities (RWAs) were created in England and Wales with responsibility for all water management matters, including sewage treatment and pollution control. However, the Secretary of State had no specific powers to set quality objectives that RWAs must apply, but excised the power under the Water Act to give general directions to the RWAs.

It was the 1974 Control of Pollution Act (CPA) that was the principal Act concerned with pollution of water. It required all discharges to inland, coastal and estuarial waters to be subject to a permit or consent. Moreover, the CPA was the main instrument for implementing the Paris Convention. The provisions of the Act were scheduled to be in full operation by 1986, which indicates that the Paris Convention had not been fully implemented by the UK until then. This also means that, under earlier legislation, discharges to coastal waters as well as some discharges to estuaries did not require authorization.

The UK did not publish national plans on water quality in this period. Due to the limited authority of the Secretary of State as well as the late implementation of the CPA, there has been a lack of coordinated national policy on water pollution. However, the 1973 Act imposes a duty on the RWAs to prepare plans for water management in general. Because of the UK's preference for environmental quality standards and objectives rather than uniform emission standards, there are no input data showing actual changes in this period. On the other hand, a series of river quality studies have been carried out in England and Wales since 1970, with a first survey in 1958. The 1985 survey was the first since 1970 to show lengths of river degraded in quality overtaking those that had improved (Kinnersley 1994). The OECD (1994) also noted that a slight deterioration was reported in the 1980s.

Relevant EC Directives had a significant impact on UK water pollution control policy, but did not affect British legislation during this period. Directives served to force RWAs to involve themselves with seawater earlier than they would otherwise have done, consequently bringing pressure to bear for the full implementation of the 1974 Control of Pollution Act (Haigh *et al.* 1986). Like the Netherlands, the UK implemented the Oslo Convention by passing its Dumping at Sea Act in 1974 (replaced by Part II of the Food and Environment Protection Act 1985).

From the 1987 Conference, international commitments were incorporated by so-called 'Guidance Notes', and a North Sea Action Plan was presented in 1990.[21] The main international targets are adopted in these documents, but the guidance notes are vague on governmental responsibilities and measures. The UK's water pollution and dumping policy as well as the institutional set-up changed radically after 1987. A new Water Act was established in 1989 and the National Rivers Authority (NRA) was set up as an independent regulatory authority. In addition, the 1989 Environmental Protection Bill introduced a system of integrated pollution control which will control emissions of dangerous substances to all media. These changes particularly affected discharges of some hazardous substances. Shortly before the 1987 Conference the UK government announced its intention to develop a *new approach* designed to reduce to a minimum inputs of the most dangerous substances. This led to the adoption of the 'Red List' in 1989. Comprehensive surveys were conducted to identify major sources of 'Red List' substances. However, the 'Red List' included only 23 of the 36 substances required. With regard to nutrient emissions, the UK government claims that there are no significant 'sensitive areas' around the UK coast, and it is not clear whether the UK government is bound by the 50 per cent targets. According to the OECD (1994: 154), the UK is committed to far-reaching measures to reach quantitative targets agreed within the Third North Sea Ministerial Declaration. In short, the UK has reluctantly accepted international obligations concerning hazardous substances and dumping and incineration at sea, whereas nutrient obligations have largely been evaded.

Concerning Level II implementation, UK data are not directly comparable with the data reported by the Netherlands and Norway.[22] However, some achievements can be witnessed although they fall short of international requirements. The UK falls short of goal achievement concerning three of the seven heavy metals for which baseline data exist. The OECD (1994: 154) generally confirms the positive trend in discharges and emphasizes the great significance of the INSC commitments, since direct and riverine inputs in 1990 were among the highest among the contracting parties to the Paris Commission.

With regard to discharges of organic substances and pesticides to the water environment, 1985 input estimates are not available and data are insufficient to determine specific reductions. Between 1991 and 1993, a positive trend in reductions has been reported. In recent years, the UK has been the only state to dump sewage sludge in the North Sea. The UK has been responsible for approximately half of all industrial wastes dumped beyond internal waters. However, the quality of the sludge in terms of heavy metal content has improved considerably. Total amount authorized for North Sea disposal of seven heavy metals were reduced from 828 tons in 1987 to 590 tons in 1993.[23] Incineration at sea has been phased out and disposal of solid and liquid industrial waste covered by OSCOM has ended.

The link between international commitments and domestic UK policy has been strongest and most direct with regard to hazardous substances and dumping at sea. The UK's acceptance of uniform emission standards came as a direct response to international commitments, and the 'Red List' was directly linked to the INSC commitments. Moreover, the UK changed its dumping policy – albeit reluctantly – in line with international obligations, and significant reductions have been achieved. Thus, we may conclude that, for the UK, inputs of regulated substances are headed in the right direction.

Change in outcomes and 'unrelated' factors

Significant, although varying, reductions have been achieved by the three countries with regard to substances covered by international commitments and national policy programmes. Let us now see whether these reductions would have been achieved in any case due to factors unrelated to relevant international commitments and related domestic regulation. Several factors may shed light on the reductions and variance witnessed: first, some actions would probably have been taken anyway, despite any international cooperation, due to purely domestic concerns and perceived damages from polluting activities. In all three countries, actions on land-based sources were based mainly on domestic concerns to the mid-1980s, with some intercountry variation particularly due to EC Directives. This picture changed significantly from the first INSC in 1987, and INSC Declarations rapidly became a core feature of the states' efforts to combat land-based sources. The situation concerning dumping and incineration at sea was different, since the Oslo Convention became operational before national legislation had been adopted and the EC did not succeed in adopting a dumping directive. National policy on dumping and incineration at sea has been influenced by the Oslo Convention and the Oslo Commission since the mid-1970s, but has changed in line with land-based sources due to the second INSC in 1987. Thus, national action has been motivated largely by transnational concerns and international cooperation except for the first decade of controlling land-based discharges.

Second, reductions in discharges from specific sectors could be due to reduced production and activity in the sectors concerned. The early 1980s were characterized by changes in the economic climate which affected all North Sea riparian states, although they differed in intensity from one country to another. Many countries experienced recession that affected particularly the older and generally more polluting industries and there were political pressures not to impose overly stringent environmental standards on industry. This situation changed between 1985 and 1995 and reductions in regulated substances took place within a fairly favourable economic context in all three countries (OECD, 1995). With regard to heavy metals, there are two examples of other causes that are not directly linked to environmental policy on water and marine pollution. Reduction of copper in Norway is partly related to abandoned mines, while reduction in arsenic discharges between 1991 and 1993 in the UK is due exclusively to the closure of a large tin smelter on the Humber. Still, most reductions are, in the view of the respective governments, due to deliberate measures in industrial sectors and product control.[24]

A third possibility is the development of new technology that may affect inputs of specific substances. Environmentally friendly technology is being developed continuously, both in relation to environmental policy and sometimes unrelated to such policy. To my knowledge, however, there has not been any major breakthrough in relevant technology since the mid-1980s that may account for the general discharge patterns witnessed. For example, effective sewage treatment technology has been available throughout the relevant time period. However, building sewage treatment plants with a nitrogen removal phase means introducing new purification technology. And indeed, the Norwegian authorities argued that such plants will not be completed in time due to limited experience with this technology. Nevertheless, in Norway the nitrogen removal programme was cancelled for reasons other than lack of technology (cf. Chapter 7 in this volume).

Fourth, the availability of alternative means of disposal may account for variance between sectors and activities. In some cases, inputs to surface water and the marine environment may simply be switched to other media, leading to what I have previously referred to as 'indirect' effects. In other cases, change in production processes and purification systems are needed in order to reduce the amount of waste. The only problem for which any 'easy' switches exist is incineration at sea. Incineration at sea has mainly been switched to incineration on land, or waste production has been reduced. Thus, we see that the availability of alternatives may contribute in understanding why such activities have been phased out by all states according to schedule. Fifth, other international commitments than those included here may cover the same substances and actually account for reductions witnessed. International agreements on ozone-depleting substances have been important for 2 of the 12 organic substances, (carbontetrachloride and trichloroethane). All North Sea states were obliged by the Montreal Protocol to discontinue production, consumption, and import of these two by 1 January 1996.

We may conclude that different unrelated factors may account for a small amount of reduction in inputs since the mid-1980s, especially concerning land-based emissions of hazardous substances. We have noted here the closure of some plants, and the fact that two hazardous substances are covered by other international agreements, in this case the Montreal Protocol. Moreover, the availability of alternative means of disposal may help to explain why incineration at sea has been phased out according to targets. On the other hand, most of the reductions witnessed can be traced back to deliberate control and regulation linked to international commitments within a favourable economic context, albeit without any major technological breakthrough in abatement technology.

Comparison between countries and sectors

International commitments have increasingly influenced the water and marine policies of all three countries, leading to a more ambitious water policy. All three states have explicitly adopted and incorporated international commitments into various domestic plans, including specific North Sea Action Plans. The turning point in Level I implementation came after the 1987 and 1990 International North Sea Declarations, and was not due to commitments adopted within the legally binding OSPARCOM and EC frameworks. These Declarations also became to a significant although varying degree included in OSPARCOM recommendations and decisions as well as EC Directives. However, in some cases, national goals have been more ambitious than the percentage reduction goals agreed upon for nutrients, hazardous substances, and dumping and incineration at sea.

The Netherlands has generally adopted domestic goals and plans that are more ambitious than those internationally required. Thus, the Netherlands appears ambitious in terms of Level I implementation. Norway has generally adopted domestic goals and plans that are in line with international obligations with regard to incineration at sea and nutrients. Thus, intermediate is the most appropriate score. The case of the UK is more problematic. However, we can exclude the ambitious category, as there has been no evidence that the UK has adopted national goals more ambitious than those internationally required. In sum, UK goals have been both in line with and less ambitious than international targets. For example, the dumping commitments were reluctantly adopted, while the UK failed to include all the 36 hazardous substances in its Red List. Thus, the UK can with a fair amount of certainty be categorized as reluctant/intermediate.

Reduction in input of regulated substances is generally headed in the right direction according to baseline year in all three countries. In the Netherlands, achievements for some hazardous substances have been more ambitious than required; phosphorus substances and dumping and incineration at sea have been reduced according to obligations, while with nitrogen and some other hazardous substances there has been less behavioural change than required. Thus, an appropriate score for the Netherlands seems to be intermediate. Since the Netherlands had adopted more ambitious goals than those internationally required, this indicates that there is a mismatch between domestic ambitions and actual achievements.

Even though Norway's ambitions were more modest than those of the Netherlands, Norway scores higher on behavioural change. With regard to hazardous substances, there has actually been a high degree of over-achievement, amounting to over 90 per cent reduction for many substances. Norway has not dumped industrial waste and sewage sludge at sea, and incineration at sea has been phased out in accordance with obligations. Phosphorus substances have also been reduced by 50 per cent, but the achievements of reduction target concerning nitrogen lags behind both national goals and international obligations. Thus, achievements are not fully in line with ambitions, but they clearly exceed ambitions with regard to hazardous substances. All in all, then, Norway may be located somewhere between ambitious and intermediate with regard to actual achievements.

Input data reported by the UK are in many cases insufficient and not directly comparable with those of Norway or the Netherlands due to different calculation methods. With these caveats in mind, we can still judge UK developments with a fair amount of certainty. In relative terms, the UK has achieved less than the Netherlands, especially if nutrients are included. The Netherlands has probably achieved more concerning organic hazardous substances, since all substances were included in the national priority lists. In addition, the Netherlands had apparently achieved more prior to 1985. Since the UK has not yet identified sensitive areas or given priority to nutrient reductions, we can assume that significant reductions have not been achieved after 1990. Thus, given that achievements concerning dumping and incineration at sea were roughly equal, the UK has probably achieved less overall as compared to the Netherlands. This indicates an intermediate/reluctant rating for the UK.

In conclusion then, the patterns in Table 4.1 have emerged concerning Level I and Level II implementation. The preceding sections have strongly indicated significant variations in achievements not only between countries, but also between sectors across countries. The general impression is that the industrial sector has been most 'successful', followed by the municipal sector, whereas the agricultural sector has apparently been least 'successful'. These indications are further supported by cases where the same substances originate from different sectors. Even though nutrient discharges from the agricultural and municipal sectors are more significant as compared to industry, all three sectors have been made subject to regulative efforts in order to reach the 50 per cent reduction targets. Behavioural change has been least significant in the agricultural sector, while the industrial sector has achieved the 50 per cent target con-

Table 4.1 *Level I and II implementation in Norway, the Netherlands and the UK*

	Level I	*Level II*
Netherlands	Ambitious	Intermediate
Norway	Intermediate	Ambitious/intermediate
UK	Intermediate/reluctant	Intermediate/reluctant

cerning both nitrogen and phosphorus. The municipal sector can be placed in between agriculture and industry.[25]

Conclusion

In all three countries, international North Sea commitments have been incorporated in national water and marine pollution policy, but there are significant variations in national policy ambitions. The Netherlands has adopted goals that are more ambitious than those required; Norway's goals have mainly been in line with obligations, while the UK has adopted goals that tend to be less ambitious than those required. However, international commitments and domestic policy must be transformed into behavioural change at target-group level in order to affect inputs of regulated substances. Actual achievements show an overall positive trend compared to baseline year in all three countries. Moreover, the reductions witnessed can only to a limited extent be traced back to factors unrelated to North Sea commitments and national regulation, which in turn indicates that most reductions are due to deliberate governmental intervention. However, actual achievements also vary across countries and sectors. Given the uncertainties involved in calculating inputs to the water and marine environment, we may say that Norway had achieved most significant reductions followed by the Netherlands and the UK. Thus, especially in the case of the Netherlands, there seems to be a significant mismatch between the level of policy ambitions and actual behavioural change provided at the level of target groups. At sector level, industry stands out as most 'successful' in terms of behavioural change, followed by the municipal sector and the agricultural sector.

The patterns identified in this chapter represent the focus for explanation in the following chapters. The first 'model' to be examined is the Unitary Rational Actor model.

Notes

1 For the number and type of decisions and recommendations adopted by the Oslo and Paris Commissions from the mid-1970s to the mid -1990s, see Oslo and Paris Commissions Procedures and Decision Manuals which are updated continuously. London: Secretariat for the Oslo and Paris Commissions.

2 Declarations up to 1990 are included in *Ministerial Declarations* (1995), *Esbjerg Declaration* (1995).
3 *Esbjerg Declaration* (1995: 18).
4 *Progress Report* (1987: 2).
5 Ministry of the Environment (1975).
6 Ministry of the Environment (1985).
7 Ministry of the Environment (1989).
8 Ministry of the Environment (1992).
9 State Pollution Control Agency (1992).
10 *Progress Report* (1995).
11 *Progress Report* (1995), and NOU (1995).
12 Oslo Commission (1990).
13 Oslo and Paris Commissions (1992a).
14 State Pollution Control Agency (1996).
15 Ministry of the Environment (1989: 119).
16 Ministry of Transport and Public Works (1980).
17 Ministry of Transport and Public Works (1980: 32).
18 NEPP (1989).
19 *Progress Report* (1995).
20 *Progress Report* (1995: 94).
21 Department of the Environment (1988); Department of the Environment (1990a); Department of the Environment (1990b).
22 With Regard to heavy metals and organic substances, Norway and the Netherlands have reported Type 2 data (point discharges) and Type 3 data (point discharges + losses from diffuse sources), while the UK has reported Type 1 discharges (riverine inputs and direct discharges to estuaries and coastal areas). See *Progress Report* (1995). I seek to minimize this problem by utilizing data presented also by other international bodies than those directly linked to the North Sea cooperation.
23 Ministry of Agriculture, Fisheries and Food (1995).
24 See *Progress Report* (1995).
25 Oslo and Paris Commissions (1992).

5

The calculus of the core cooperating states

According to the Unitary Rational Actor model, change in the stringency of joint commitments, as well as change and variance in compliance, can be traced back to change and variance in problem-related interests. This perspective sees actions of the states as motivated by costs and benefits; states choose options believed to maximize net gains. Thus, states will accept regulations, only if they expect to reap benefits, and joint commitments will under certain conditions be largely determined by the interests and preferences of the 'least ambitious' actors. Moreover, a state will comply with an agreement it has signed as long as compliance costs remain lower than the costs it would incur by defecting. In addition, compliance is always a matter of choice: there is no such thing as domestic implementation 'failure'. In order to challenge this model seriously, we should ideally be able to identify joint commitments that depart significantly from what would have been adopted on the basis of unilateral action and compliance levels that seem inconvenient with regard to the interests of actors.

I shall restrict the discussion to Norway, the Netherlands and the UK – three states that have all been active participants with significantly different interests in North Sea pollution control. It may indeed be argued that these states are representative of the major groups of interests that have been present in the international cooperation, since they represent the net exporters, net importers and the 'balanced' in terms of exchange rates of marine pollution. In essence, an agreement between these states would in many ways represent an agreement between *all* the North Sea states.

Applying this to the case of transfrontier marine pollution, we need a reference point against which any changes in interests can be compared. In line with Chapter 4, the situation at the end of the first decade, i.e. before the 1987 International North Sea Conference, is taken as the point of departure. Concerning the stringency of joint commitments, I will focus on the 1987 and 1990 North Sea Declarations with regard to both land-based (nutrients and hazardous substances) and ocean-based (dumping and incineration) activities. As previously noted, these obligations have to a significant extent also been adopted by the Oslo and Paris Commissions. Compliance refers to compliance with the 50 per cent targets on land-based sources and the targets aimed at phasing out dumping and incineration at sea adopted at these conferences. Chapter 5 is structured as follows. In the first section, I focus on joint commitments, while the second section centres on incentives for complying with these commitments. The model under scrutiny here is evaluated in the third section, and concluding remarks are presented in the final section.

Expected joint commitments

The stringency of joint commitments will be determined by three factors. First, decision rules and procedures are crucial to aggregate preferences, particularly when problems are 'hard' – i.e. when the interests and preferences of the actors diverge significantly, as in the North Sea cooperation. Some version of agreement represents the most demanding and commonly used decision rule in international politics. Second, coupling or de-coupling of issues could stimulate the adoption of joint commitments that would not otherwise be possible. For example, one actor can be compensated on one issue in return for that actor's compensating to its partners on another issue. If we combine the requirement of agreement among all parties in a given group with a requirement of absence of issue-linkages, i.e. that commitments are considered only on their own merits, collective action will be limited to those measures acceptable to the least enthusiastic party. Thus, the third factor is the actual positions of the parties.

The positions of the parties are in turn conceived of as a function of three determinants. First, abatement costs represent a motivation to avoid stringent regulations as long as they are approached as (short-term) costs. Second, damage costs represent the most important motivation for adopting stringent regulations. Since marine pollution is also a transfrontier pollution problem, the 'balance of pollution exchange' (the rate of 'export' and 'import') is likely to determine the extent to which joint action is advocated. Thus, according to P_1 (see p. 40), we would expect that net-exporters facing low damage costs and high abatement costs are candidates for the position as the least enthusiastic states. International cooperation is risky for exporters since importers will try to persuade them to cut discharges. Conversely, highly affected net importers facing low abatement costs have incentives to advocate stringent joint commitments. For an importer, joint action is crucial since own abatement efforts will be insufficient to reduce damage costs. Those with a balanced exchange rate of pollution facing high damage costs and abatement costs will have incentives to take an intermediate position and to support joint commitments in between the reluctant and the ambitious. Let me commence by analysing the incentives and positions of Norway, the Netherlands and the UK.

Incentives and positions

Norway can be expected to take a quite ambitious position within the North Sea cooperation. Knowledge concerning the direction of the North Sea currents that has been available since the 1970s shows that Norway is clearly a net importer of marine pollution. The counter-clockwise direction of the North Sea currents (Figure 5.1) places Norway downstream to other North Sea states.

Norway became increasingly aware of its role as 'victim' of transnational pollution. We may note the opening speech made by the Norwegian Minister of the Environment at the 1987 North Sea Conference: 'Ocean currents carry pollutants, specially from the southern part of the North Sea into Norwegian waters. This gives us grounds for deep concern.'[1] Pollution of watercourses and the marine environment conflicted with drinking water, water for irrigation purposes, water used by industry, fisheries, fish-farming and recreation interests.

Dumping of industrial waste at sea has not been viewed as a viable disposal option in Norway. Hence, Norway would have virtually nothing to lose and everything to gain from advocating stringent joint commitments concerning dumping. This expectation matches well with Norway's actual position within the Oslo Commission (Skjærseth 1991). Since coping with land-based discharges also involves significant abatement costs, however, the picture becomes more complex. Total investment costs for implementing the North

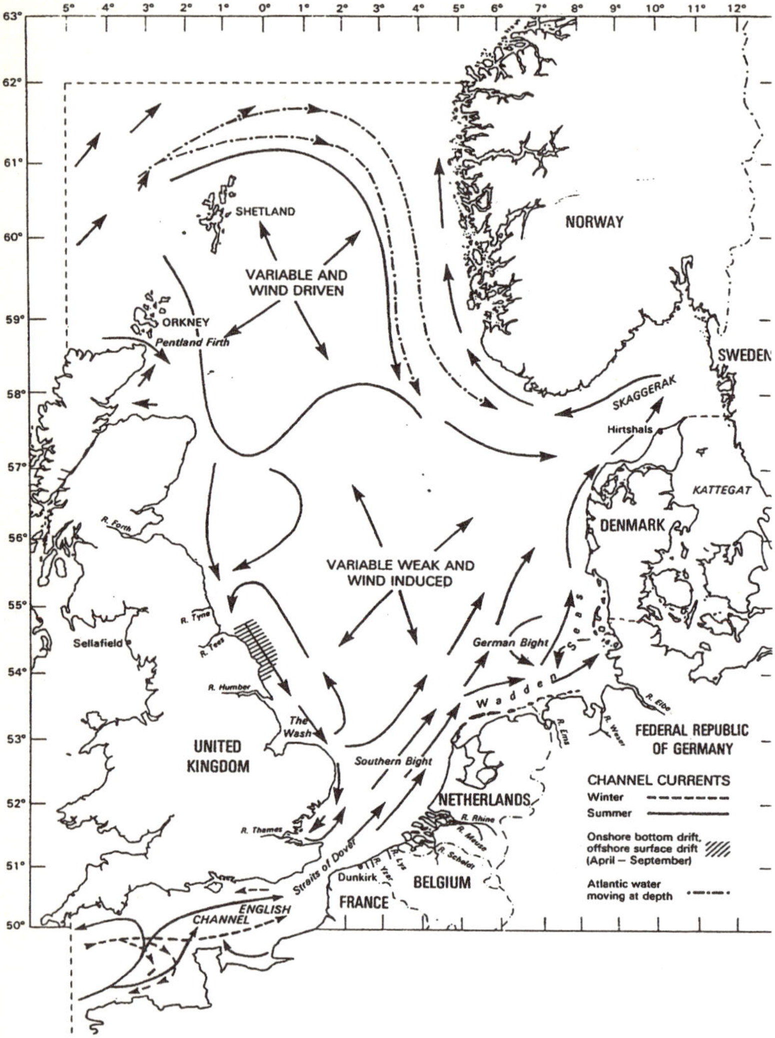

Figure 5.1 *Movement of surface water currents in the North Sea*

Source: Quality Status of the North Sea 1987

Sea Declarations were estimated at NOK10 billion between 1985 and 1995.[2] On the one hand, stringent joint commitments would reduce the share of pollution caused by other states. On the other hand, Norway would only have incentives to adopt unilateral regulations that matched expected benefits from own discharges. As we saw in Chapter 4, Norway's goals on land-based discharges have mainly been in line with the international obligations.

The Netherlands would have incentives to take an intermediate position. The counter-clockwise direction of the North Sea currents places the Netherlands in the 'middle' of the current chain, importing pollution from the upstream states (Belgium, France and the UK), and exporting it further downstream to Germany, Denmark and Norway. The Wadden Sea and the North Sea are linked by strong ecological ties, with every tide bringing a flow of North Sea Water into or out of the Wadden Sea (Zwiep 1990: 203). However, the Netherlands to a large extent suffers the consequences of its own discharges since water circulation is restricted along other parts of Dutch coastal waters.[3] Export or import of North Sea pollution did not feature on the agenda in the Netherlands and central policy documents paid no attention to this dimension. While Norwegian problems were confined to some few sources only, waterways and fjords mainly in the western and southern part of the country, Dutch water pollution sources are scattered throughout the country. Thus, Dutch policy programmes talked about the battle against water pollution. A comprehensive state of the environment report published in 1988 – *Concern for Tomorrow* – confirmed the perception of the Netherlands as heavily affected by inland and coastal pollution. The most important environmental problems identified concerning water were eutrophication and pollution of the Rhine, Meuse and Shcelde and their basins, as well as the North Sea and the Wadden Sea.[4] Abatement costs were also high and raising. According to the OECD (1996), pollution abatement and control expenditure increased in general from 1.4 per cent of gross domestic product (GDP) in 1985 to 1.7 per cent in 1990 and 1.9 per cent of GDP in 1992. This tendency is also reflected in expenditures on water pollution, which were 3.4 billion guilder in 1985 as compared to 4.3 in 1992 at 1991 prices. Thus, the Netherlands fits into the intermediate category of balanced exchange of pollution, high affectedness and high abatement costs.[5] Accordingly, the Dutch position was more ambitious than expected (cf. Chapter 4).

The UK is the candidate for the role as the least ambitious party. The UK is clearly a *net exporter* of marine pollution. Water circulation may transport inputs from the coastal areas of the UK to the eastern, southern and northern part of the North Sea. Conversely, inputs from other North Sea states are not likely to affect the UK coastal waters, due to the counter-clockwise circulation patterns. And indeed, UK coastal areas were perceived to be – and probably were – little affected. Both land-based discharges and inputs from dumping at sea were transported away from the UK coast. According to the British Minister of the Environment in 1984, UK pollution was under sufficient control, and polluting sources in the UK were mainly a thing of the past. With regard to dumping and incineration at sea: 'our sea-dumping operations take place only under licence and under carefully controlled conditions ... If we had any reason to believe that our limited programme of controlled sea dumping caused or was likely to cause environmental damage, we would stop'.[6] The practice of discharging industrial waste water through the sewage system generated huge amounts of contaminated sewage sludge that were dumped at sea. Changing this practice would be very expensive. The government held that such dumping had no negative consequences for the marine environment, but that: 'The social and economic consequences of radically changing disposal policy in each case for which dumping at sea had been used were considerable.'[7]

One major conclusion from the surveys on water quality is that the proportion of rivers, canals and estuaries categorized as 'good', 'fair' and 'unpolluted' has remained high. In 1985 for example, 91 per cent of freshwater rivers and canals were classified as 'good' or 'fair', and 92 per cent of estuaries achieved the same score (Kinnersley 1994: 125). However, the 1985 survey was the first since 1970 to show lengths of rivers degraded in quality overtaking those that had improved. Investments in public water supply and sewerage decreased steadily from the early 1970s until 1982. In 1974, total investments were about £2 billion as compared to less than £1 billion in 1982 at 1989 prices (OECD 1994: 63). Lower investments affected the performance of sewerage works and are probably an important reason for the degradation in river quality. Moreover, this development revealed that significant capital investments would be needed to cope with the situation. In 1990, the government calculated that £13.7 billion would be needed up to the year 2000 to improve sewerage works.[8] Thus, the UK had minor incentives for advocating joint action on marine pollution, since potential damage costs would be caused entirely by own discharges, which were partly exported. Moreover, abatement costs were quite high. These incentives also matched well with the actual position taken by the UK (cf. Chapter 4).

Decision rules and issue-linkages

The requirement of agreement and absence of issue linkages is frequently left to the realm of theoretical assumptions. However, our conclusions would become more robust if these assumptions could be checked against empirical observations. With regard to decision rules, we should note that the joint commitments adopted on the 50 per cent reductions from land-based sources and the phasing out of dumping and incineration at sea were not only consensual, but actually based on unanimity – which is the most demanding of all decision rules. Whereas consensus merely requires the absence of objections, unanimity requires the positive approval of all actors. Up to 1990, the North Sea Declarations required the positive approval of all North Sea states. Prior to the INSC process, the Oslo and Paris Conventions and Commissions were also explicitly based on the requirement of unanimity. However, the Paris Convention is formally open to the possibility of qualified majority in the Paris Commission if unanimity is not attainable. One may argue that the INSC Declarations actually introduced a more demanding decision rule on land-based discharges as compared to the Paris Commission.

The second requirement is more difficult to assess empirically since issue-linkages frequently occur tacitly. Nevertheless, we may argue that the likelihood of this possibility is minor within this substantive issue-area. Leaving aside the possibility that combining issues may reduce the possibilities of agreement, Sebenius (1983) argues that issue addition, separation or combination may enhance or create a zone of possible agreement. However, this would require that the positions of the actors varied on different issues that could be added, subtracted or combined. This requirement is not fulfilled, since the UK was the 'reluctant' actor on *all* issues included here. In essence, cleavages were cumulative, since the UK would find itself in the same situation on all sub-problems. As an exporter of marine pollution, the UK would probably adopt the same position towards any other relevant issues. Thus, we can conclude with a fair amount of certainty that the stringent joint commitments adopted were not due to issue-linkages in this case.

In short, we would expect the 'law' of the least ambitious actors to apply. This proposition matches very well with the first decade of the OSPARCOM cooperation. The lenient decisions and recommendations adopted in the Oslo Commission represented the positions of those states that preferred to regulate dumping activities rather than alter dumping behaviour. The leader among the laggards has been the UK, while Norway and the other Nordic states have explicitly aimed at phasing out dumping of hazardous substances since 1971.[9] The same appears to be the case within the Paris Commission, where outcomes could in some instances even be characterized as 'less than the least ambitious' (Sætevik 1988: 112).

However, the proposition fails to predict the *changes* that occurred in the stringency of commitments in the second decade, for three reasons. First, the basic decision rule did not change. In fact, this model would even predict that more lenient commitments would be adopted at the INSC due to a more demanding decision rule. Second, presence of issue-linkages is not very likely. Third, the position of the UK was assumed to be generally reluctant, thus representing a stable 'least ambitious party'. In short, we would not expect any significant changes in joint commitments in the second decade, since those factors assumed to determine any changes remained constant. The overall conclusion then is that P_1 (see p. 40) corresponds reasonably well with observed patterns in the first decade, but not in the second. And this result strongly suggests that something other than the core variables included in this model must have changed prior to the increase in stringency.

Another possibility compatible with this model was suggested in Chapter 3: the 'law' of the least ambitious programme may be sensitive to the range of positions that are present. Let me briefly recapitulate the main argument. The ambitious and reluctant represent the two opposite poles assumed to have strong interests and preferences in opposite directions. The ambitious may go too far, while the reluctant may fall short in relation to the Pareto frontier, i.e. when no further increase in benefits to one party can be obtained without thereby leaving others worse off. Both the ambitious and the reluctant may actually leave others worse off. The intermediates may be particularly important in this situation since they represent a compromise position in following their self-interest. Intermediates may be capable of forging compromise solutions and activating indifferent actors by means of entrepreneurial leadership.

Since the Netherlands was categorized as an 'intermediate', we would expect that it could act as a mediator by following its interests. This assumption conforms with realities. The Netherlands has acted as active mediator in the Paris Commission and the Oslo Commission since the 1970s. The Dutch strategy has on several occasions been to express sympathy with the position of the most ambitious subsequently combined with proposals aimed at moderating specific proposals. For example, this behaviour was clearly exposed during the Oslo Commission meeting in 1987: 'The Netherlands delegation also expressed sympathy for the Nordic proposal [on dumping], but intended to keep open the possibility of dumping relatively harmless wastes at sea in certain cases ... The Netherlands delegation expressed sympathy with the Nordic proposal [on incineration at sea] ... but the date proposed by the Nordic countries was too early.'[10] In essence, the Netherlands aimed at keeping the proposals from the ambitious at a politically realistic level in between the reluctant and the ambitious.

The existence of an active mediator has probably been important for the parties' ability to adopt joint commitments in general. On the other hand, the Dutch role does not appear to be an important explanatory factor for the *change* in joint commitments, since the Netherlands has acted as an entrepreneur since the 1970s. In short, the joint commitments adopted from 1987 diverge from what we could expect on the basis of the URA model.

Expected versus actual compliance

This section takes as its point of departure the joint commitments on the percentage reduction of land-based discharges and the phasing out of dumping and incineration at sea. Compliance is here assumed to be a function of two major determinants (cf. P_2, see p. 42). First, of major importance is the link between each actor's abatement costs and damage costs in complying with the commitments. The more important other's compliance is for oneself, the more will incentives for compliance depend on the effect of own contribution upon the behaviour of others. Under conditions of net import or net export of pollution, the link between own damage costs and abatement costs following from compliance is weak, so there may be weak incentives for compliance. Conversely, if compliance implies a strong link between own abatement costs and damage costs, there will be strong incentives for complying. This condition is likely to be fulfilled whenever there is a balanced export and import rate. Second, the link between the behaviour of partners to an agreement is also sensitive to the size of contributions. The more one party contributes, the more sensitive will its partners be to its level of compliance, except when the link between own abatement costs and damage costs is strong

Incentives for compliance

Both Norway and the UK represent cases where the link between AC and DC is weak. As an exporter of marine pollution, the UK clearly had incentives to defect from the North Sea commitments. The UK had full control over events important to domestic and coastal pollution problems, and was not affected by the behaviour of other states. With regard to land-based discharges, the UK had incentives to comply with the international commitments up to the point where the degradation of rivers could be counterbalanced. However, the degradation of river quality from the beginning of the 1980s was insignificant and the situation was generally classified as satisfactory. There was virtually nothing to suggest, or justify, the joint obligations to cut discharges of nutrients and hazardous substances by 50 per cent. The situation was even clearer concerning dumping and incineration at sea. These activities affected neither the state of inland water quality, nor the quality of the marine environment around the coast. A positive link between abatement costs and damage costs was completely absent: indeed, there was even a danger that the link was negative, i.e. that increased abatement costs could increase damage costs. Measures to combat dumping of sewage sludge at sea might well transform a sea-based 'non-problem' in subjective terms to an inland pollution problem. Land-based alternatives to cope with sea dumping of such waste could cause pollution problems since such alternatives include farmland, landfill, and onshore incineration. In short, the UK had strong incentives to defect on the basis of the link between abatement costs and damage costs following from North Sea commitments.

As a significant source of marine pollution, the UK would not easily be accepted as a 'free-rider' by its partners. All North Sea states were potential 'victims' of UK discharges, since the UK represented the first part in the current chain. Obviously, then, UK consent would be needed for any commitments to have a significant effect on the state of the North Sea. Further, the UK was forced to weigh the problem-related cost-benefit calculations against calculations of the political costs of not signing an agreement. Subsequent defection from an agreement would be more costly for the UK since it represented a large contributor of marine pollution. Thus, the size of UK contribution would work in the opposite direction of the AC–DC link and probably push its compliance position from reluctant towards intermediate.

The Norwegian situation paralleled the UK situation in the sense that the link between Norway's abatement and damage costs was weak. As a net importer of marine pollution, the compliance of others was crucial to Norway, whereas Norway's behaviour was not likely to affect the behaviour of its partners. Thus, other states were not sensitive to Norway's compliance. Norway's contribution of nutrients to the North Sea was only about 3 per cent of the total. Norway's share of inputs of hazardous substances has not been quantified, but they would probably be of the same order of magnitude, in view of the relatively low-level industrial activity. Moreover, Norway represented the final link in the current chain, so Norwegian discharges were likely to be transported out into the wider North-East Atlantic. Norway would clearly prefer others to contribute more, since damage costs were partly caused by import of pollution. In essence, the North Sea commitments were more stringent than Norway would itself have chosen. As a small victim, Norway would also be accepted as a 'free-rider' since its own minor discharges did not affect other states. Thus, Norway had apparently incentives to push for and defect from North Sea commitments.

In contrast to the UK and Norway, the Netherlands had strong incentives to comply. Due to its balanced import and export situation, the benefits that would accrue from the compliance of others would probably equal the benefits that others would enjoy from Dutch compliance. In addition, a significant proportion of Dutch damage costs was caused by Dutch discharges, so the link between abatement costs and damage costs was strong. Moreover, the Netherlands was highly affected by both marine and inland water pollution. This indicates that the Dutch needs were closer than those of Norway and the UK to the reduction targets. The ambitious Dutch position on land-based discharges supports such an interpretation. Although the size of contributions is of little relevance since the Netherlands had no incentives to defect, we should also note that the Netherlands can be categorized as a large contributor. Due to its considerable contribution of nutrients in particular, progress in Dutch implementation of the North Sea Declarations has been seen as essential to ensure a healthy North Sea (Vertegaal 1993). Thus, if the Netherlands for some other reason decided to defect, it would hardly be accepted as 'free-rider'. Hence, we would expect the Netherlands had strong incentives to comply with joint North Sea commitments.

Actual compliance

If we combine the expectations outlined above with the data on Level II implementation presented in Chapter 4, we get the patterns set out in Table 5.1. The aggregated compliance data show that two cases have achieved compliance with joint commitments contrary to expectations, while one case roughly matches expectation. Thus, overall, the model has not been able to predict actual compliance well. The Netherlands had strong incentives to comply with commitments; moreover, the Dutch government has also been very ambitious in terms of national positions on land-based sources. Thus, the mismatch between positions and actual compliance record appears to be the result not of a deliberate choice, but rather of a lack of domestic implementation ability. As a downstream victim, Norway would prefer that other states adopted and implemented stronger measures than itself. However, Norway has the highest relative compliance rate, representing a level of compliance apparently beyond Norwegian interests.

One possible explanation for this situation could be the exceptionally toxic algae blooms in 1988–89, which hit Norway hard compared to the UK and the Netherlands. The blooms killed fish in aquaculture enclosures to a value of NOK30 million in 1988

Table 5.1 *Predicted positions v. actual compliance record*

	Predicted positions	*Actual compliance record*
Netherlands	Ambitious	Intermediate
Norway	Reluctant	Ambitious/intermediate
UK	Reluctant/intermediate	Reluctant/intermediate

alone.[11] The algae blooms were taken very seriously by the Norwegian government, which brought the case to the 1988 Paris Commission meeting. The blooms were related to inputs of nutrients and the Norwegian delegation stressed that all North Sea states should strictly follow the 50 per cent agreement on nutrients reached at the North Sea Conference in 1987.[12] However, Norway failed to do so itself. Norwegian defection occurred with regard to nitrogenous substances that contributed in causing the algae blooms. This does not necessarily imply that the blooms had no effect on Norwegian compliance. It does imply, however, that the level of reductions in nutrients achieved in Norway would probably have been even lower in the absence of the algae blooms.

Overall, the UK has behaved in accordance with predictions. As a net exporter with high abatement costs and low or moderate damage costs, the UK could be expected to 'cheat'. The UK position on the nutrient target seems a classic example. Since the UK could not be accepted as a 'free-rider', it agreed to the 50 per cent reduction target in order to avoid the political costs of blocking an agreement. This calculation was probably reinforced by the fact that the 1987 Conference was held in London, and it would definitely not look good if the host country were to block the agreement. Subsequently, the UK government argued that they had no sensitive areas and were thus not obliged to comply. Even though the actual existence of sensitive areas around the UK coast continues to be a matter of dispute, this seems a classic example of defection by deliberate choice.

However, the UK had also strong incentives to 'cheat' concerning joint commitments on dumping and incineration at sea. As with nutrients, the political costs of blocking an agreement in 1987 would have been high for the UK. However, the UK had absolutely no incentives to comply: this practice did not affect the UK, and abatement costs would certainly be high and perhaps negatively related to reduction in damage costs. Thus, dumping and incineration at sea conducted by the UK stand out as another example of compliance with inconvenient commitments. The measures to combat hazardous substances were more lenient than internationally required, but stronger than previous efforts. Thus, they may have matched actual needs in light of the worsening river quality.

Assessing the Unitary Rational Actor model

Judged on the merits of pattern-matching, the URA model proved capable of predicting reasonably well the basic positions prior to the breakthrough at the North Sea Conferences. The main weakness of the URA model lies in its capacity to explain the *changes* that occurred in the stringency of joint commitments and variance in compliance. The basic variables assumed to determine such changes did not change significantly, so we must conclude that this model is clearly insufficient to explain these changes. This also implies that a general positive trend in inputs of regulated substances is difficult to understand on the basis of the URA model. The assumption that intermediates would serve as mediators and entrepreneurs gained partial support. However, the Netherlands has fulfilled this role ever since the 1970s, so Dutch behaviour is not likely to explain changes.

The data appear sufficiently robust to seriously weaken the first part of the hypothesis we wish to refute – that joint commitments and compliance would be the same if the states merely pursued their material interests. Especially the UK, but also Norway, serve as examples of states that have agreed to joint commitments that deviate from those they would have adopted on the basis of unilateral action. As an exporter of marine pollution, the UK generally had scant incentives to support joint commitments and definitely not the stringent commitments adopted in 1987 and 1990. As a net importer of marine pollution, Norway had incentives to pursue more ambitious joint solutions than it would have adopted on the basis of unilateral action. The stringent commitments adopted seem more in line with the interests of the Netherlands, a highly affected actor likely to suffer the consequences of its own actions. We have also identified various situations where compliance with the commitments actually adopted would prove inconvenient, especially for the UK and Norway. The clearest example is perhaps the dumping and incineration conducted by the UK, where there was nothing to gain and everything to lose for the UK. In relative terms, the Netherlands had the highest incentives to comply, but actual compliance was lower than for Norway. In short, we have found joint commitments and compliance levels clearly different from what we could expect according to this model.

As a heuristic device, however, the model cannot be deemed

invalid. We should note that a low score on pattern-matching does not necessarily imply that the behavioural mechanisms underlying the model are irrelevant. We have clear indications that cost/benefit calculations have been central to all three states. The action plans presented from the mid-1980s are highly influenced by this line of thought. For example, the Norwegian government explicitly states that the benefits of measures should, ideally, be equal to or higher than the costs incurred in implementing them.[13] The preceding analysis does not suggest that cost/benefit rationality is unimportant, since it matters in understanding the basic positions of the actors. However, the results strongly suggest that factors other than those included in the URA model may have affected the calculus of actors. Moreover, other behavioural mechanisms such as norms of environmental behaviour may have played an important role.

There are in fact several possible explanations of the mismatch observed between expectations and behaviour. First, there is always the possibility that the data utilized to measure the core dimensions are invalid, especially in cases where the match between 'objective' characteristics and 'subjective' perceptions is weak. However, the main impression is that the link between these dimensions has been generally good here. Second, we have no indications of 'hidden agendas' and significant ulterior motives, i.e. that changes occurred in order to achieve other purposes than pollution control. North Sea pollution control has never been strongly contaminated by 'high politics' or strategic foreign policy considerations. The former superpowers have never participated and the participating states have all belonged to the same defence alliance (or have been neutral). Thus, the general impression is that the actors have considered the problem mainly on its own merits.

Other remaining possibilities are left for the remaining chapters. First, international institutions may have been important. The way of organizing the cooperation has clearly changed and possibly affected cost/benefit calculus through various institutional factors that have not been included in the URA model. Moreover, if we relax the assumption of cost/benefit rationality, institutions may also have contributed in developing norms of environmental behaviour and cooperation. A second possibility lies in relaxing the assumption of unity while retaining the assumption of cost/benefit rationality. This would take us to an analysis of the relative support and opposition of those sub-national actors that have to change their behaviour in accordance with national goals following from international commitments. A third possibility is to relax both the assumption of unity and rationality, and study the impact of national institutions. The two latter options would be particularly attractive in cases of domestic implementation failure. We have strong indications that particularly the general level of Dutch achievements and Norway's compliance with the nutrient target may be traced back to lack of implementation ability. Moreover, the UK has experienced problems concerning land-based discharges of hazardous substances.

Conclusion

The purpose of this chapter has been to assess the URA model on the developments witnessed within the North Sea cooperation. Evaluated in terms of pattern-matching, the model was able to predict the basic positions of Norway, the Netherlands, and the UK reasonably well. On the other hand, the model largely failed to predict the significant changes that occurred in joint commitments and compliance. Basic damage costs, abatement costs, and the 'balance of pollution exchange' would not suggest any significant change in national positions and joint commitments, simply because these dimensions did not change significantly. Against the above conclusions it may be argued that these results rely heavily on one particular way of operationalizing the model. The theoretical core of the model is abatement costs and damage costs, and these dimensions may clearly be operationalized in different ways. Norway's incentives to comply with the North Sea Declarations represent a clear example in this respect. Other states may have been more sensitive to Norway's compliance than a purely material cost/benefit assessment would suggest. However, inclusion of political and symbolic significance in the model should be weighed against the danger of watering out the model. As a heuristic tool, the model proved valid in the sense that cost/benefit calculations have been central to all actors in this issue-area. However, we have strong indications that such calculations are not all that matters for policy-makers.

Nevertheless, the data appear as sufficiently robust to seriously weaken the first part of the hypothesis we wish to refute – that commitments and compliance would remain the same even if states merely pursued their own rational interests. But we do not yet know the extent to which this is attributable to the impact of institutions. If we relax the various assumptions linked to the URA model, several other factors may explain the observed patterns. The first candidate is the potential impact of international institutions, to which we now turn.

Notes

1 *Summary Record* (1987: 1).
2 Ministry of the Environment (1992).
3 *North Sea Quality Status Report* (1993: 108). London: Oslo and Paris Commissions
4 NEPP (1989: 52).
5 The most comparable figures are OECD pollution abatement and control (PAC) expenditure as percentage of GDP from 1990. Total PAC for Norway is 1.2 per cent as compared to 1.7 per cent in the Netherlands. However, these figures are not confined to water pollution in particular. Even though figures presented in the countries' action plans are not directly comparable, they indicated that there was a significant difference. Dutch expenditure on water pollution only in the municipal and industrial sectors was approximately 0.5 per cent of gross national product (GNP) in 1985. Total Norwegian abatement costs (water and air) in the municipal and industrial sectors amounted to the same in 1982.
6 *Summary Record* (1984: 2).
7 Oslo Commission (1989: 33).
8 *This Common Inheritance* (1990: 27).
9 Ministry of Foreign Affairs (1972).
10 Oslo Commission (1988: 18).
11 *Interim Report on the Quality Status of the North Sea* (1990: 14).
12 *Summary Record* (1988: 12).
13 Ministry of the Environment (1985: 39).

6

The functioning and consequences of international institutions

The North Sea institutions were established to come to grips with collective action problems characterized by different interests and preferences. Consequently, we cannot explain the development towards more stringent joint commitments and actual behavioural change going in the right direction merely by the saying that states had common interests in coping with these problems. In Chapter 5, we observed that very little of the significant change in joint commitments and behaviour from the late 1980s could be traced back to changes in problem-related interests of the states concerned. In addition to differences in material interests, both ocean- and land-based problems were 'infected' by the dispute on Uniform Emission Standards (UES) and Environmental Quality Objectives (EQO). This controversy was linked to both varying material interests – including principles of competition between states – and different norms concerning the basic philosophy of pollution control. The UES/EQO dispute led to cumulative conflict by pitting the same actors against each other on different issues. In short, it made the problem even more difficult to solve through voluntary cooperation.

According to the international institutional perspective, we would expect significant changes to have occurred in the institutionalization of the cooperation from the first to the second decade. More specifically, international institutions are assumed to promote cooperative environments and provide aggregation and integration capacity, as well as stimulating implementation and compliance by reducing discretion. Fulfilment of, and change in, these functions might affect the willingness of states to adopt and implement stringent joint commitments.

The functioning and consequences of international institutions will be assessed according to different phases in which the stringency of joint commitments is affected by institutional change that in turn may affect domestic implementation. In the first decade – from the mid-1970s to the mid-1980s – the cooperation took place within the framework of the legally binding Oslo and Paris Conventions and Commissions (see Figure 6.1). In the second decade – from the mid-1980s to the mid-1990s – the 'soft law' International North Sea Conferences were added to the co-operation and they took over as the goal-producing engine. There has been a very close relationship between these 'hard' and 'soft' law institutions since the mid-1980s even though they are clearly distinct in the sense that each makes its own priorities and adopts its own agendas.

The first argument pursued in this chapter is that these 'hard' and 'soft' law institutions to a large extent have fulfilled different functions, and the key to understanding the impact of institutions in this issue-area lies in their symbiotic nature and combined influence. The second argument is that the relevant institutions have changed over time, and that these changes have influenced both joint decision-making and implementation.

Cooperative environments: specific and diffuse reciprocity

In international environmental politics, reciprocity is an effective strategy for maintaining cooperation between states. Essentially,

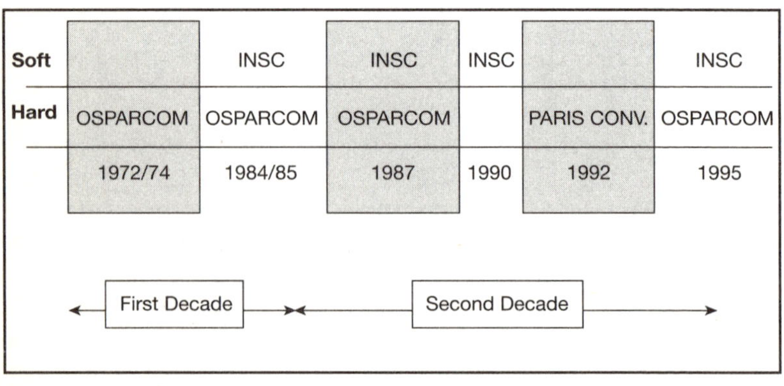

Figure 6.1 *Time phases and institutional development*

reciprocity represents exchanges of roughly equivalent values in which the actions of each party are contingent on the prior actions of the other. Reciprocity may be either specific or diffuse, depending on the degree of economic self-interest and common norms of cooperative behaviour involved. While specific reciprocity is related to mutual suspicion, diffuse reciprocity rests upon the good faith of others and cooperative norms of obligation. In general here, we will expect that the larger the element of diffuse reciprocity, the more cooperative will the environments be. Cooperative environments are characterized by institutional factors that provide the actors with opportunities to adopt and pursue a constructive approach to making and implementing joint commitments. The basic assumption is that diffuse and specific reciprocity may serve different functions and affect joint commitments and implementation differently. More specifically, the unstable, malleable and flexible features of specific reciprocity may provide the actors with greater capacity to affect the adoption of stringent joint commitments. Conversely, diffuse reciprocity, characterized by stability, persistence and mutual confidence, may provide a basis for solutions and ensure that the parties behave in accordance with the agreements reached.

The cooperative environment index presented in Table 3.2 will be examined in accordance with the following institutional factors:

- formal fora;
- systemic actors;
- frequency of meetings and interpersonal relationships;
- level of cooperation;
- decision-making procedures and systems;
- access granted to outsiders;
- bindingness of prescriptions.

Note that these seven factors may also serve other purposes than affecting cooperative environments. We start with the first decade of the Oslo and Paris Commissions.

The first decade: towards diffuse reciprocity

According to the Oslo and Paris Conventions, various *formal cooperative fora* were to be established. At political decision-making level, the Oslo and Paris Commissions were established as permanent decision-making bodies in 1974 and 1978 respectively. The Oslo and Paris Commissions very soon became aware of the complementary nature of their tasks and decided to establish a joint meeting of the Commissions. This convened for the first time in 1979. The joint meetings have mainly dealt with procedural tasks common to both Commissions. At scientific/technical level, each commission set up a standing scientific group. In the case of the Oslo Commission, this was the Standing Advisory Committee for Scientific Advice formed at the first meeting of the Commission. In the case of the Paris Commission, it was the Technical Working Group set up at the first meeting of the Interim Commission. These permanent groups were assisted by more or less permanent working groups. For example, the Paris Commission established a working group on oil pollution in 1978 that is still in existence. At the first joint meeting of the Commissions in 1979, a Joint Monitoring Group was established and a Joint Monitoring Programme (JMP) became operational in accordance with Articles 13 and 11 of the Oslo and Paris Conventions respectively. The JMG and the working groups report to the standing scientific groups, which in turn advise the Commissions.

In addition to the political and scientific/technical standing groups, two permanent *systemic actors* were established. The Commissions set up a permanent secretariat in London comprising a secretary, two vice-secretaries and a small office staff. The Commissions also set up a standing group, titled the Group of Chairmen and Vice-Chairmen (CVC). As the name indicates, this group consists of the Chairmen and Vice-Chairmen of each Commission, assisted where necessary by the Chairman of the standing scientific/technical groups. The tasks of CVC were to deal with administrative problems arising between meetings of the Commissions and to offer advice which could promote their efficient operation.

With regard to the *frequency of meetings*, the Oslo and Paris Conventions state in Article 16 that the Commissions shall meet at regular intervals and at any time when due to special circumstances. In practice, both Commissions have normally met annually, both separately and jointly. Each of the scientific/technical groups and the Joint Monitoring Group also holds an annual meeting, while the Group of Chairmen and Vice-Chairmen holds two meetings per year. The various working groups also meet annually. Taken together, meetings are convened throughout each year in different member-countries at scientific/technical and political level, while the Secretariat serves as the truly permanent core. No wonder, then, that malicious tongues have described the early years of the Oslo and Paris Commissions as a 'travel club' (Andresen 1996: 74).

The Oslo and Paris Commissions were composed of civil servants at a relatively low *level of participation*. Governmental political representatives were completely absent from national delegations. The cooperation was also marked by strong and close interpersonal relationships and high consistency in terms of participation between the Secretariat, the CVC group and national delegations. In short, there was always a core of key persons that carried the history with them.

Formally, the *decision-making procedures* differ between the Oslo and the Paris Commission. The Oslo Commission is explicitly based on unanimity. Also the Paris Commission is to draw up its own Rules of Procedure by unanimous vote. However, should unanimity not be attainable, the Paris Commission may none the less adopt a programme or measure by a three-quarters majority of its members. In practice, however, the difference between Oslo and Paris Commissions has been minor. When it comes to decision-making procedures 'in use', unanimity has been the basic rule for both Commissions in this period. In the Oslo and Paris Commissions' 'Strategy for the Future' (Paris Commission 1984), adopted by the Commissions in 1984, the wider *decision-making system* is described as a dynamic and rolling programme that undertakes various stages of identifying problems, action in the form of joint decisions and implementation and reappraisal in order to identify additional needs. In practice, however, the system may be described as quite static, administrative and incremental. The parties have frequently agreed to delegate, agreed to postpone, or agreed to disagree. Agreement to delegate unresolved problems to further examination by working groups has been common. In 1981, the Contracting Parties to the Oslo Commission agreed that they should take a decision concerning incineration at sea in the 1990s. Moreover, in 1978, the parties agreed to disagree on the UES/EQO approaches and the Commission decided to retain a dual approach for the following five years.

The Oslo and Paris Commissions were essentially state driven and closed to the outside world. The Rules of Procedures that were adopted unanimously contain strict *access procedures* for non-parties and are coloured by a wish to work in privacy. Until 1990, NGO involvement was limited to the occasional brief presentation to the delegations to the Commissions before their annual meetings (Sadowski 1996). Commission documents were largely regarded as confidential and access was restricted to such documents, including Summary Records and meeting documents. The general rule was that documents submitted by the Contracting Parties should be released only with prior authorisation. As late as in 1987, the Commissions agreed that the Secretary should issue a press notice in advance of the annual Commission meetings. It was stressed that the press notice should be brief and neutral and contain no details of proposals for Recommendations or Decisions.

The Oslo and Paris Conventions are *legally binding* instruments within the framework of international law. Of particular interest in this section is that legally binding instruments, being hard to amend, provide stability in institutional procedures. In practice, the framework for cooperation was altered very little in the first decade, although some clarifications were subsequently needed. Thus, legally binding instruments may hamper the dynamic elements emphasized by the Commissions. For example, a new protocol on incineration at sea was negotiated and opened for signature in Oslo in 1983. That protocol did not come into force until September 1989.

We may conclude that the first decade scores high on the co-operative environment index. Various formal fora were established, systemic actors were present, the cooperation took place at a low level of participation, the decision-making procedures in use were based on unanimity, decision-making systems were incremental and administrative, access to 'outsiders' was largely denied and the actors cooperated within a legally binding framework that was difficult to amend and that altered very little in practice. Meetings were also convened frequently, at both political and scientific level. Moreover, the cooperation was marked by close and consistent personal relationships between the Secretariat, the CVC group and national delegations. In short, the institutionalization of the first decade points towards diffuse reciprocity and highly cooperative environments.

We also have strong indications that a highly cooperative environment actually emerged. If contingency rests on good faith in the actions of other, we expect that there is no need to monitor and verify performance. Although both the Paris and Oslo Conventions place a clear duty on the Contracting Parties to assess the effectiveness of measures, there was almost no monitoring of performance in the first decade. With regard to the assessment of measures, the parties had not developed any common and mandatory implementation report routines. The monitoring practice developed by the Commissions appear to have been *ad hoc* and based essentially on each party's freedom to report on whatever they wish. As late as in 1987, this practice was still applied by the Paris Commission; the Commission recognized that there were shortcomings in Contracting Parties' reporting performance, even in those cases where mandatory obligations existed.[1] The Oslo Convention also includes a general requirement of evaluation of measures according to Article 17. However, monitoring was given equally low priority as in the Paris Commission, with the exception of input data. In the late 1980s, the Commission had a good idea as to who was dumping what, where and how much. However, this information was not collected in order to assess implementation, but due to the general licensing requirements included in the Oslo Convention. Various independent participants with long experience from the cooperation also emphasize that the cooperation climate can be described as a 'club culture' characterized more by administration than by negotiation.[2]

The second decade: towards specific reciprocity

The organization of the North Sea conferences deviates significantly from the cooperation within the framework of the Oslo and Paris Conventions. From 1984 to 1995, the conferences had no standing, formal cooperative fora. These conferences were *ad hoc* in the sense that each conference had to decide whether there would be a follow-up conference. As noted, the first 1984 Bremen Conference was originally envisaged as a unique event; the question of whether to proceed with the conferences has frequently re-entered the agenda. In fact, the conferences have become more permanent over time and have been held at a regular basis. At the 1995 Esbjerg Conference, it was decided to establish a permanent committee of North Sea Senior Officials to meet on a regular basis.

Preparations for each conference have been conducted by a secretariat appointed by the host country and various political and technical/scientific preparatory groups specifically linked to each conference. Conferences were convened approximately every three years. The scientific and political working groups met quite frequently during the last year before each conference; for example, during the preparation of the 1987 Conference the Scientific Technical Working Group met five times between January 1986 and February 1987. This way of organizing work promoted a kind of periodic stability in interpersonal relationships leading up to each conferences. At political decision-making level, Ministers of the Environment, accompanied by a secretary of state or a high-level civil servant, would normally head the national delegations. Ministerial representation implied a higher level of participation as compared to OSPARCOM. Most countries sent large and diversified delegations to the conferences, including national representatives in the political and technical working groups. Negotiations were based on Draft Declarations prepared by the political working groups in which unresolved problems were left to the Ministers. Ministerial representation led to low stability in interpersonal relationships. Since ministers come and go as governments change, the level of representation would in itself make close personal contacts more difficult. This was reinforced by three-year period between the conferences. For example, Denmark and the Netherlands were the only states represented by the same minister at both the Bremen and London conferences.[3]

The North Sea conferences operated without any formal decision-making procedures. However, the Declaration texts in which the ministers either 'decide to' or 'agree to' show that unanimity has served as the basic decision rule in use. At Bremen and London, all decisions were unanimous. However, a new 'footnote' practice developed during The Hague Conference, whereby resistance from one country would not necessarily block the efforts of all the others. The wider decision-making system underlying the Conferences was based on the same logic as OSPARCOM. Quality Status Reports on the North Sea were prepared in order to identify problems, and the Conferences aimed at joint solutions to the problems, while the next follow-up Conference would evaluate progress in implementation and identify additional needs. However, the Ministers had limited possibilities to delegate or postpone decisions, as there were no standing subordinate bodies. Moreover, each minister would have to bring some results back home from each conference, since a second chance was unlikely. Negotiations were more political than in OSPARCOM, due to the high level of representation. The decision-making practice and system would probably lead to tough 'across the table' negotiations as opposed to the administrative decision-making style of the Oslo and Paris Commissions.

The North Sea Conferences also gradually opened access to the outside world, attracting broad public attention and intensive media coverage. While the OSPARCOM meetings were largely ignored by the media – as indeed deliberately intended by the procedures adopted – the INSCs reached the news headlines in most North Sea capitals. In preparation for the 1984 Conference, a hearing was held in August 1984 at which non-governmental organizations presented their views. This hearing represented the first ever official attempt to consult with NGOs in the North Sea/North-East Atlantic cooperation. In 1987, NGOs were, for the first time, permitted to attend the opening session only and make brief statements. At The Hague 1990, NGOs had again the opportunity of delivering an oral statements at the beginning of the conference, and their access to information was improved. France and the UK had insisted that the preliminary 1989 reports on implementation of the 1987 Declaration as well as other preparatory documents should not be sent to any NGO. However, the Danish Parliament decided unilaterally in 1989 that all preparatory documents should be public. As a consequence, Greenpeace received – albeit anonymously – preparatory documents from most North Sea capitals (MacGarvin 1991). Over the years, participation of environmental non-governmental organizations and target groups has increased (Skjærseth 1998). At the 1995 Conference, there were 36 delegates representing ENGOs, and 32 from target groups.

In contrast to the Oslo and Paris Conventions, the North Sea Declarations are not legally binding instruments (Mensbrugghe 1990: 21). The core difference in terms of reciprocity between these forms of international instruments lies in the fact that the North Sea Declarations contain no legal procedures that hold any implications for the desire of decision-makers to change course, or determine the 'rules of the game' on a case-by-case basis. The 'footnote' and 'access' practice that developed are examples of the latter. Moreover, as these Declarations are not subject to formal national ratification, they can take instant effect. In essence, the INSCs represent truly dynamic and unstable institutional instruments. Moreover, the INSC did not 'mature' in the same way as OSPARCOM. Since there was no legal text underlying the cooperation, the parties did not have to invest time and energy to agree on earlier loosely defined concepts.

To conclude, the INSC process scores low on the reciprocity index both in absolute and relative terms – i.e. compared to the index and the cooperation within the framework of the Oslo and Paris Conventions. Within the INSC, cooperation has taken place in the absence of formal fora and systemic actors; decision-makers have been represented at political level; and decision-making systems have been essentially political, and probably marked by real 'across the table' negotiations. Moreover, the INSC has developed closer contact with 'outsiders' and the actors have cooperated within a 'soft law' framework which allowed for swift action that could take immediate effect. Compared to OSPARCOM, the Conferences have been convened less frequently than the Commission meetings, and personal relationships have been more loose. Hence, the institutionalization of the INSC process points towards specific reciprocity and less cooperative environments. Thus, it seems reasonable to assume that the parties would put more emphasis on monitoring performance. In order to make own actions contingent to the actions of others, the actions of others must be clearly revealed.

In contrast to OSPARCOM, assessment of implementation was immediately accorded high priority within the INSC process. The second INSC had two main purposes according to the Conference agenda. First, it was to review the implementation and effectiveness of the decisions taken in Bremen. Second, it should adopt further measures. A progress report on the implementation of the Bremen Declaration was prepared by the working groups and presented to the Conference.[4] The London Declaration underlines that the third INSC should evaluate the measures agreed in 1987, especially concerning hazardous substances, nutrients, and dumping and incineration at sea. A comprehensive implementation report was prepared for the 1990 Conference.[5] In contrast to the 1987 evaluation, this 1990 report focuses mainly on national implementation. The progress report presented at the 1995 Esbjerg Conference was explicitly guided by the principle of transparency, i.e. it should be clear where there have been failures in implementation.[6] In essence, the INSC developed a comprehensive and systematic programme for assessing implementation and compliance of a significantly different order of magnitude, compared to the sporadic assessments conducted within OSPARCOM up to 1990s.

In addition to new emphasis placed on monitoring implementation, the difference in cooperative environments is also evident if we look at how similar problems like dumping at sea were approached by essentially the same state actors in OSPARCOM and in the INSC. In 1984, cooperation within the Oslo Commission was still marked by tacit disagreement, and the parties were occupied with developing Codes of Practice to control dumping operations in line with the preferences of the 'least enthusiastic'. The same year, dumping at sea became a major topic at the 1984 Bremen Conference. That conference was marked by significant disagreement and open conflict. The majority at the Bremen Conference held – as a principle – that dumping at sea represented an unacceptable disposal method. The minority tried to work out a compromise, but the Nordic countries preferred having no solution to giving in on their positions.[7] This example shows that similar problems could be approached very differently by the same actors at the same time within two different institutional contexts. Independent participants have also emphasized that the cooperation 'climate' at the Conferences in general was significantly different from that at OSPARCOM in terms of the level of conflict, mutual confidence and real bargaining involved, not least since all outstanding issues had to be resolved within one and a half days.[8]

Consequences of different modes of reciprocity

To recapitulate: a cooperation based on specific reciprocity has probably a larger capacity to cut through different positions to enable collective solutions. Conversely, highly cooperative environments based on cooperative norms may provide a necessary basis of mutual confidence underlying joint action. In essence, the most significant consequences of different cooperative environments lie in their combined effect.

These assumptions will be analysed by narrowing in on the single most important and perhaps the most difficult issue – Uniform Emission Standards versus Environmental Quality Standards – that has been on the agenda since the cooperation commenced in the 1970s. It is important because an agreement to apply UES would constitute a necessary first step towards adopting the principle of precautionary action, technology standards aimed at curbing pollution at source and the percentage reduction goals on land-based and ocean-based sources. The UES/EQS issue is also clearly difficult in the sense that it involves significant elements of both externalities and competition. In addition, the UES/EQS controversy touches upon normative elements concerning the basic philosophy of pollution control. The latter is probably best illustrated by noting that Portugal preferred EQS while Spain preferred UES, even though these countries have had quite similar material interests and preferences within OSPARCOM. If expected consequences bear some significance according to this issue they will probably affect less 'malign' issues as well. In line with the assumptions presented above, we would suspect that the solution to this controversy would have come within the INSC process and not the OSPARCOM cooperation.

Towards a solution The UES/EQO dispute appeared immediately on the agenda in the Paris Commission. At the first meeting of the Interim Paris Commission in 1974, the parties discussed which approach should serve as the basic principle for the cooperation. Although the first discussion was linked to mercury pollution, it was clear that the approaches exceeded the framework for the study of a single substance. The majority supported the UES approach, stressing the preventive aspect of their approach, the fact that it could be based on Best Available Technology and that it opened for equal international standards for all parties. Uniform Emission Standards supporters felt that the latter would also have a stabilizing effect on competitive situation between the states, since UES was based on equal standards for all actors. Conversely, quality objectives and standards might distort competition, since the quality of one region can differ from that of a neighbouring region. Portugal and the UK supported the EQO approach, emphasizing that the final objective of the Convention is the protection of the marine environment and of man as a consumer of seafood. They quoted Article 6 of the Convention, according to which the Contracting Parties should take account of various criteria including the quality and *absorptive capacity* of the receiving waters of the maritime area.[9] In short, UES advocates emphasized that discharges of substances known to be toxic, persistent and bioaccumulative and listed in the Convention's 'black lists' should be limited as far as possible at source, whereas the EQO defenders maintained that standards set should be determined by observable negative effects in the marine environment for each particular substance.

This discussion continued the first four years, and the parties did not succeed in adopting any common basis for action. While the Contracting Parties continued to agree to disagree within the Paris Commission, the UES/EQO controversy became a major topic at the first INSC in Bremen 1984. The Ministers tried to forge a compromise based on four different text proposals, but they were unable to agree on a final solution. Nevertheless, some progress was made. The Declaration hinted at the precautionary principle, which in effect would imply common recognition of the UES approach, since it involves taking action prior to observable damaging effects. The core scientific argument of UES advocates was linked to the fact that current scientific knowledge would not permit indisputable causal links to be established between inputs, concentrations and effects.

In the wake of the Bremen Conference, an *ad hoc* working group was established by the Paris Commission in 1985 aiming at evaluating the EQO and UES approaches. On the agenda of the first meeting of the group the same year were the positions of the parties according to scientific, economic and environmental basis and consequences.[10] Portugal did not participate at the meeting. This indicated that its preference for EQO was not a matter of high priority, and left the UK alone as a dedicated defender of EQO. The parties proved unable to agree on any of the above dimensions. With regard to the scientific basis, the parties could not agree on how to define an 'acceptable risk'. No firm conclusion could be reached about the cost consequences of the two approaches, and the UK did not accept that the use of UES would prevent distortion of competition. Concerning environmental effects, available data did not permit for a systematic assessment.

The Policy Working Group preparing the 1987 Conference in London set out to find a solution. The Chairman of the working group prepared a paper in which he emphasized the *complementary* nature of the EQO and UES approaches. The paper did not include any new arguments, but the different approaches strengths and weaknesses were systematically discussed. Although the paper indicates a growing recognition of the complementary nature of the two approaches, acceptance by all parties would nevertheless imply a change in the position of the UK. Many other states actually applied a combination of the two approaches domestically and were not in opposition to quality standards as such. The main limitation to an agreement was that the UK did not accept the UES approach.

The breakthrough came at the 1987 London Conference. Here the Ministers agreed on the precautionary principle, that emissions should normally be limited at source taking into account the best technical means, and, further, that quality objectives should be fixed on the basis of latest environmental data. This agreement paved the way for the uniform percentage reduction targets on hazardous substances, nutrients, and dumping and incineration at sea. Subsequently, a second meeting of the *ad hoc* working group on the EQO and UES approaches was convened in 1988 under the auspices of the Paris Commission.[11] Here the UK presented a paper 'Up-date of the UK Position as Regards the Use of Environmental Quality Objectives and Uniform Emission Standards', reaffirming that EQO/Environmental Quality Standards (EQS) still remains a basic principle for water and marine pollution control. On the other hand, the UK explicitly accepted the UES approach. This change in UK policy was to have far-reaching implications for both the UK and the North Sea/North-East Atlantic cooperation. First, the UK government followed up by declaring a new approach to hazardous substances aimed at reducing them at source (the Red List). Second, the Paris Commission followed up in 1989 by adopting two recommendations, on the principle of precautionary action and on the use of Best Available Technology. This opened the way for a number of decisions and recommendation on BAT to be applied within specific industrial sectors. These principles were in turn written into the 1992 Paris Convention for the Protection of the Marine Environment of the North-East Atlantic.

Assessment of the process The UES/EQO dispute infected most discussions and hampered joint action in the Paris Commissions from 1974 to 1987. Moreover, it served as the basic idea behind the 'control' of dumping approach. The Contracting Parties within the Commissions agreed to disagree on the matter, and some decisions and recommendations were actually adopted based on a two-track approach. The cooperative environment developed within the Commissions appears to have prevented a complete stalemate, which could otherwise easily have occurred. The Contracting Parties acknowledged and respected each others' positions. The chief disadvantage was that this cooperation 'climate' made it difficult to solve the matter, since a clearly defined minority of the parties would have to yield.

The first real attempt to solve the dispute took place at the 1984 INSC in Bremen, where the cooperative climate permitted a more 'coercive' political approach directed against the UK. However, even the Ministers initially had limited success, although the Bremen Declaration hinted at the precautionary principle which would imply UK acceptance of the UES approach. Moreover, the Ministers decided to convene a follow-up conference to continue to address the problems. Thus, the Bremen Conference sent a clear political signal that the majority of the North Sea states wanted to end the dispute by identifying a common ground. Against this backdrop, the Paris Commission established the *ad hoc* working group in 1985. Despite signals sent from Bremen, this group was not able to make any significant progress or come up with a suggestion for solution to the Commission. However, the work of the Commission in this period contributed towards keeping the issue within an inclusive approach at the Commission level. The breakthrough came with the preparations for the 1987 London Conference and the final adoption of the precautionary principle. One may indeed wonder why the UK offered to host the second INSC, since it risked heavy political pressure to change its course. Although this is hard to verify, a likely interpretation is that the UK wanted to control the process and sought to ensure that the UES approach did not get its breakthrough.

While the principle of precautionary action has been criticised for its elusiveness, it did put an end to the UES/EQO discourse and ensured that future negotiations would stem from the same premise concerning the basic philosophy of water and marine pollution control. The Commissions continued to address the issue by including the new principles in various recommendations. Eventually, these principles were included in the new 1992 Paris Convention, thereby gaining a firm footing in international law. Thus, due to the work of the Commissions, the new agreement did not merely end up as an occasional political declaration sensitive to the current views of the UK government.

The case of dumping industrial waste at sea can illustrate the specific consequences of putting and end to the EQO/UES dispute. The adoption of the precautionary principle reversed the basic principle which had guided international policy on dumping for the previous 15 years. The Convention negotiated in the early 1970s had provided a regulatory framework for dumping subject to certain restrictions to minimise environmental damage. After 1987, this principle was turned upside down by a requirement that the dumpers had to prove through a Prior Justification Procedure (PJP) that such activities would cause no harm in the marine environment. In essence, the limitations in knowledge concerning cause-and-effect relationships became the burden of those who wanted to dump waste at sea.

The combined efforts of the Commissions and the INSCs illustrate the strengths and weaknesses of the cooperative environment stimulated by two types of institutions. Each institution could provide something that the other could not provide. The solution to the UES/EQO dispute came as a result of the combined effect of necessary conditions fulfilled by OSPARCOM and INSC. The Commissions provided an important basis for the solution as well as a means to promote persistence for the future. The INSC provided the necessary political impetus to reach the solution.

Institutional aggregation and integration capacity

International institutions may affect joint decision-making by aggregating and integrating the parties' interests and preferences. Moreover, the relative balance between aggregation and integration capacity may impact on the parties' incentives to implement joint commitments. Integration capacity is first and foremost conceived of as a function of institutional factors capable of influencing the interests and preferences of the parties and of overcoming asymmetrical interests by designing political feasible agreements. First, integration capacity may be stimulated by designing politically feasible agreements given the interests and preferences of the parties. Adaptive solutions from which at least some actors benefit and no actor lose may be provided by various 'fast-track' options. Second, the parties' interests can be influenced and combined by the production and sharing of damage and abatement knowledge. In addition, integration capacity may be stimulated by the establishment of selective incentives provided by specific institutional arrangements aimed at increasing access to funding, resources, markets and technology. In contrast to some other environmental regimes, such arrangements have not played any important role in the North Sea cooperation.

While the essence of integration is to influence and combine interests, aggregation capacity is a matter of establishing priorities and cutting through deadlocks. Aggregation capacity reaches its maximum in purely hierarchical systems and its minimum in systems requiring unanimity, while high-level conferences and summits may forge trade-offs that reach beyond the authority of low-level officials. Significant *imbalance* between these functions may lead to a mismatch between the stringency of joint commitments and incentives to implement them (cf. P_4, p. 53).

The first decade: low integration and aggregation capacity
The Paris Convention makes provision for both 'abatement' and 'damage' science. However, the bodies established to serve these functions did not function well in the first decade, when judged against the goals set out in the Convention. According to Article 10, the contracting parties shall establish complementary or joint programmes of scientific and technical research: including research into the best methods of eliminating or replacing noxious substances so as to reduce marine pollution from land-based sources, and to transmit to each other the information so obtained. Article 11 requires that the parties shall set up joint monitoring programmes in order to assess the existing level of pollution. The Technical Working Group and various *ad hoc* working groups focused first and foremost on identifying sources of pollutants. Less effort was invested in joint research on means to cope with such sources. Although the TWG did produce some relevant data during the first decade, a report on cadmium, mercury, and PCB inputs prepared by an *ad hoc* working group in 1984 concluded that there was a general lack of information about the methodologies used by the Contracting Parties in measuring inputs and the analytical limits of detection varies markedly.[12] The Oslo Convention also includes requirements for abatement and damage science, in line with Articles 12 and 13 respectively. At its first meeting in 1974, the Commission agreed on the terms of reference for the Standing Advisory Committee on Scientific Advice. The SACSA focused particularly on the development of various Codes of Practice to be followed in order to control dumping activities. There was almost no systematic research on alternative disposal methods, with the exception of sewage sludge where alternative disposal options were identified.

The Paris and Oslo Conventions aimed at 'diagnosing' problems through environmental monitoring. The Joint Monitoring Group was to coordinate the monitoring programmes of the Commissions and advise on how, when, where and what to sample and measure. Monitoring of environmental quality had significant shortcomings with regard to land-based sources. According to Wettestad (1998) the JMG was malfunctioning. Likewise, Ducrotoy (1997: 177) claims that the group was unable to tackle the existing shortfall in knowledge about the North Sea. Input studies of regulated substances were inadequate and indeed lacking in most cases. In 1987, the Joint Monitoring Group was still preoccupied with developing monitoring methodology, and was not able to indicate to the Commission any clear trends with regard to any substance.[13] Monitoring of dumping grounds was also insufficient. Monitoring of dumping grounds for dredge materials was still inadequate and even non-existent in 1990.[14]

While uncertainty concerning inputs, concentrations and effects was high, the level of scientific disagreement was quite low. According to the Annual Reports from the meetings, scientific arguments occasionally surfaced in the Commission. However, discussions were mainly related to the lack and relevance of data, and not the reliability of the assessments and recommendations of the technical/scientific bodies. Thus, we may characterise the quality of the scientific basis in the first decade of the cooperation as high in uncertainty and high in consensus.

While the production and sharing of scientific knowledge can affect the interests and preferences of the parties, another set of institutional factors has the potential to develop politically feasible agreements given the interests of the parties. Of significant importance concerning the latter was the fact that the Conventions did not include any procedures that could differentiate among its members, or allow others to proceed by 'fast-track' options. Spain and Portugal do not border on the North Sea, but they could not be treated differently from the North Sea states albeit other parts of the Convention area had needs different from those of the North Sea owing to geographical, hydrographic, and ecological circumstances. On the other hand, different systemic actors acted as mediators and served as bridge-builders to overcome the polarized situation within the Oslo Commission.

The tiny Secretariat for the Oslo and Paris Commissions with its five or six staff in the mid-1980s represented the 'engine' of the cooperation in the first decade. One way of measuring the *involve-*

ment of the Secretariat – and thus its potential to influence the course of actions – is by looking at the number of documents prepared by the Secretariat for the Commission meetings in relation to those prepared by the Contracting Parties and other actors. The preparation of documents for the various agenda items provides the Secretariat with the possibility to affect the premises for subsequent discussions.

The level of involvement of the Secretariat was very high in the first decade (Table 6.1). On average, 71 per cent of all documents prepared for the Commissions meetings stood in the name of the Secretariat, while the remaining 29 per cent stood mainly in the name of the Contracting Parties and, to some extent, international governmental organizations. Although the Secretariat operated under quite restrictive formal procedures in terms of political initiatives, it should perform any task remitted by the Commissions or by the Chairman. The latter opened up for its role as an active mediator in practice. In some cases, the Secretariat came up with compromise proposals based on the parties' preferences. In other cases, the Secretariat would propose its own solutions (Sætevik 1988: 117). Especially in those cases where the Secretary and the Chairman were able to work closely together, their behaviour could promote outcomes that would otherwise probably not have materialized.[15] These observations show that activism is not necessarily linked to size in the sense that very small secretariats may have significant influence.

The requirement of *unanimity* had two important consequences within the Oslo Commission. First, it provided the 'laggards' with

Table 6.1 *Documents prepared for Paris Commission by the Secretariat, 1978–84*

	Total	*Secretariat*	*Share of total(%)*
1978	45	33	75
1980	18	13	72
1981	11	11	100
1982	18	13	72
1983	26	17	65
1984	30	13	43

Source: Skjærseth (1999).

veto power over proposals which they opposed. Of the North Sea states, this procedure equipped especially the UK with the necessary power to block any joint initiatives. Second, it led to protracted decision-making, due to the need to negotiate compromise agreements acceptable to all parties. Initially, the inclusion of qualified majority procedures in the Paris Commission had been viewed as a 'victory' for the cooperation. However, unanimity came to serve as the basic decision rule in use since little can be achieved unless decisions are supported by those significantly affected by the decision.

The major 'blocker' was the EC Commission, which blocked six proposals followed by the UK which blocked two (Sætevik 1988). Since the EC Commission had adopted Uniform Emission Standards as the preferred approach, this behaviour was probably more a reaction to the EC system than any opposition to the content of the proposals. The distribution of competence between the Commission and the member-states was unclear and defined as an 'internal' matter. However, in those cases where binding decisions were proposed by the Paris Commission, the Council of Ministers would have to take the final decision. For example, recommendations on cadmium and mercury had to be postponed due to EC reservation and could not be adopted as decisions in the Paris Commission until the Council of Ministers approved the proposals, which it did in 1985.

While the low level of participation in the Oslo and Paris Commissions promoted diffuse reciprocity, it hampered joint decision-making. Delegation leaders were sometimes worried about reactions from their respective superior authorities with regard to proposals for decisions (Sætevik 1988: 117). In order to avoid any mismatch between joint commitments and national preferences, the delegations operated under restrictive domestic mandates, which in turn meant that each delegations had minor leeway for making compromises. Thus, in the first decade, the aggregation capacity of OSPARCOM was low in terms of both decision rules in use and the level of cooperation.

We may conclude that cooperation within OSPARCOM was equipped with some procedures that would allow for a certain degree of integration and aggregations capacity that could have been utilized to overcome the interests and preferences of the 'least ambitious' actors. However, the cooperation was based on unanimity in practice, and lacked the will to provide new information as to ways of reaching and implementing joint decisions and 'diagnosing' problems. In addition, the cooperation was based on low level of participation, and there were no procedures allowing for 'fast-track' options. However, the systemic actors provided some impetus and acted as mediators as well as proposers of integrative solutions. With this reservation in mind, we may say that the first decade was marked by low integration and aggregation capacity, which in turn indicates scant possibilities to adopt and implement stringent joint commitments.

The second decade: increasing aggregation and integration capacity
In the second decade, both TWG and SACSA focused more on abatement science. At the joint meeting of the Oslo and Paris Commissions in 1987, it was decided to exchange information on abatement technology. Against this backdrop, the Paris Commission established the Industrial Sectors Working Group in 1989 (INDSEC). The INDSEC identified 13 industrial sectors, and lead countries with expertise in the field were appointed to prepare assessment on each sector as a basis for joint action in the Commission. The lead country approach promotes an integrative effect, since the lead country principle reduces the possibility that countries that lack a given sector will insist on regulating it to the discomfort of those countries with the sector (Haas 1993: 144). As of 1992, seven studies had been concluded and six of them actually led to joint action in the Paris Commission.[16] Two other permanent 'abatement' working groups were also established in the second decade with relevance for land-based inputs of nutrients and hazardous substances. At its eighth meeting in 1986, the Paris Commission established a Working Group on Nutrients (NUT) and approved its terms of reference. The work of NUT led to a comprehensive report on inputs from different sources, eutrophication symptoms and problem areas as well as a detailed scrutiny of the existence, practicability and effectiveness of measures.[17] Several new recommendations were adopted in the wake of NUT. For example, in 1988 the commission adopted a recommendation on the 50 per cent reduction target. At its twelfth meeting in 1990, the Paris Commission also agreed to establish a Working Group to consider *diffuse sources* of hazardous substances reaching Convention waters, irrespective of their route to these waters. Of the six sources identified in 1990, three have been covered by joint commitments as of

1995: agricultural pesticides, toxic chemicals from aquaculture and household and consumer goods.

In contrast to the Paris Commission, the Oslo Commission did not establish any new permanent working groups after 1987. However, the Commissions agreed in 1987 that SACSA should follow up the requirements on technology by reviewing alternative means of disposal for the industrial wastes being dumped. The SACSA undertook similar activities concerning incineration at sea and dumping of sewage sludge. Both types of activities were to be phased out. For example, with regard to incineration at sea, both alternative options and cost aspects were scrutinized. The information provided appears to have had an integrative effect. Studies conducted in Germany concluded that the cost difference between incineration at sea and incineration on land would be insignificant and remain within acceptable limits.[18] In contrast to Germany, the UK had estimated a cost difference between sea- and land-based incineration in the order of 3–4:1. Even though costs may differ from one country to another, it seemed clear that the UK had overestimated, and the UK delegation informed the *ad hoc* working group on incineration at sea that estimates would be recalculated in the light of the German results. Thus, the information provided on the economic consequences of switching from ocean-based to land-based incineration changed the problem to one of cost-efficiency.

In 1993, a more systematic scrutiny of alternative measures and means was introduced by the replacement of SACSA and TWG by the programmes and Measures Committee (PRAM) linked to the new 1992 Convention. The function of PRAM is to draw up programmes and measures for the prevention and elimination of pollution. According to its terms of reference, PRAM is to initiate technical studies and keep under review the progress of scientific and technical knowledge. Moreover, it is to advise the Commission on these matters, as well as preparing proposals for Decisions and Recommendations for consideration in the Commission.

Damage science was also intensified significantly in the second decade, thanks to the initiatives taken by the 1987 INSC. The first international report on the *quality status* of the North Sea had been compiled by a Group of Experts commissioned to prepare a synthesis of the scientific material submitted by the North Sea riparian states and the EC to the 1984 Bremen Conference. This 1984 Quality Status Report (QSR) merely represented a compilation of the national reports and opinions of the North Sea states and was thus closely related to political interests. The 1984 QSR painted a picture of high uncertainty concerning inputs, concentration and effects.[19] In line with the policy that the Second North Sea Conference in 1987 should be science based, a revised and updated QSR was prepared in 1987.[20] This was the first attempt at a synthesized overview of the entire North Sea ecosystem. The only disagreement hinted at was related to the relationship between PCBs and fish populations. The second QSR demonstrated both that much was known about the North Sea ecosystem and that there were significant shortcomings in the data. In particular, it was still not possible to prove causal links between contaminant levels and environmental changes.

The major concern of the Ministers was the high level of uncertainty revealed by the 1987 QSR. Against this backdrop, the London Conference concluded that there was a need to enhance the scientific knowledge and understanding of the North Sea. The Oslo and Paris Commissions and International Council for the Exploration of the Sea (ICES) were charged with establishing a new joint working group, which subsequently became the North Sea Task Force. In contrast to the previous Quality Status Reports, the NSTF was charged with the task of producing new knowledge by organizing a coordinated scientific programme that should lead to a dependable and comprehensive statement in 1993 of inputs, concentrations and effects. For example, the Task Force developed a new monitoring plan (Monitoring Master Plan) utilizing newly developed measurement and techniques.[21] Moreover, the NSTF represented a new way of organizing damage science. Previously, the responsibility of monitoring and assessment work had been split among the JMG, the INSC working groups and partly the TWG and SACSA. The NSTF brought coherency into this fragmented environment (Reid 1990: 87–8).

The NSTF completed its task and published an updated North Sea Quality Status Report in 1993. This 1993 report gives a comprehensive account of the characteristics of the North Sea as well as of man's impact on the ecosystem. The 1993 QSR does not reveal any significant disagreement: 'the report that follows represents a best practical overall assessment of and a consensual opinion on the present status of the North Sea in physical, chemical, and biological terms'.[22] The report was welcomed by the Ministers at the Intermediate Ministerial Meeting in 1993 and was debated by the scientific community, including representatives of NGOs, at a Scientific Symposium in April 1994. In broad terms, the conclusions reached in the 1993 QSR parallel those of the 1987 QSR. Uncertainty with regard to cause–effect relationships was still significant and there were remaining issues of concern that would require further action. Despite the remaining uncertainty, the 1993 QSR can be said to have reduced the degree of uncertainty in at least two ways. First, uncertainty was reduced especially with regard to input data. These data became essential in assessing compliance with the 50 per cent reduction targets adopted at the INSC conferences. Second, and probably more importantly, the degree of uncertainty as to cause–effect relationships changed in a rather peculiar direction. Previously, it had been believed that gaps in knowledge concerning the relationship between inputs, concentrations and effects could be filled through more effective scientific research and monitoring. A major new element in the 1993 QSR involved the recognition that significant uncertainty would probably be permanent. Thus, we may say that uncertainty was decreased with regard to the prospects of reducing uncertainty. This made more 'robust' the scientific basis for the commitments on hazardous substances in particular based on the need of precautionary action and emission standards, since these commitments had been based on insufficient knowledge.

Capacity to identify feasible solutions also grew in the second decade. The German initiative to organize the first INSC in 1984 represented in itself a *regionalization* of the original cooperation within the framework of the Oslo and Paris Conventions, excluding the wider North-East Atlantic and narrowing in on the North Sea and the North Sea states. Iceland, Ireland, Spain and Portugal were decoupled from the North Sea cooperation and France became marginalized. Even though France is an official party to the INSC Declarations and borders on the English Channel, which clearly falls under the body of water defined as the North Sea by the Parties, its main coastline borders on the North-East Atlantic and the Mediterranean. In very few cases has France reported on achievements according to percentage reduction targets adopted in 1987 and 1990. This indicates that it never had any serious intentions of implementing the Declarations. Indeed, France has largely and tacitly been accepted by the other parties as a mere 'bystander' in the sense that its lack of enthusiasm has not hampered the progress of others. As a response to INSC regionalization, the integrative capacity of OSPARCOM also increased by means of changing procedures. As we have seen, previous arrangements had prevented those bordering on the North Sea from proceeding through 'fast-track' procedures. In 1988, the Dutch delegations to the Oslo and Paris Commissions presented a proposal that could open the way for differentiated obligations in the light of the North Sea Conference process. Portugal and Spain in particular emphasized that the problems of the North Sea were not necessarily reflected in other parts of the Convention area.

New procedures that allowed for different routes and timetables became operational immediately and they were to prove crucial in OSPARCOM's efforts to implement the North Sea Declarations. For example, the recommendation adopted in 1989 on a coordinated programme for nutrient reduction applied only to the North Sea states, while the parties would consider similar actions in other Convention waters. The new procedures adopted by OSPARCOM in 1988 were subsequently included and expanded to cover economic considerations in the 1992 Paris Convention for the Protection of the Marine Environment of the North-East Atlantic.

The systemic actors continued as bridge-builders in the second decade. The size of the Secretariat almost doubled from the mid-1980s – from a staff of 5–6 to 11–12 in the 1990s. However, since the scope of the cooperation (and consequently the workload) also increased this does not necessarily imply an increase in net administrative capacity available for integrative activities. In fact, the level of involvement of the Secretariat in relation to other actors decreased somewhat in the second decade. The average share of documents prepared by the Secretariat was 52 per cent in the second decade as compared to 71 per cent in the first (Skjærseth 1999). Thus, the level of involvement was still significant, albeit lower than between 1978 and 1984. One important reason for this development was an increase in documents prepared and presented by NGOs. In the second decade, more types of actors were able to have their say, and the relative level of involvement of the Secretariat became lower, although it still played an important role. For example, the Secretariat was the driving force in pushing for and developing the new procedures on implementation reporting in the early 1990s.

While the OSPARCOM provided higher integration capacity in

the second decade, the International North Sea Conferences provided higher aggregation capacity. However, this change was only to a minor extent related to changes in decision-making rules. The main change in aggregation capacity introduced by the INSC occurred due to the change in level of representation – from the middle-level civil servant representation in OSPARCOM to Ministers of the Environment at the INSC. While the basic mechanism at work is relatively clear in the case of changing from unanimity to majority rules, the consequences of changing the level of representation are more complex. At least the following factors seem to play a role in combination. First, politicians are more sensitive to social demands and public pressure than bureaucrats, since they are accountable to their domestic electorates. Accordingly, their willingness to cut through deadlocks and adopt ambitious commitments is likely to be sensitive to changes in such demands. Second, while lower-level civil servants appear very cautious about exceeding their mandate, ministers are under greater pressure to have something to show back home. We may perhaps say that lower-level civil servants are under pressure to minimize domestic obligations in order to avoid negative reactions from higher-order decision-makers, whereas ministers are under pressure to maximize domestic obligations in order to avoid reservations or blocking of agreements. This mechanism is closely related to the high media attention that has surrounded the Ministerial Conferences, in contrast to the annual meetings of the Oslo and Paris Commissions.

While the integrative capacity of OSPARCOM increased as a response to the Ministerial Declarations – especially with the introduction of the principle of differential obligations – this change was insufficient to ensure international implementation of the Declarations. Although the Paris Convention opened the way to majority decisions, agreement prevailed as the decision rule 'in use' in the first decade. However, this practice changed in the early 1990s. There was an increase in reservations to the decisions and recommendations, especially with regard to commitments to combat hazardous substances. For example, 18 reservations were filed in 1994 of which the UK was responsible for eight (Skjærseth 1999).

We may conclude that aggregation and integration capacity increased significantly in the second decade, due particularly to a higher level of representation combined with regionalization provided by the INSC. The change to ministerial representation magnified pressure, especially against the UK, which remained the main 'laggard' once Spain and Portugal had been decoupled from the INSC cooperation. Moreover, France became marginalized, as it has only to a limited extent borders on the North Sea. The OSPARCOM responded to this change by increasing aggregation and integration capacity as well by adopting the principle of differential obligations and by changing the decision rules in use.

Consequences of change in aggregation and integration capacity
The first decade of OSPARCOM was marked by low aggregation and integration capacity. According to P_4 (see p. 53) we would thus expect scant possibilities of reaching and implementing stringent joint commitments. With regard to commitments, we find a high degree of convergence between expectations and observed patterns. As concluded in Chapter 4, relatively few commitments were actually adopted in the first decade, and these tended to be lenient. In essence, the joint commitments adopted largely reflected the interests and preferences of the 'least ambitious' actors. According to the latter part of the proposition, we can also expect scant possibilities for implementing measures that significantly affect behaviour in line with the joint commitments actually adopted. This is particularly due to the low integration capacity provided by OSPARCOM in the first decade. From the poor data provided by the cooperation itself, we see that lenient commitments did not lead to widespread implementation. For example, in one of the rare cases where the Commission tried to assess compliance, the conclusion is that:

> The Commission took note that the TWG had reviewed information submitted by the United Kingdom, the Netherlands, Denmark, Ireland and Portugal, which had summarised the situation with respect to the usage of the 'drins' in their respective countries. The Commission took note with regret that there had been no substantial progress in the phasing out of the drins.[23]

However, the preceding analysis has shown that the patterns observed are not necessarily causally related to aggregation and integration capacity procedures. The EC Commission was seen to be the main 'blocking' party in the OSPARCOM in the first decade. Thus, the behaviour of the Commission as part of the EC system may represent an important explanation of the lenient outcomes.

Perhaps one explanation behind the joint commitments lies in Commission reluctance caused by the distribution of competence between the Commission and the EC member-states. The Council of Ministers had to take the final decision in those cases where legally binding decisions were proposed by the Paris Commission. It is further clear the EC did not formally allow for majority procedures on environmental Directives or Decisions until the Single European Act was adopted in 1986 and entered into force in 1987. Thus, single member-states could in principle block PARCOM proposals in the Council of Ministers.

The crucial question then becomes the degree of match between 'laggards' participating in OSPARCOM and the EC. Greece did not participate in OSPARCOM, but joined the EC in 1981. Moreover, Greece has generally behaved as a laggard in international environmental cooperation independent of issue-areas, frequently together with Spain and Portugal, which joined the EC in 1986 (Skjærseth, Andresen and Wettestad 1992). Thus, in theory, Greece had the formal possibility to block PARCOM Decisions at EC level. In other words, the behaviour of Greece in the Council of Ministers might explain a reluctant EC behaviour, if that Greece represented a less enthusiastic party than Spain and Portugal *and* was willing systematically to veto PARCOM initiatives at EC level. Neither of these conditions is very likely. Spain and Portugal were not EC members in the first decade, so it actually seems more likely that the EC had higher capacity to adopt joint commitments since OSPARCOM had two 'southern' laggards, while the EC had only one. In any case, the UK participated both in the EC and in OSPARCOM and represented the most powerful laggard with regard to emission standards, also in the EC. In short, then, while the behaviour of the EC Commission on some occasions has protracted PARCOM decision-making, it does not appear as a major cause of the few and lenient commitments actually adopted. In fact, the EC Commission has also been identified as a 'pusher' in the Paris Commission, since the Paris Commission in some instances – like mercury – could base its work on existing EC legislation (Sætevik 1988: 101–2).

These considerations point toward the following main conclusion: high integration and aggregation capacity constitute necessary, though not sufficient, conditions for stringent joint commitments in situations characterized by asymmetrical interests and preferences. Participation by systemic actors that are part of other institutions –

in this case the EC Commission – may hamper joint decision-making. Where such institutions include other 'laggards' than those involved in the cooperation, this may lead to a deadlock if unanimity is required. On the other hand, such participation may also have a positive effect if other institutions have developed more advanced rules and procedures.

Both aggregation and integration capacity increased significantly in the second decade. Accordingly, we would expect better possibilities for adopting and implementing stringent joint commitments. The patterns observed conform with the expectation that joint commitments were significantly strengthened (cf. Chapter 4). Change in aggregation capacity was due to a combination of change in level of participation and change in decision-making rules in use. As in the first decade, however, factors other than those directly linked to aggregation capacity influenced the course of events. First, high-level conferences are very sensitive to changes in societal demands in the countries concerned, as ministers are accountable to their electorates. Since the UK remained the major lowest common denominator within the INSC, a significant change in social demands for environmental protection prior to the 1987 North Sea Conference may indicate that change in public attitudes does represent the fundamental explanatory factor. Chapter 8 presents a scrutiny of changes in societal demands. To anticipate, a central finding is that changes in social demands increased most significantly *after* the 1987 Conference, where the original breakthrough came not only in the UK, but generally in the North Sea states. Thus, change in societal demands does not appear as sufficiently significant to render change in level of participation spurious.

The EC Commission did not represent the main potential 'blocking party' in the second decade. The Commission was a party to the INSC and agreed with the INSC Declarations without tabling any 'footnotes'. Thus, since the Commission probably protracted joint decision-making in the first decade, this effect decreased in the second decade. Moreover, in the 1990s relevant EC Directives became increasingly important (cf. Chapter 4.). Important reasons for this change may be found in institutional changes at EC level. In particular, the aggregation and integration capacity of the EC itself increased in the area of the environment after the adoption of the Single European Act in 1986 and the Maastricht Treaty, which came into effect in 1993. As in the first decade, the change in aggregation capacity appears as a necessary, though not sufficient, condition for the change in joint commitments in the second decade.

Since integration capacity also increased, we would expect implementation to have increased as well. From the data presented in Chapter 4 we can see that the level of implementation increased significantly compared to the first decade. This strongly indicates that integration capacity has increased apace with the increase in aggregation capacity. With regard to 'abatement science', OSPARCOM significantly intensified joint efforts to assess *how* the joint commitments could be achieved. This was accomplished mainly by establishing new and permanent scientific/technical working groups based on the 'lead country' approach. Integration capacity through identifying political feasible solutions also increased in the second decade. This change was first and foremost related to a change in OSPARCOM procedures allowing Spain and Portugal to be treated differently from the North Sea states in terms of joint commitments. Since these two clearly had needs different from those of the North Sea states, this change represented a necessary condition for OSPARCOM's ability to transform the North Sea Declarations into decisions and recommendations.

As noted in P_4 (see p. 53), balancing integration and aggregation capacity may be crucial to ensure both the adoption and the implementation of stringent joint commitments. While high aggregation capacity may stimulate the adoption of stringent commitments, incentives for implementing them may be scarce. Conversely, high integration capacity may affect incentives to implement joint commitments, but such capacity will not necessarily ensure that such joint obligations are adopted. At a general level, the combination of integration and aggregation capacity appears roughly balanced within the cooperation in both decades. We also see a clear pattern of different institutions fulfilling different functions. The North Sea Conferences provided mainly aggregation capacity, while the standing OSPARCOM cooperation was crucial in providing integration capacity. The Conferences had the necessary capacity to cut through and establish clear priorities, while OSPARCOM combined and influenced the interests of the parties. Thus, each institution provided something the other could not provide, and the consequences lie largely in the combined effect.

International commitments: constraining the behaviour of states

Given the existence of cooperative environments and some combination of aggregation and integration capacity, collective outcomes in the form of international commitments are likely to be produced. International commitments may constrain the activities of states and limit discretion. Thus, international commitments may be characterised along a continuum from discretion to constraint. Discretion centres on the degree of freedom actors have to judge independently whether certain activities are permissible, while actors are constrained to the extent international commitments do not leave room for them to decide for themselves whether an activity is permissible (Nollkaemper 1993). Discretion and constraint are here conceived of as a function of strength and compliance control. Strength is determined by legal status and specificity, while compliance control is determined by verification and enforcement. This point of departure permits for two different views on the behavioural mechanisms at work when actors comply or defect from their international obligations. On the one hand, some argue that states violate obligations whenever it is in their economic interests to do so. In this case, international commitments may constrain behaviour as long as they affect the incentives underlying such interests. On the other hand, some argue that states will not necessarily defect under such circumstances due to the authoritativeness of joint obligations. In this case, it is the authoritativeness of joint commitments that triggers behavioural response rather than calculations of anticipated costs and benefits associated with different options. In both cases, however, the interlink between institutional factors and behavioural mechanisms has the capacity to reduce discretion.

The first decade: low constraint and high discretion

The commitments adopted in the first decade provided the parties with significant discretion. We may distinguish three main categories of joint commitments that apply to North Sea/North-East Atlantic cooperation. First, we have water quality standards and objectives that set general or specific minimum values for the quality of receiving waters. The second category consists of emission standards and percentage reduction standards. Obligations to apply particular technological processes and certain environmental practices represent the third category. These three categories may be conceived of along a means–ends dimension in which the latter category is more confined to means. Crudely speaking, a development from quality standards via emissions standards towards technological processes and environmental practices represents in itself a development towards greater specificity: from controlling pollutants at sea towards controlling processes and practices at source. Specificity is enhanced by linking obligations more directly to the specific sources of pollution.

The commitments included in the Paris Convention and adopted during the first decade of the Paris Commission centred mainly on quality standards. The Paris Convention itself focused on water quality – to reduce pollution in the maritime area. In the case of mercury and cadmium, the parties could choose between quality and emission standards. In addition, some commitments aimed at prohibiting and phasing out substances were adopted. While prohibition may eliminate discretion completely, the commitments for phasing out substances included loopholes that, in effect, did not place any clear obligations on the states. For example, in 1978, the parties agreed that the drins should be phased out of use as soon as ecologically less harmful substitutes were available for each of the present uses of these substances. A similar type of wording was adopted for PCBs and PCTs: they were to be phased out by new equipment *as soon as possible*. The elasticity of these concept means that they contain hardly any substantive obligations.

The Oslo Convention was more precise than the Paris Convention in two ways. First, although Article 1 of the Oslo Convention also focused on pollution, it was stipulated that all possible steps should be taken to prevent such pollution by substances *liable* to create hazards. Second, this liability prescription led to the following obligation included in Article 5: the dumping of substances listed in Annex I to the Convention is prohibited. At first glance, Article 5 would seem straightforward. However, other provisions in the Convention opened the way to dumping of Annex I substances which 'rapidly converted into substances which are biologically harmless' and if they were 'non-toxic'. Moreover, Annex I substances could be dumped if they appeared as merely 'trace contaminants'. In addition, Annex II substances required a permit only if they were dumped in 'significant quantities'. Aware of the dangers of these potential loopholes, the Contracting Parties tried to operationalize these qualifiers during the first decade. While procedures were approved at the first meeting of the Oslo Commission regarding the terms 'non-toxic', 'trace contaminants' and 'significant quantities', only the latter was defined with sufficient precision. Annex II substances are said to be present in significant quantities if they represent more than 0.1 per cent of the weight of the waste disposed of. Nevertheless, the commitments adopted did not clearly oblige the parties to do anything – at least not in the short term.

In general, there is a conviction in both the legal literature on international obligations and more specifically among the OSPARCOM parties that joint commitments should preferably be legally binding on states. These views are based on the assumption that states will be more inclined to comply with legal than with non-legal obligations. In other words, the constraint imposed by commitments will be greater. A state is seen as legally bound by a certain commitment as long as it consents to a legally binding obligation. This point of departure implies that the Oslo and Paris Conventions are binding, whereas the INSC Declarations are not. However, the bindingness of commitments adopted in the Oslo and Paris Commissions is somewhat unclear. Until 1984 an explicit distinction was not made between recommendations and decisions. Given this uncertainty, about half of the commitments adopted up to 1985 were legally binding decisions.[24]

Verification refers to institutional procedures for controlling compliance with internationally adopted goals (Andresen 1992: 102). Both the Paris and Oslo Conventions include provisions related to this function. As previously noted, the Paris Commission and its working groups did not develop any systematic verification procedures in the first decade. The monitoring work was aimed at assessing general pollution trends, not whether the parties were meeting their environmental quality standards. The work of TWG focused mainly on identifying sources of pollution, and not the measures taken to comply with emission standards or prohibition. Thus, the verification obligations included in the Paris Convention were in fact not complied with. Concerning the Oslo Convention pollutants in the Convention area are to be monitored, and records of permits and approvals issued by the Contracting Parties shall be reported to the Commission. Compared to the Paris Commission, the verification system functioned well in the Oslo Commission. By the early 1980s, the Commission and the Secretariat had a good overview over who was dumping what, where and how much

(Skjærseth 1991: 63). Although the Oslo Commission verified performance, it did not utilize this information to assess compliance. This was related to the fact that OSCOM had not adopted specific commitments that included standards against which compliance could be assessed.

If that non-compliance were verified, what were the possibilities for holding a state responsible and bringing the case before an international court or tribunal? In theory, this would depend on the legal nature of obligations since only non-compliance with legal rules can involve state responsibility (Nollkaemper 1993: 237). In practice, however, the difference is minor if not totally absent. Throughout history, enforcement has always been the weakest part of international efforts regulating marine pollution (IJlstra 1986; Somers 1990). The theoretical possibility that international legal action carries any deterrent effect does not seem very reasonable, due to lack of practice. This is supported by the fact that the parties to the Paris Commission have recognized that an effective international enforcement system is lacking. The Paris Convention does not include any explicit procedures for cases of non-compliance.

The situation is more complex with regard to dumping and incineration, since they represent vessel-source pollution. According to Article 15 of the Oslo Convention, each Contracting Party shall take in its territory appropriate measures to prevent and *punish* conduct in contravention of the provisions of the Convention. The courts of the flag-state are competent to institute proceedings, irrespective of where a violation has occurred. In practice, the requirement of issuing permits within the framework of the Oslo Convention was formally implemented by the adoption of national legislation requiring dumpers to apply for such permits. If the dumpers fail to comply with the conditions underlying the permits, national authorities can take legal action. For example, UK authorities have fined non-compliance with their national dumping Acts. Thus, while the enforcement procedures do not constrain state behaviour in any significant way, they may constrain target-group behaviour in the case of dumping at sea.

We may conclude that the first decade of OSPARCOM left the participating states with significant discretion. Specificity was low, verification of compliance nearly absent, and possibilities for enforcement meagre. On the other hand, the Conventions and commitments adopted were legally binding. In terms of enforcement, however, this seems to have had minor practical consequences for possibilities to constrain state behaviour.

The second decade: towards higher constraint and lower discretion

The INSC Declarations of 1987 and 1990 included percentage reductions to combat dumping and incineration at sea, hazardous substances and nutrients. These commitments share three features. First, the commitments set forth an unequivocal objective concerned with limiting a certain percentage of discharges. Second, the discharges are to be reduced according to a baseline year. Third, the discharges are to be reduced within a specified deadline. Thus, we may generally argue that commitments included in the INSC Declarations served to increase specificity significantly. Most obligations adopted within PARCOM from 1989 were based on Best Available Technology, or other measures directed against specific industry sectors. Best Available Technology clearly removes discretion as to the means to be applied and will consequently carry a significant potential for actual prevention. Moreover, BAT shifts the focus from 'end-of-pipe' emissions to processes that can prevent the production of regulated substances. Requirements to apply Best Environmental Practices (BEP) represent a variant of BAT to be applied on diffuse sources. As with BAT, Best Environmental Practice focuses on measures. In contrast to BAT, there is not *one* best practice, which means a higher level of discretion as compared to BAT. However, obligations to apply BEP may also be made more specific by linking such obligations to specific sectors. For example, a PARCOM Recommendation adopted in 1992 on the reduction of nutrients from agriculture applies this approach. A list of 40 specific measures is included and the Contracting Parties agree to apply all, or some, of these measures. Thus, discretion may well be high, but it is not unlimited.

Any doubts about the legal nature of decisions and recommendations were removed by the new 1992 Paris Convention on the Protection of the North-East Atlantic. According to Article 13, decisions are legally binding, whereas recommendations shall have no legally binding force. In general, increase in specificity went hand in hand with a tendency to adopt non-binding obligations. The INSC Declarations including obligations on percentage reductions were not binding within the framework of international law. In addition, of the 12 commitments adopted from 1989 within

PARCOM that explicitly refer to BAT and BEP, none were legally binding. Most of the legally binding decisions in this period had a general focus on reduction in discharges and pollution from specific industry sectors.

Verification procedures and practice improved significantly in the second decade. As noted the INSCs systematically reviewed the achievements of each preceding Conference by preparing comprehensive implementation and progress reports on legal and administrative measures taken as well as on reductions in inputs of regulated substances. Verification procedures remained poorly developed in the Paris Commission until the new Paris Convention on the Protection of the North-East Atlantic was adopted in 1992. In contrast to the old Paris Convention, the new Convention includes separate articles (22 and 23) dealing exclusively with reporting and compliance. While both the Oslo and Paris Conventions explicitly placed the responsibility for assessing and securing compliance on the Contracting Parties, the new Convention makes it clear that this is to be the duty of the Commission. Moreover, implementation problems are addressed as a concern. The requirements included in Articles 22 and 23 were immediately brought into operation by the establishment of the Programmes and Measures standing working group in 1993. In turn, PRAM developed specific reporting procedures on implementation that were agreed upon at the 1994 OSPARCOM meeting. This change significantly raised the level of transparency as to compliance.

The new 1992 Paris Convention does not include any specific Articles on enforcement. However, there are some signals indicating slightly more weight given to this function. The Contracting Parties shall report on particular measures taken to prevent and punish conduct in contravention of those provisions. However, this general obligation apparently refers to national authorities' enforcement against sub-national target groups, and not enforcement on the part of states.

We may note that discretion was reduced in two important ways in the second decade. First, the specificity of the joint commitments increased significantly. Second, procedures and practice to verify implementation and compliance increased correspondingly. Concurrent with this development, there has been a tendency to resort to non-legal binding commitments especially for the most specific commitments adopted on land-based sources. Procedures and practice with regard to international enforcement have, however, remained constant and weak.

Assessing the consequences of reduced discretion

The first part of P_5 (see p. 55) generally states that reduced discretion will increase the probabilities of behavioural change going in the right 'direction'. While implementation clearly increased in the second decade, it is very difficult to single out the effect of reduced discretion from other factors. In general, one may argue that vagueness results from problems of achieving agreement. Conversely, if the level of agreement is high, there will be no need to adopt vague commitments. Consequently, there is reason to suspect that high aggregation capacity leads to high specificity. If this assumption is correct, specificity will by itself represent a spurious factor. However, an equal degree of specificity may go hand in hand with variation in agreement. In the case of land-based discharges for example, we found no clear variations in specificity in the first decade, in the sense that all commitments adopted within the Paris Commission appeared vague in one way or the other. Since the level of agreement concerning each commitment varied, there was no automatic relationship between degree of consensus and degree of specificity. We have strong indications that the reason may at times be the case due to scientific and technical complexities. While quality standards and emission standards both may be formulated in terms of unequivocal numerical limits, these approaches vary significantly in terms of constraint. Even if all parties agreed to apply a stringent quality standard for substance X in fish flesh, the parties would still not know exactly what to do, when and how, due to scientific uncertainty as to the causal link between discharges, concentrations and effects. Thus, while level of agreement clearly matters for specificity, it does not follow automatically from agreement that commitments maximising constraint will be chosen.

One way of approaching the *consequences* of specificity is to compare variations in different sub-problems within one decade. This strategy would help us to control for change in other variables from the first to the second decade. Take, for example, dumping at sea in the first decade. In general, all OSPARCOM parties had agreed to prevent pollution by substances liable to create hazards. However, obligations concerning Annex I substances were not only more demanding than those covering Annex II substances, but also more specific. Thus, if specificity matters, we would expect more significant reductions in Annex I substances than in Annex II substances. This conforms with realities. Concerning dumping of sewage sludge, a Recommendation from 1980 obliged the parties to reduce heavy metals included in both Annexes. Annex I substances were actually reduced to a significant larger extent than Annex II substances (Skjærseth 1991).

In the second decade, verification procedures and practice improved concurrent with a reduction in vagueness. Our general assumption related to the consequences of verification centered on its capacity to stimulate mutual expectations that cheating will be detected, which in turn could remove incentives for free-riding. First, verification has affected the relationship between states by exposing the laggards to international pressure. At a general level, increased transparency between states has put pressure on the UK. While the UK tried to get rid of the sobriquet 'the dirty man of Europe' after the 1987 Conference, the 1990 North Sea Conference in The Hague was the first international event to present a comprehensive assessment of implementation. According to the host, the Dutch Minister of the Environment, the Conference revealed three large problems: 'nutrients, dumping of radioactive substances and the UK' (MacGarvin 1991: 129). It is reasonable to assume that political agitation directed against laggards will have more effect when it rests on verified performance than when based on sheer rhetoric. The second way in which verification matters concerns the relationship between states and ENGOs. Here, verification has worked through other institutional changes – the most important being increased access for non-state actors to receive documents and increased access for ENGOs to the international decision-making bodies. The combination of these factors enables ENGOs to act as 'watchdogs'. For example, Greenpeace used verification data to put pressure on the UK particularly in the case of dumping at sea.[25]

The second part of P_5 (see p. 55) postulates that reduced discretion affects implementation partly due to the authoritativeness of the commitments. The authoritativeness of commitments may trigger behavioural response not because they affect incentives, but simply because they are perceived as authoritative and to be followed, in line with the norm of *pacta sunt servanda*: treaties are to be obeyed. In short, legally binding commitments may constrain activities simply because they are legally binding. It is extremely difficult to study this phenomenon empirically with precision. However, two assumptions may help to elucidate this phenomenon. The first relates to whether and why the parties consider the distinction between binding and non-binding commitments to be important. The most obvious answer would be that binding obligations are linked to positive or negative sanctions that may affect incentives. If this is not the case, there must be something else. The distinction between binding and non-binding commitments has actually been perceived as important in the cooperation. In OSPARCOM, and particularly the Paris Commission, the legal nature of commitments has been discussed repeatedly. For example, in 1984, the parties decided that, as a general rule, binding legal decisions were to be preferred to recommendations. While the distinction between legally binding and non-legally binding commitments is perceived as important, we have strong indications that this perception is not dependent on possibilities for international enforcement. We have found virtually nothing to suggest that this possibility is perceived as a real threat in cases of non-compliance. Thus, the significance attached to the legal nature of obligations is probably due to factors other than international enforcement.

The second assumption states that if the parties consider it is less acceptable to breach binding rules than non-binding rules, we would expect that increased preciseness and verification would tend to produce fewer legally binding decisions whenever incentives to defect cannot be ruled out. There has clearly been a development in this direction. First, the INSC Declarations that included the percentage reduction targets linked to comprehensive assessments of compliance were not legally binding. Developments within the Paris Commission provide us with even stronger indications, since there has been a change over time. The most specific commitments adopted within the Paris Commission on BAT and BEP have consequently been adopted as recommendations, while some other and less specific commitments have been adopted as decisions.

To recapitulate then: the OSPARCOM parties and INSC actors perceive the legal nature of commitments as important. Moreover, there are strong indications that this perception has influenced the nature of joint commitments when verification and preciseness improved. In addition, the difference between the two types of instruments can probably not be explained by the different consequences of non-compliance between states. However, there remains one possibility conforming with this assumption. As previously noted, legally binding decisions would in some cases have to be adopted by the Council of Ministers of the EC. Thus, implementation of EC Directives would be made subject to EC enforcement. The enforcement procedures of the EC concerning the environment are unique in the sense that cases of non-compliance may be submitted to the European Court of Justice. The Court has authority to initiate proceedings, and recent changes in EC enforcement procedures have led to heavy fines in the case of water pollution.[26] Although this possibility cannot be ruled out, another argument points in the opposite direction: the European Court of Justice has also considered non-legally binding rules (Nollkaemper 1993: 239).

These observation do not necessarily prove that the states feel more committed to legally binding instruments simply because these carry more authoritativeness. There are other – and more instrumental – motives that may affect the preferences for legally binding commitments. First, legal commitments may impose greater constraints on states since they are immune to changes of political leadership. In theory, this could explain the importance attached to transforming the Ministerial Declarations into legally binding decisions within OSPARCOM. However, this possibility does not shed any light on the difference between recommendations and decisions adopted within OSPARCOM. Both types of commitments are adopted by the Contracting Parties to the Conventions and not by politicians representing specific governments.

Second, legally binding decisions and conventions have to be implemented in legislation, which means involving national parliaments. Formal ratification may in turn raise a state's commitment to actually implement the obligation. This presupposes that legally binding obligations trigger the involvement of Parliaments, whereas non-legally binding obligations do not. However, this assumption is by no means correct. At least in the UK, Norway and the Netherlands, the INSC Declarations have triggered substantially more parliamentary activity in response to White Papers than OSPARCOM recommendations and decisions. Third, obligations should be legally binding instruments because of the possibility to invoke such obligations before national courts. As mentioned, the relevance of the Paris Conventions is practically nil in this respect, but the Oslo Convention may have greater relevance. On the other hand, national courts have granted legal effect to non-legal international rules in the case of dumping and incineration at sea (Nollkaemper 1993: 245).

All in all, then, it seems reasonable to assume that legally binding decisions have constrained state behaviour due to their authoritativeness. This implies that in the case of dumping and incineration at sea, state behaviour became constrained by three factors: verification, preciseness and bindingness. Commitments covering land-based sources were mainly constrained by the first two factors.

Conclusion

I commenced this chapter by arguing that the functioning and consequences of international institutions may contribute to explaining the development of joint commitments and implementation witnessed. The Unitary Rational Actor model assessed in Chapter 4 was clearly insufficient for explaining the significant changes that have taken place in the North Sea/North-East Atlantic cooperation. International institutions were assumed to affect the adoption of joint commitments, as well as the implementation of these commitments. This could be accomplished by three crucial functions ensured by the OSPARCOM and INSC institutions. First, they could provide cooperative environments based on different types of reciprocity. Second, they could provide capacity to integrate and aggregate the interests and preferences of the states. Third, they could constrain state behaviour and promote compliance and implementation.

The first function centered on the degree of cooperative environments. We argued that different ways of designing international institutions would lead to different types of cooperative environments based on diffuse or specific reciprocity. This assumption was based on the idea that institutions stimulating different types of reciprocity would have differing strengths and weaknesses. Most positive effects on outcomes could be expected where these types of institutions operated simultaneously within the same issue-area. We saw that the organization of the OSPARCOM cooperation pointed in the direction of diffuse reciprocity and highly cooperative environment, while the organization of the INSC process pointed in the direction of specific reciprocity. Second, the empirical data indicated that these institutions had actually led to different cooperation climates: OSPARCOM based on common cooperative norms of behaviour, INSC more marked by economic self-interest based on contingency relationships. The strongest indication of different cooperative climates was perhaps the observation that similar problems could be approached very differently by the same actors at the same time within two different institutional contexts.

The assessment of consequences were guided by some crude conceptions that specific reciprocity had the capacity to establish priorities and reach solutions, while diffuse reciprocity could provide a basis of mutual confidence for solutions as well as persistence once solutions had been reached. We assessed these ideas by focusing in on the role of OSPARCOM and INSC in solving the UES/EQO dispute, as this represented perhaps the most important and difficult issue within the cooperation. As expected, the solution was found within the INSC process, while the OSPARCOM provided a basis and ensured that the solutions achieved were given a firm footing in international law. We have strong indications that two different types of reciprocity have been complementary and in sum have provided functions that probably affected the resolution of the conflict. This implies that the absence of the INSC process would have made a resolution significantly more difficult. Likewise, the absence of OSPARCOM would probably have had the same effect.

The first explicit proposition linked to international institutions focused on *integration* and *aggregation* capacity and the relative balance between these functions (P4). High aggregation capacity was assumed to promote stringent joint commitments by cutting through deadlock, while high integration capacity was assumed to carry a potential to combine and affect the interests and preferences of actors. Significant imbalance between these functions was expected to lead to a corresponding imbalance between the stringency of commitments and implementation. We noted that the first decade of the cooperation was marked by low integration and aggregation capacity as well as lenient commitments and minor implementation. The development in this decade also showed that integration and aggregation capacity may be sensitive to participation by systemic actors from other institutions – in this case the EC Commission. The lesson from overlapping participation is that where such institutions include other 'laggards' than those already part of the cooperation, this may lead to a deadlock, or protract decision-making whenever unanimity is required. Conversely, other institutions may have a positive impact if they possess comparatively higher aggregation and integration capacity. Changes in these functions may shed light on why relevant EC Directives have become increasingly important in the 1990s.

The second decade witnessed a significant increase in aggregation and integration capacity, together with more stringent commitments and a significantly higher degree of implementation. Thus, the empirical patterns roughly match expectations. Several specific causal pathways were also identified. Higher aggregation capacity was provided first and foremost by higher level of participation in the form of ministerial representation that forged trade-offs reaching beyond the authority of lower level officials. The effect of high-level participation was conditioned by a certain level of societal demands for environmental protection – but only partly. The most significant change in societal demands came after the 1987 Conference, thus indicating an independent effect of changing level of participation. Second, change in decision rules in use within the Paris Commission affected international implementation of previous commitments. Higher integration capacity was provided by a combination of the design of politically feasible solutions and new knowledge and information that affected actors' interests. As to the former, particularly important were the regionalization of the co-operation provided by the INSC process and new procedures that allowed differential solutions. Concerning the latter, new information on abatement and damage science identified new solutions and promoted new insights. The evolving recognition that uncertainty as to cause/effect relationships would probably be permanent significantly strengthened the argument for precautionary action. In particular, it contributed to a change in the position of the UK. We should also note that a rough balance between aggregation and integration capacity was provided largely by different institutions. The INSC process mainly provided aggregation capacity, while the OSPARCOM provided integration capacity.

The second proposition focused on the consequences of reduced discretion and the underlying behavioural mechanisms (P_5). In line with expectations, we found that discretion was reduced by more specificity and improved verification in the latter decade. We have strong indications that these changes affected the incentives of 'laggards' by exposing them to political pressure from other states and ENGOs. On the other hand, possibilities for international enforcement remained constant and weak in both phases. Nevertheless, the parties perceived the distinction between binding and non-binding commitments as important; binding commitments – as in the case of dumping and incineration at sea – have apparently further constrained state behaviour due to their authoritativeness, not to their capacity to affect incentives. Thus, the international implementation of the INSC Declarations has further reduced discretion by transforming non-binding Declarations into commitments within the framework of international law.

Viewing the above propositions together, we see a relatively clear pattern of differing functions fulfilled by the various institutions operating in the North Sea. Moreover, the main impact of these institutions lies in their 'symbiotic' nature: each institution has been able to contribute with something the others could not provide. The OSPARCOM cooperation based on legally binding treaties has provided a highly cooperative environment, high integration capacity as well as legally binding commitments. The 'soft-law' INSC cooperation has provided a less cooperative environment that – in combination with other factors – has yielded high aggregation capacity by cutting through deadlock. Moreover, the INSCs have provided specific commitments and verification of performance. The establishment of the INSC also appears perfectly *timed*, in the sense that OSPARCOM had provided a solid basis for cooperation before it stagnated in terms of capacity to produce joint commitments with 'teeth'. The dynamic development and relationship between OSPARCOM and INSC will be further explored in Chapter 9. Until then, however, we shall leave the international level and concentrate on domestic implementation. Chapter 7 is concerned with the relevant groups of sub-national actors and how they behaved and responded to international North Sea commitments and national water and marine pollution policy.

Notes

1 Paris Commission (1987).
2 Interview with Stig Borgvang and Stan Sadowski, deputy secretaries OSPARCOM secretariat, 7 December 1996, London. Interview with Dik Tromp, former secretary and chairman to the Paris Commission, 10 December 1996, the Hague.
3 *Summary Records* (1984; 1987).

4 *Progress Report* (1987).
5 *Implementation Report* (1990).
6 Progress Report (1995).
7 Ministry of the Environment (1984).
8 Ibid.
9 Oslo and Paris Commissions (1984).
10 *Summary Record* (1985).
11 *Summary Record* (1988).
12 Paris Commission (1984).
13 Paris Commission (1987).
14 Oslo and Paris Commissions (1990).
15 Interview with Dik Tromp, 10 December 1996, The Hague.
16 Oslo and Paris Commissions (1992b).
17 Oslo and Paris Commissions (1992a).
18 Oslo Commission (1988: 44).
19 *Quality Status of the North Sea* (1984).
20 *Quality Status of the North Sea* (1987).
21 North Sea Task Force (1990).
22 *North Sea Quality Status Report* (1993: 5).
23 Paris Commission (1987: 16).
24 This calculation is based on the Procedures and Decision manuals of the Oslo and Paris Commissions.
25 Greenpeace International (1990).
26 For example, the Commission has slapped heavy fines on Germany and Italy for disregarding the rulings of the European Court of Justice on breaches of EC environmental legislation concerning surface water. Germany has been told to pay fines of US$188,520 for each day that it violates the EC law. *Down to Earth* (1997: 5). Polluters pay! February 28.

7

The calculus and mobilization of sub-national actors

This chapter is concerned with the incentives, positions and behaviour of sub-national actors in implementing the national goals that follow from international North Sea commitments. Previously, we have seen that governments sometimes defect from international commitments by deliberate choice. This chapter focuses on Level II implementation and introduces domestic implementation 'failure' as an additional reason for defection.

There is significant variation in implementation between countries and sectors even though discharges are generally headed in the right direction (cf. Chapter 4). Since it is the target groups who normally control the behaviour that has to be modified, governments depend on their active or reluctant 'cooperation'. Thus, we must look into the extent to which target groups have incentives to defect from, or comply with, higher-order goals. Target groups and governments do not, however, interact in a vacuum. Under certain conditions, environmental non-governmental organizations tend to mobilize in favour of stringent national goals. Such mobilization may counterbalance the influence of reluctant target groups and reduce the likelihood of vertical disintegration of environmental policy. Hence, ENGO mobilization represents the second topic under scrutiny in this chapter. According to this perspective, we may say that environmental policy is formed and implemented in the area of tension between ENGO mobilisation on the one hand, and the distribution of costs and benefits among target groups on the other hand.

It may perhaps seem strange to place, say, large and powerful industrial confederations on an equal footing with the green movement. Here, however, target groups are considered more important for implementation in the sense that it is they who control the behaviour that has to be modified. On the other hand, the mobilization of ENGOs may be crucial in bringing about necessary changes. Suffice then to recall that approximately 4 million Britons, or nearly 8 per cent of the population, had joined the green movement by 1990. By comparison, the political parties in the UK had less than 2 million members (Rawcliffe 1995: 29). Moreover, previous research has recognized the important role played by both target groups and ENGOs in environmental policy, even though earlier studies have tended towards a biased focus on the 'reactive' or 'proactive' role of industrial firms (Jänicke 1997). Target groups within sectors other than industry have been largely neglected, even though the need to change behaviour may be a more profound challenge within the agricultural and municipal sectors.

Decision-makers acting on behalf of target groups are assumed to evaluate options in terms of costs and benefits to their organization, and only in those terms, and choose whichever option (is believed to) maximize net gain. The extent to which they are willing to pay the price of regulation is first and foremost assumed to depend on whether costs and benefits are concentrated to their activities or distributed widely throughout society. In addition, the size of the costs involved may be important. Here we will also examine the behavioural mechanism underlying this line of reasoning. Inherent in the conception of norm-guided behaviour is the potential to render the above logic insufficient to understand the positions and behaviour of NGOs.

This chapter will be structured around the distribution of costs and benefits among target groups and the mobilization and presence of counterbalancing forces respectively. In the first section, I introduce the main characteristics of the various target group sectors in the three countries. The second section will take us to a discussion of the mobilization, presence and role of the relevant ENGOs, and concluding comments are presented in the last section.

Target groups: incentives for changing behaviour

In order to fulfil the international North Sea commitments on hazardous substances, nutrients and dumping/incineration at sea, target groups within three principal domestic sectors have to change their behaviour: these are industry, agriculture and the municipal sector. Let us start with the industrial sector.

Industry: concentrated costs and widespread benefits
The structure of the industrial sectors seems clear enough. The fundamental actors that have to change their behaviour are individual firms within different branches of industry. Different branches normally have 'their' interest organizations, which in turn are organized into national confederations such as the Confederation of British Industry (CBI), the Confederation of Netherlands Industry and Employers (CNIE), or the Norwegian Confederation of Business and Industry (NCBI). Also important are branch organizations controlling significant inputs of hazardous substances, like the associations for the chemical industry.

Incentives to change behaviour Manufacturing industries represent a major source of hazardous substances in all three countries and a minor source of nutrient inputs to the water and marine environment. This sector has also been responsible for the earlier practice of industrial waste dumping and incineration at sea. Environmental expenditure on water and marine pollution has increased significantly in all three countries since the mid-1980s. These expenditures have mainly been born by the industrial sector itself. A large share of the expenditures has been directly linked to the implementation of the North Sea Declarations.

The Netherlands Central Bureau of Statistics has been conducting surveys on environmental expenditure for several years now. A significant increase has been found in such expenditures since 1985 related to surface water and marine pollution in the industrial sector (OECD 1996). This tendency is also reflected in estimates made by the Confederation of Netherlands Industry and Employers. Net environmental costs (capital and operating expenses) in industry have risen continually. In 1992, net environmental costs were some 2.5 times higher than in 1984.[1] As we have seen, Norway has estimated the total costs of implementing the North Sea Declarations in Norway at NOK10 billion. Total costs connected to the part of the North Sea Declaration dealing with hazardous substances were estimated to amount to approximately NOK1 billion for the period 1991–95. These costs are borne mainly by the industrial sector. There are examples of positive side-effects in the form of new technology due to environmental regulation in the industrial sector. However, a study of 200 Norwegian industrial firms indicates that savings in the form of reduced need for raw materials and energy were insignificant compared to actual environmental investments.[2] However, positive side-effects are extremely hard to measure and the data are surrounded with high uncertainty. In 1990, the Department of the Environment in the UK presented its first estimate of pollution controls. Total industry expenditure on pollution control was estimated at £1.55 billion, in 1986 prices, with capital costs accounting for 48 per cent of the total. The chemical industry's share was 25 per cent. Firms were also asked how they benefited financially from controlling pollution. On average, financial benefits were equivalent to 7 per cent of gross costs. However, these figures are regarded as underestimates, since many firms could not quantify the benefits of pollution control.[3] According to the OECD (1994: 139), pollution control expenditure by the chemical industry in the UK rose from £482 million in 1988 to around £830 million in 1991 and £1.03 billion in 1992. The phasing-out of industrial waste dumping at sea meant additional costs for 25 companies licensed to dump liquid and solid industrial waste in 1989. Imperial Chemical Industries (ICI) was the largest dumper, licensed to dump 165,000 tons of liquid waste. The costs of implementing 'no-waste' technology for this company alone were significant.[4]

We may conclude that the costs of water pollution abatement borne by the industry have increased in all three countries since 1985. Although industry may benefit directly from environmental investments, studies indicate that a large proportion of total expenditure represents net costs. Discharges from industry to rivers or directly to the sea are transported and liable to benefit other users downstream of industrial activities. In other words, the costs incurred in curbing discharges to water are concentrated to the individual companies, whereas the benefits are distributed widely throughout society. Thus, industrial decision-makers will have incentives to oppose implementation of stringent measures in order to fulfil higher-order goals.

Positions taken by industrial organizations The positions of target groups will be categorized according to whether they oppose, support or are willing to go further than required[5]. If we look at the actual positions of industry organizations, we see that they have been more ambitious than expected. The Confederation of British Industry is the most powerful NGO in British environmental policy-making and implementation. Moreover, the CBI was assigned a key role at the North Sea Conference in 1987 as the representative of industrial confederations in all North Sea states. Founded in 1965, the CBI describes itself as an independent, non-party political organization funded entirely by its members in industry and commerce. Although health, safety and the environment have been topics of interest since the organization was founded, a special environment, health and safety group was established in the latter part of 1980s. Today, the CBI represents companies from every sector of UK business – some 250,000 companies and more than 200 trade associations, employer organizations and commercial associations. The main goal of the CBI is straightforward: 'The CBI's objective is to help create and sustain the conditions in which business in the UK can compete and prosper'.[6]

The general position taken by the CBI concerning inputs of hazardous substances to the water and marine environment largely accords with the traditional environmental quality approach of the UK government. The CBI does not oppose stringent standards *per se*, but claims that any regulation should be based on scientific risk assessment that will ensure an appropriate balance between environmental and economic factors. Accordingly, the CBI does not accept zero discharges of hazardous substances as it appears in the 1995 North Sea Declaration.[7] However, the CBI has supported the introduction of Statutory Quality Standards for rivers – a core element of the UK North Sea Action Plan – since this takes river use and quality as its point of departure. As we shall see in Chapter 8, these standards have failed to become implemented, but not because of opposition from the CBI.

Following the 1987 North Sea Conference where the first Declarations concerning the phasing out of dumping were taken, pressure started to build up within the UK concerning the licensing of industrial waste dumping. The CBI defended one of large dumpers, Sterling Organics, arguing that without sea deposition, production is threatened and employment of hundreds is at risk.[8] However, there are indications that the CBI softened its position on industrial waste dumping between 1987 and 1990. The CBI did not lobby actively against the decision taken in 1990 to phase out dumping of industrial waste.[9] A more proactive role in pollution policy is also underlined by the CBI as a general change in recent years. A concrete example of this change may be found at branch level. The UK chemical industry is a major emitter of hazardous substances such as chlorinated substances and heavy metals. Around 200 of the larger companies, accounting for approximately 75 per cent of the industry's capital expenditure, are members of the Chemical Industries Association (CIA) (OECD: 1994). In 1989, the association launched the first Responsible Care programme in Europe aimed at improving performance in safety, health, and environmental protection. This programme represents a voluntary initiative unique to the chemical industry. By 1995, all members of the CIA had become members of Responsible Care and the amount of Red List substances discharged to water has been reduced by 89 per cent since 1990.[10]

The official position taken by the Confederation of Netherlands Industry and Employers signals a somewhat more ambitious attitude as compared to the CBI. The CNIE is organized along roughly the same lines as the CBI with its own Environment Group. In addition to industrial interests, the CNIE explicitly acknowledges what it terms the industry's own social responsibility to reduce environment impacts within the limits set by the concept of sustainable growth.[11] The CNIE accepts emission standards and generally supports the Dutch North Sea Action programme concerning the hazardous substances included in The Hague list. Wherever targets have not been met, the CNIE blames other sources (than industry) and inputs from other countries. The largest emitter of hazardous substances – the Dutch chemical industry – also participates in the Responsible Care programme. Of the 150 chemical sites, 105 are involved in the programme. Since all the major companies participate, this represents more than 85 per cent of Dutch chemical production. The entire chemical industry has reduced heavy metals emissions to water on an average from about 275 tons per year in 1985 to below 50 tons per year in 1995.[12]

The positions adopted by the Federation of Norwegian Industries (FNI) and, from 1989, the Norwegian Confederation of Business and Industry parallel those of the Dutch Confederation. The FNI established an environment committee in the late 1960s and a permanent section for environmental matters in 1970. The FNI explicitly prefers that Norway adopt a position among the most ambitious states in the North Sea cooperation. Moreover, the FNI has urged its members to comply with their discharge consents since breaches from single firms will negatively affect the reputation of the industry as a whole. The basic principles underlying the position of the

FNI are cost/benefit considerations, cooperation with authorities and social responsibility. The branch organization controlling the largest sources of hazardous substances in Norway is the Federation of Norwegian Process Industries (PIL), which has 660 member companies within 14 industrial sectors including pulp and paper, metallurgical and chemical industries. In 1993, PIL launched the Norwegian version of the Responsible Care programme including a majority of the members. The official goal of PIL's work is explicitly rooted in a zero line of thought implying continuous improvements towards zero environmental damage. We should note that this ambition appears as almost a copy of Greenpeace's North Sea policy goal. Almost, since there is still a difference between the goals of Greenpeace and PIL. Greenpeace focuses on zero discharges, while PIL is concerned with zero damage. Between 1985 and 1995, emissions of hazardous substances (including heavy metals and organic substances) fell by 87 per cent.[13]

We may conclude that the positions taken by industry in the three countries appear generally more ambitious than expected. Industrial organizations tend to encourage their members to support, or even exceed the goals and standards adopted by their respective authorities.

Agriculture: concentrated costs and widespread benefits
The individual farms represent the fundamental actors required to change their behaviour within the agricultural sector. Like industrial firms, farmers are organized in different interest or lobby organizations established to protect their particular interests. The agricultural sectors in Norway and the Netherlands are significant emitters of nutrients as well as pesticides. The UK will not be dealt with in this section since the UK government has failed to identify any eutrophication problem areas. This has meant that British agriculture has not been obliged to take action towards achieving its share of the percentage reduction targets.[14]

Incentives to change behaviour The approximately 90,000 farms in Norway and the 120,000 farms in the Netherlands control a type of behaviour that has to be changed in order to reduce inputs of nutrients in the agricultural sector. These units vary considerably in terms of size and production methods, from large agro-industrial entities to 'one family farms'. Largely due to the North Sea commitments, environmental investments in agriculture have risen since the mid-1980s. Environmental investments in Dutch agriculture have risen rapidly since 1985, mostly for manure storage facilities (OECD 1995). According to the government, the drastic increase over a short period justifies a major contribution through the government. Increasing environmental expenditure is expected to bring about continuity problems for many enterprises, and planned environmental policy is expected to cause problems above all for the cattle-breeding and dairy sectors (Hegeman *et al.* 1992).

According to the Norwegian North Sea Action Plan, NOK0.8 billion was invested in the agricultural sector between 1985 and 1990; investments between 1990 and 1995 have been estimated at NOK1.0 billion. The shares of these investments and operating costs that has to be borne by the private or by the public sector is very difficult to estimate. Norwegian agriculture is heavily subsidized, and product prices are determined by negotiations between the farmer organizations and authorities through the Agreement on Agriculture. Although the agricultural sector is more heavily subsidized as compared to industry there are net costs involved. For example, the Bank of Agriculture provides loans at normal interest rates for up to 35 per cent of total costs with regard to improvement of technical facilities. Benefits in the form of reduced environmental damage are rarely concentrated on the individual farms, since nutrient surplus drains into watercourses and into the sea, where it may lead to eutrophication and algae blooms. Hence, nutrient emissions from the agricultural sector can be characterised by concentrated costs and widespread benefits following from the implementation of the North Sea commitments. This means that farmers would generally have incentives to oppose implementation of adequate measures as long as these involve net costs.

Positions taken by farmers' organizations

In general, the farmer organizations have reluctantly accepted the joint commitments on nutrients. The basic diverging interests between agriculturalists and environmentalists in Western Europe have largely remained that same over time (Conrad 1993). On the other hand, polarization has lessened. In the Netherlands, farmers' organizations have reluctantly accepted the policy on the reduction of nutrients. Compared to industry, there are few signs of any pro active behaviour. Originally, the Dutch Agricultural Board did not want any environmental regulations, arguing that it was 'unfair' to require environmental investments since the government had encouraged the use of intensive production methods. Nevertheless, the Manure Act was introduced in 1987 aimed at the stabilisation of manure production. A new critical union (Dutch Agricultural Youth Contact) was formed in the 1980s and this organization together with the Agricultural Board published its first environmental action plan in 1989. The ambitious targets set for the agricultural sector in the National Environmental Policy Plan of 1989 were partly based on the positions of the Agricultural Board.

With regard to a wide range of specific measures included in various PARCOM Recommendations towards implementing the 50 per cent reduction goals, the strategy of the Agricultural Board has been twofold. First, the types of measures identified have largely been reluctantly accepted, with the exception of regulatory levies which have encountered strong opposition. Second, farmers' organizations have subsequently sought to water down the specific requirement included in the general measures.[15] For example, they were able to reduce the period of non-application of manure and change the initially high standards set for nutrient content in excretion.

The Norwegian farmers' organizations appear more split than their Dutch counterparts. The Norwegian Farmers' Union is the largest of the agricultural organizations in Norway, with approximately 66,000 members. The other organization of some significance is the Norwegian Small-Holders' Union with about 13,500 members (Mydske and Steen 1994). The Norwegian Farmers' Union generally emphasizes traditional economic sector interests, while the Small-Holders' Union tends to give greater priority to environmental concerns (Klausen 1996). The Farmers' Union established a committee on pollution control in 1971, but it was not until 1988–89 that attention attached to environmental problems increased significantly. The union has generally accepted the North Sea commitments. The union is positive to most measures suggested except taxes on input factors, such as fertilisers. According to the union, in a situation where farm income is under pressure, such taxes will only lead to further reduction in income. Still, the North Sea Declarations and governmental plans to implement the 50 per cent reduction target have not been met with much enthusiasm. In a commentary to the State Pollution Control Authority's 1990–93 action plan, the Union states that Norway's 50 per cent reduction obligation should be reconsidered in light of Norway's minor contribution to the total load of nutrients draining into the North Sea.[16]

We may conclude that the large farmers' organizations have reluctantly accepted relevant goals and measures. In contrast to industry, there are few signs of any serious voluntary, or proactive initiatives.

The municipal sector: widespread benefits and costs

Nutrients and some hazardous substances represent the main inputs from the municipal sectors in Norway, the Netherlands, and the UK. The target groups here are not immediately obvious, so a brief description is in order.[17] Household and industrial waste water is discharged into surface water. Policies to reduce phosphorus and nitrogenous substances may follow two lines: (1) treatment of discharges; (2) reduction of discharges. Relevant authorities collect household and industrial waste water via the sewer systems and remove compounds before discharging it into the sewer system or into surface water (route 1) as well as reducing the industrial inputs by imposing limits to the discharges into the sewer system, normally in the form of permits (route 2). Since the latter route is dealt with by regulation directly placed on industry, we will focus on route 1. The treatment of discharges via wastewater treatment works (WTWs) may be regarded as a kind of 'end-of-pipe' measure. Prevention is thus limited to recycling of nutrients in the form of reuse of sewage sludge, e.g. in agriculture, instead of incinerating or dumping the sludge at sea.

Incentives to change behaviour Private households are clearly affected by regulation, since the financing of waste water treatment is based on *water charges* in all three countries. Moreover, in principle households control the behaviour that has to be modified. The Dutch North Sea Action Plan has prepared estimates of the costs of complying with nutrient goals. The abatement operation programme was expected to involve some 1.5 billion guilders in investment costs, and between 230 and 320 million guilders in annual operating costs.[18] Measures for denitrification and dephosphating of waste water will have to be paid for directly or indirectly through the Pollution of Surface Water Act levy. The pollution levy administered by the water boards is used to finance new investments in phosphorus and nitrogen removal. The levy has increased significantly since 1985 and is expected to double on an average up to year 2000. The main reason is linked to the new requirements concerning nutrient removal.[19]

In the Norwegian North Sea Action Plan, estimated costs and investments in WTWs amounted to NOK3.6 billion between 1991 and 1995. According to the Pollution Control Act of 1981, the municipalities are responsible for drainage of waste water, and for the necessary purification. Such measures would affect about 80 of Norway's 435 municipalities situated in sensitive area. In 1991, the average level of municipal sewerage charges was about NOK1,100 per household per year. Preliminary calculations of expected increase in sewerage charges as a result of implementing the measures show that in about 85 per cent of the affected municipalities along this stretch of coast, charges will rise by about NOK1,000, with 1991 as base year. As part of the North Sea Action Plan, an investigation was carried out on people's willingness to pay higher municipal sewerage charges for the measures required to fulfil the targets of the North Sea Declarations. The results indicated a willingness to pay an extra average sum of NOK1,000–2,000 per year: this would be sufficient to implement relevant measures.[20]

In the UK, many programmes have been launched since the late 1980s to improve WTWs in order to meet new requirements related to both EC Directives and the North Sea commitments. Water companies in England and Wales plan to invest £28 billion (at 1989 prices) between 1990 and 2000: £13 billion for water supply and £15 billion for sewerage treatment (OECD 1994: 62). Actual investment by the water companies rose sharply after 1989; from 1989 to 1995, £14 billion was in fact invested.[21] In the same period, the average water bill in England and Wales had risen from £140 just before privatization to £170 in 1992, at 1992 prices.[22]

Implementing the North Sea commitments in the municipal sector will involve significant costs in all three countries. A significant proportion of these costs will have to be paid by households in the form of increased water charges. Such charges have risen significantly in all three countries and are expected to increase steadily up to year 2000. Thus, costs are clearly more distributed to the public at large, as compared to the industrial and agricultural sectors. On the other hand, the costs will not be shared equally throughout the municipalities, regions and provinces of the three countries. They will depend on investments already undertaken, local natural conditions as well as the pattern of settlement. For example, in England and Wales, the largest increase is expected in south-west England, where large investments are needed and where the customer base is small. Benefits in the form of improved water quality will also probably be widespread. Since WTWs are based locally and serve the local population, they also reduce local and regional problems of eutrophication. As costs, however, local benefits may vary significantly, depending on local use and the natural conditions of the area. The Norwegian willingness-to-pay study revealed that direct benefits were not the main motivation of affected households. Only 20 per cent of willingness to pay was based on people's own use of fresh and salt water, whereas about 60 per cent was motivated by the necessity to preserve water bodies for the future, and about 20 per cent by the wish for Norway to be a leader in environmental protection. In short, costs and benefits are widely distributed in the municipal sector and we may thus expect that target groups will be unlikely to have any strong incentives, either in support of or opposition to implementation of North Sea commitments.

Positions taken by organizations representing the 'municipal sector'
Since the Dutch Pollution of Surface Waters Act came into force in 1970, provinces have in most cases authorized WTW tasks to water boards which finance almost all expenditures including the construction and operation of WTWs. The regional water boards in the Netherlands have their own lobby organization: the Union of Water Boards, which exists to protect the interests of the water boards *vis-à-vis* the central authorities. The coverage and quality of WTWs in the Netherlands rank among the highest in OECD. In 1994, 97 per cent of the population was connected to waste water treatment, of which almost all plants had secondary (advanced) treatment capacity or more (OECD 1995). According to one union official: 'We thought we had a perfect system before the new requirements were included in the Dutch North Sea Action Plan.'[23] Although the pollution levy is based strictly on the 'polluter pays' principle, the regional water boards have become increasingly worried about the significant increase in water charges. The Union has adopted a twofold strategy pointing both 'downwards' and 'upwards'. First, it reluctantly accepts the standards since these are international, and

the Union then tries to persuade the regional boards to take the necessary steps. Second, it seeks to influence central authorities as to timing, seeking to postpone the investments required.

In contrast to the Netherlands, Norway delegates significant competence in this field to municipalities. In Norway, only 57 per cent of the population was served by waste water treatment in 1990, a slightly lower proportion than the OECD average of 63 per cent (OECD 1993). According to the government, investments in many municipalities have lagged far behind the need indicated by the actual pollution status. However, there has been fierce opposition at local level, especially concerning the need for nitrogen removal. All affected municipalities sent appeals to the Ministry of the Environment concerning the obligations for nitrogen removal issued by the county governor offices. Concerning sewage treatment requirements other than nitrogen removal, a case study of three Norwegian municipalities show them generally reluctant to central government instructions, based upon Norwegian goals following from the North Sea commitments (Harsheim and Hovik 1996).

In the UK, WTW construction and operation was privatized in 1989. After privatization, responsibility for sewerage (as well as water supply) was transferred to ten private water companies. However, limits for water charges are not set by the companies themselves, but by the Office of Water Services (OFWAT) after consulting with regulatory agencies. In 1990, 87 per cent of the population in Great Britain was served by waste water treatment plants, a level far above the OECD average. However, many of the plants have low capacity and a low level of purification efficiency (primary or less) (OECD 1994). Thus, the problems lie more in the quality and operation of plants than in the coverage as such. Increasing demands for investment in the privatized water industry have led to a 'turf of war' between regulators and target groups. As in Norway and the Netherlands, this 'war' centres on customers' (un)willingness to pay higher water charges.

Crudely put, on the one side stands OFWAT calling for lenient standards and low charges. OFWAT's duty is to ensure that the water companies have sufficient financial means to enable them to carry out their functions in sewerage satisfactorily. On the other hand, it is also obliged to protect customers' interests. For the latter purpose, it has a network of regional customer service committees as well as a national body in which public opinion is articulated and aggregated. At the other pole stands the National Rivers Authority which, according to its director, will seek to ensure: 'that excessive regulatory caution is avoided while insisting that necessary and appropriate standards are met' (Maloney and Richardson 1994: 133). These opposing positions have led to an open and bitter conflict in which compliance with international commitments has been central. For example, the UK North Sea Action Plan identified the introduction of statutory surface water quality objectives as one important measure. OFWAT's scenario does not include the financial resources needed to implement these objectives.

The patterns we have identified concerning the positions taken within the 'municipal' sector do not match expectations. Although costs and benefits are more widely distributed as compared to the agricultural and industrial sectors, the goals and measures following from the North Sea commitments have been repeatedly opposed by target-group organizations.

Incentives, positions and behavioural change of target groups

To recapitulate, P_3 postulated that different target-group positions could be expected on the basis of distribution of costs and benefits. This proposition was based on the Rational Actor model applied to sub-national target groups. The main results – including actual behavioural changes in line with obligations – are presented in Table 7.1

Table 7.1 *Distribution of costs and benefits: predicted v. actual**

Sectors	*Costs*	*Benefits*	*Predicted incentives*	*Actual positions*	*Behavioural change*
Industry	Concentrated	Distributed	Low	Ambitious	High
Agriculture	Concentrated	Distributed	Low	Intermediate	Low
Municipal	Distributed	Distributed	Medium	Reluctant	Medium

* In relative terms

From Table 7.1, we see that the proposition derived from the subnational Rational Actor model gains little support judged on the merits of pattern-matching. Target groups within both the industrial and agricultural sectors have had incentives to oppose and defect from domestic goals linked to North Sea commitments, probably even when state subsidies are involved. However, available data concerning their actual positions indicate that both sectors have been more supportive than expected. Moreover, there are indications that these sectors react differently to the same situation. Industry has in general articulated a more proactive position as compared to agriculture, which has reluctantly accepted new requirements. Various explanations may shed light on the difference in position between the industrial and the agricultural sectors. First, the industrial sector is more likely to trigger ENGO mobilization than the agricultural sector. Industrial discharges often flow from point sources that are visible and easy to identify. Such activities serve as ideal targets for ENGO campaigns. Second, positive side-effects may play a more important role in the industrial sector. Porter and Linde (1995) argue that the static view with regard to a fixed trade-off between ecology and economy is simply wrong since it ignores the more important offsetting productivity benefits from *innovation*. In their view, properly designed environmental standards make companies more competitive, not less so, since innovations allow companies to make more productive use of a range of inputs, from raw materials to energy to labour.

The third possibility goes beyond the Rational Actor perspective and focuses on the development of environmentally related norms. In particular, the Norwegian Process Industry has adopted a long-term target paralleling the original aim of Greenpeace, while the Dutch CNIE has explicitly acknowledged a social responsibility for Dutch industries exceeding narrow cost/benefit considerations by arguing that industry changes behaviour due to both self-interest and social responsibility. A potential for the latter is also emphasised as a part of the Responsible Care programme. Thus, while cost/benefit calculations are indisputable and fundamental for any company, we also have indications that new norms of environmental behaviour have developed. The industrial input of hazardous substances has been regulated for a long time and environmental concerns are today seen as a natural part of business activities.

We would expect the municipal sector not to oppose governmental implementation initiatives actively, in contrast to industry and agriculture, since both costs and benefits are more widespread. However, the results are contrary to what we had expected. Relevant actors within this sector have actively resisted core elements of domestic plans to implement North Sea commitments. The Norwegian willingness-to-pay investigation indicated that cost/benefit considerations were not the chief motivation for willingness to pay for higher water charges. To the extent these results also bear some significance for the Netherlands and the UK, changes in public attitudes towards environmental regulation may actually be the key for understanding why this sector has opposed national goals.

As a heuristic device, however, the sub-national Rational Actor model cannot be deemed invalid. Cost/benefit considerations appear as one fundamental behavioural mechanism for all affected actors, ranging from households via farmers' organizations to industrial confederations. On the other hand, cost/benefit calculations are not all that matters. Since environmental norms are extremely hard to measure in any precise way, we cannot judge whether the relative importance of norms and cost/benefit calculations varies systematically between sectors.

If we look at the relationship between positions and behavioural change, we first see that actual positions match well with actual behaviour with regard to industry. Although industry has experienced problems concerning some hazardous substances, behavioural change has been high in relative aggregate terms. The agricultural sector has achieved less than the actual positions would suggest. Inputs of nutrients from the Dutch agricultural sector have remained unchanged compared to 1985 even though the Dutch government agreed to the 50 per cent cut target. More progress can be witnessed in the Norwegian agricultural sector, but achievements still lag far behind goals with respect to both nitrogenous and phosphorus substances. Conversely, the municipal sectors have achieved more than could be expected against the backdrop of actual positions. The municipal sector in the UK has actually taken a major initiative to improve sewerage treatment, while phosphorus inputs from the municipal sector have been reduced significantly in Norway and the Netherlands. On the other hand, only about half of the reductions required have been achieved concerning nitrogenous substances.

The mismatch between positions and behavioural change strongly indicates that differences in the organization of pollution control is important to understand national implementation of joint commitments (see Chapter 8).

Mobilization of environmental organizations as counterbalancing forces

Environmental non-governmental organizations constitute a heterogeneous population of organizations which use both formal and informal channels for mobilizing the public as well as influencing governmental policy and target group behaviour. In general, we assume that ENGOs have mobilized to a more significant extent around visible industrial pollution as compared to diffuse agricultural run-offs. In particular, dumping and incineration at sea of industrial waste are highly visible and concrete. Such activities serve as ideal targets for ENGO campaigns. Second, ENGO mobilization with regard to the 'municipal sector' may be even lower as compared to agriculture, since it has been characterized by widespread costs and benefits. The lack of visibility and the nature of activities also point in the same direction.

ENGO activities and priorities

There has been a general development from traditional nature conservation ENGOs to more policy-oriented ENGOs predominantly occupied with pollution problems at both national and international level (Hägerhäll 1993). The latter type of organization is of greatest relevance for water and marine pollution. Such organizations experienced significant growth in all three countries in terms of membership and income, particularly in the late 1980s. The growth in the green movement is further examined in Chapter 8. Although ENGOs in Norway, the Netherlands and the UK differ in terms of composition and development they share some striking similarities concerning priorities. Agricultural pollution in general and nutrient inputs in particular have traditionally been given far less attention than has industry and hazardous substances. In the case of pesticides, ENGOs have generally defined the producers and exporters – chemical industry – as their main targets (Dinham 1993). It is generally claimed that agriculture in Western Europe was almost free of environmental pressures until the late 1980s (Tinker 1989: 8). The growing environmental awareness and the initial policy regulations seldom addressed agriculture (Conrad 1993: 81). Moreover, municipal waste water and nitrogen removal have virtually escaped any direct ENGO attention.

The UK In the UK, the conservationist groups have remained strong and close to conservation issues (Boehmer-Christiansen and Skea 1991). The British ENGOs commenced paying serious attention to pollution issues from 1987 (McCormick 1991: 93). As noted in Chapter 6, the UK Government has clearly been exposed to pressure within relevant international institutions to change its policy on sea dumping and incineration. The major shifts in UK policy on dumping before the 1987 and 1990 North Sea Conferences have been accompanied by statements showing that the UK decisions have had nothing to do with change in the perception of the seriousness of the problem. The government has consistently argued that there were no scientific reasons to phase out dumping at sea. For example, when the Minister of Agriculture, Fisheries and Food (MAFF) declared in December 1989 that dumping of industrial was to be phased out, the declaration included the following statement: 'At no stage has evidence been produced that any of these wastes cause harm in the marine environment. Detailed scientific work in the UK has shown that no harm is caused by sea disposal. Indeed the presence of the wastes in the sea cannot be detected by the most sensitive means of analysis a few minutes after disposal.'[24]

However, both companies and authorities have also been challenged internally by the ENGOs. From 1986, especially Greenpeace has targeted UK dumping policy. Prior to the North Sea Conference in 1987, a joint Greenpeace and National Union of Seamen campaign was launched. The group threatened the UK government with direct actions against vessels operating from the UK unless policy was changed. The group also succeeded in persuading local authorities to oppose plans for new terminals to serve marine disposal operators. An application for a new waste storage terminal in Sunderland was refused.[25] Shortly after, it was reported that: 'Ocean Combustion Services (OCS), operators of the incineration vessel Vulcanus II, have been losing the public perception battle during a two-week fight in the North Sea with Greenpeace and Danish fishermen'.[26]

Greenpeace continued direct action campaigns up to the 1990 Conference. In late 1989, the Ministry of Agriculture, Fisheries and Food decided to support applications for licensing renewals for four dumping operations through the OSCOM Prior Justification Procedure, which states that licences could be approved if it could be shown both that the materials caused no harm to the environment, and that there were no practical alternatives on land. Several North Sea states protested against the decision, and Greenpeace brought the case to the media. To MAFF's embarrassment, one of the firms involved, Fisons, then withdrew its application because it had suddenly discovered a land-based disposal option.[27] On 22 February, Agriculture Minister John Gummer announced that all but two licences would be cancelled by 1992, while the other two would be extended into 1993 if absolutely necessary. The two remaining cases were ICI and Sterling Organics. In 1987 the Confederation of British Industry defended industrial dumpers by arguing that employment of hundreds was at risk, if dumping were to be phased out. By 1992, liquid industrial waste was phased out even though Sterling Organics were granted an extension of their license for the early part of 1993 (Table 7.2).

Table 7.2 *Liquid industrial wastes licensed and disposed of at sea in the UK, 1988–93*

	Licenses issued	*Licensed quantity (t)*	*Tonnage deposited*
1988	19	311,411	249,744
1989	16	292,968	248,454
1990	5	228,000	209,961
1991	2	205,000	191,945
1992	2	75,604	180,725
1993	0	0	0

Source: Ministry of Agriculture, Fisheries and Food (1994).

Besides campaigning against dumping and incineration at sea, British ENGOs have focused on the large industries such as British Coal and ICI. Many environmentalists see industry as their irrevocable enemy. According to a Confederation of British Industry Senior Adviser with responsibility for water and marine affairs, ENGOs can match the industry when it comes to real influence, especially at the international level.[28]

Greenpeace's campaign against Albright and Wilson in 1991 may illustrate how ENGOs can have a direct impact on the behaviour of target groups and authorities. In order to challenge the authorization and enforcement practices of the National River Authority, Greenpeace chose to focus on Albright and Wilson's work in Whitehaven, Cumbria. This firm, the largest single source of heavy metals in the UK, was permitted to discharge 500 tons of heavy metals into the Irish Sea annually. On 31 August, Greenpeace won a private prosecution against the company for breaches of its licence limits for zinc, chromium, copper and nickel, and the company was fined. This case was special in the sense that the prosecution was based on sampling evidence which Greenpeace had collected itself (Mumma 1993: 194). Two weeks later, Greenpeace blocked the works' effluent outfall. Facilities were damaged and several plants were forced to shut down. The same month, the NRA announced that it was prosecuting the company over copper and chromium spills. This prosecution led to another fine. Greenpeace then targeted the NRA and asked the High Court to allow a judicial review of the NRA's negligence of the plant. In October, the company announced the planning of a landfill site. According to the company, the new site would remove 90 per cent of the heavy metals and lock them up in a non-leachable form. In December Greenpeace pulled out, declaring its satisfaction with the new plans, whereas the NRA claimed that the clean-up agreement had been well advanced before the Greepeace action.[29]

The focus on industry prevailed in the early 1990s. An indication of the relative priorities given to various sectors can be found in the Environmental Data Services (ENDS) reports (see Table 7.3). As expected, most articles have focused on ENGO activity in relation to industry. The most active organizations have been Friends of the Earth (FoE) and Greenpeace. Nine of the articles are concerned with Greenpeace activity, while FoE figures in 11 of the 32 articles. While industry has been a prime target for British ENGOs with regard to pollution, conservation groups have a long tradition of mobilization against farmers. However, these groups have traditionally focused not on pollution, but on land use, species and habitats.

Table 7.3 *ENDS articles on ENGO activity in the UK, 1990–95*[30]

	1990–95
Industry	17
Agriculture	0
Water companies	2
Other	13
Total	32

Source: ENDS Report *Index* (1990–95).

Norway and the Netherlands In Norway, the development from nature conservation to pollution took place in the form of new organizations established in the 1960s, 1970s and 1980s, and within the already established conservationist organizations. For example, the most prominent ENGO in Norway – the Norwegian Society for the Conservation of Nature (NSCN) – adopted a more pollution and policy oriented approach from the late 1960s (Jansen and Osland 1996). Conflicts over the regulation of waterfalls for hydro-power dominated the ENGO agenda in Norway in the 1970s, while pollution issues became more important in the 1980s. In 1986 the ENGO Bellona was established to trace and expose pollution from industry. Bellona focused mainly on water and marine pollution caused by hazardous substances and industry. The Norwegian Society for the Conservation of Nature also mobilized against industrial pollution, particularly in the late 1980s. By contrast, agricultural pollution has never been given priority by Norwegian ENGOs: indeed, there has even been close cooperation between some ENGOs and agricultural organizations.

Seen from the industry's point of view, Norway's ENGOs have represented a significant counterbalancing force. According to the Norwegian Confederation of Business and Industry, they have had direct impact on industrial behaviour, but even greater impact on governmental policy through the media.[31] After the first-generation abatement programme for industry was concluded in 1985, a wide range of illegalities and breaches in connection with discharge permits was revealed by the State Pollution Control Authority (SPCA). However, observed breaches did not automatically lead to reactions from the authorities. In this situation, ENGOs targeted reluctant companies. In turn, this raised the willingness of the authorities to enforce regulations. According to Gundersen (1991: 27), Bellona stood forth as a militant version of the State Pollution Control Agency. By contrast, Norwegian farmers and their organizations have never been exposed to significant ENGO pressure. The Norwegian Farmers' Union emphasizes that Bellona has shown virtually no interest in agriculture, while the union's relationship to the Norwegian Society for the Conservation of Nature has been constructive.[32] The Farmers' Union and the NSCN have actually joined forces against the government and industry.

Most nature conservation ENGOs in the Netherlands were established around the turn of this century, while policy oriented organizations such as the 'Stichting Natuur en Milieu' (SNM – Society for Nature and Environment) were established in the late 1960s and early 1970s. There has traditionally been little cooperation between these types of organizations in the Netherlands. In the 1980s the pollution-oriented ENGOs became a political power in their own right (Jamison, Eyerman and Cramer 1990: 171). Some 70 per cent of the Netherlands consists of farmland, so Dutch ENGOs may have paid more attention to agricultural pollution than in Norway and the UK. However, fertilizer policy has until recently largely escaped ENGO attention, whereas industrial pollution has long been in focus.

In the course of the 1960s, a number of 'single-issue' ENGOs arose, each dealing with very specific environmental topics. These groups were the first to put pressure on government and industry concerning pollution policy. Those that later developed into large and stable organizations tended to focus on manufacturing industry, nuclear energy, the construction of new highways and the treatment of animals within bioindustry. The SNM, founded in 1972, has been characterized as rather pragmatic in the sense that it tended to focus on large-scale technical objects combined with improvement of their scientific expertise. Thus, specific and visible targets formed the core of activities. Other organizations focused on agriculture, but not on pollution as such. For example, the Kleine Aarde (Small Earth) founded in 1971 was concerned with promoting small-scale ecological methods of agriculture and a more environmentally sound lifestyle. While pollution from industry has received attention from the ENGOs since the early 1970s, agricultural fertiliser policy has been given somewhat more attention only from the early 1990s. The 'Waterpact' – a coalition of Dutch water-environmental organizations, the SNM and Greenpeace Netherlands, formed a grouping to pressure especially the Minister for Transport an Public Works to be more involved in fertilizer policy (Vertegaal 1993).

We may conclude that all three cases generally support the expectation that industry has been the focus of significantly more ENGO mobilization than has agriculture. In addition to visibility, this phenomenon may also be related to what Tinker (1989) describes as the 'public mind'. Since farming is concerned with something as positive as food production and is a function of the countryside, it could not harm the environment. For example, farmers in the UK could defend themselves against charges of pollution by showing that they acted in accordance with 'good agricultural practice'. The Environmental Committee of the House of Commons noted their surprise at this fact and concluded: 'As a chemical company in this country is expected – indeed required – to safely dispose of its toxic wastes, we see no reason why agriculture should not be expected to have safe slurry and silage stores and disposal routes' (Tinker 1989: 8).

Conclusion

Evaluating the Rational Actor model applied at sub-national level in terms of the tenability of the propositions derived from it, we can conclude that we have had only a limited degree of success in predicting the positions and behaviour of relevant actors. Concerning expected incentives and positions based on P_3, we could not observe any 'perfect' fit. Industry and agriculture varied in their positions, and both were more ambitious than could be expected, while the municipal sector was less ambitious than expected. With regard to the relationship between positions and actual behavioural change, the achievements of industry paralleled actual positions. Agriculture had achieved less than actual positions would suggest, whereas the 'municipal' sector had achieved more.

One possible explanation is that the model is insufficiently valid in terms of the underlying behavioural mechanisms. Evaluating the model as a heuristic tool, however, we can conclude that costs and benefits have been a significant element in how target groups have responded to the domestic goals and measures linked to North Sea Action Plans. Both industry and agriculture are concerned with competitiveness and efficiency and they articulate a general concern for a trade-off between economic concerns and new environmental requirements. Moreover, actors within the municipal sector are concerned that increased water charges may not result in a comparable increase in benefits. On the other hand, we have indications that one explanation may lie in our assumption that actors have dual utility functions made up of norms in addition to rationality. Although this is very hard to verify, we have found indications that considerations exceeding a narrow cost/benefit calculation may be important in explaining the positions taken by target groups. Thus, the mismatch identified between expected and actual patterns may rest on the possibility that the model is based on an insufficient behavioural assumption.

ENGO mobilization may also contribute towards understanding the performance of industry in general, and dumping and incineration at sea in particular. ENGOs have mobilized significantly more with regard to industry than agriculture. Moreover, in some cases, mobilization appears to have had a direct impact on target group behaviour. Still, ENGO mobilization frequently aims at affecting governmental pollution policies and regulation, and the governments ability to 'deliver' pollution control may be equally important, if not more. In addition, variation in ENGO mobilization is unlikely to explain why the municipal sector has achieved more than the agricultural sector, since the municipal sector has been virtually free of any ENGO pressure. And finally, the various target-group sectors have shown more similarities than differences across states. Hence, variance in implementation and compliance between the individual states can only to a limited extent be traced to variation in positions at the target-group level. For example, the major farmers' organizations in Norway and the Netherlands have reluctantly accepted national goals based on North Sea commitments. However, the achievements witnessed in agriculture vary significantly between these countries. Consequently, there are good reasons to proceed beyond this model to understand 'success' and 'failure' in domestic Level II implementation of international commitments. So far, we have said little about the organization of pollution control and the regulation of target groups. The demand for and supply of pollution control will be on the agenda in the next chapter.

Notes

1 CNIE (1995).
2 Næringslivets Hovedorganizasjon 1992.
3 *ENDS Report* 1990a: 3–9.
4 Up to 1991, ICI had already invested £ 25 million.
5 Measuring general positions or more specific preferences among target groups is complicated. First, official positions may differ from real preferences; then there is the problem that the positions of NGOs are not systematically made explicit according to relevant national goals and international commitments. What I aim for is first to present data indicating general positions of the target groups with regard to official goals and key principles as they appear in 'their' sections within the North Sea Action Plans, or related national plans.

6 Confederation of British Industry 1995a.
7 Confederation of British Industry 1995b.
8 *ENDS Report* 1990b: 13–16.
9 Interview with Graham Boyes, Ministry of Agriculture, Fisheries and Food/Environmental Protection Division, 6 December 1996.
10 CEFIC 1996: 16.
11 CNIE (1995).
12 CEFIC (1996: 21).
13 CEFIC (1996: 24).
14 We should note that inclusion of British agriculture would fit well into the general patterns observed in Norway and the Netherlands. First, the National Farmers' Union (NFU) has had a very close relationship with the Ministry of Agriculture, Fisheries and Food. Second, the NFU has traditionally proved sceptical to environmental regulations. See McCormick (1991: ch. 4).
15 Interview with Harm Smith, Ministry of Agriculture, 9 December 1996.
16 Norges Bondelag 1989–90: 102–6.
17 This description is based on Hegeman *et al.* (1992).
18 Ministry of Transport and Public Works (1990).
19 Interview with W.G.M. Heldens and G.R.M. van Dijk, Union of Water Boards, 10 December 1996.
20 Ministry of the Environment (1992).
21 Environment Agency (1996: 121).
22 *ENDS Report* (1992b: 18–20).
23 Interview with W.G.M Heldens.
24 Ministry of Agriculture, Fisheries and Food (1989).
25 *ENDS Report* (1987a: 8).
26 *ENDS Report* (1987c: 7).
27 *ENDS Report* (1990b: 13).
28 Interview with Amanda Bradley, Confederation of British Industry, 4 December 1996.
29 *ENDS Report* (1992a: 10–11).
30 Articles have been categorized on the basis of the *ENDS Report Index* rubric labelled Environmental Lobby, the General Index, and Agriculture and Forestry.
31 Interview with Bjørn Sveen, Norwegian Confederation of Business and Industry, 12 September 1997.
32 Interview with Finn Edland, Norwegian Farmers' Union, 17 Setember 1997.

8

The functioning and consequences of domestic institutions

The main purpose of this chapter is to scrutinize the extent to which and how domestic institutions have affected implementation of the North Sea commitments in Norway, the Netherlands and the UK. Differences and change in domestic institutional procedures and rules can be expected to have affected the various stages linking domestic policy (output) to change in the behaviour of target groups (outcome). I expect that this perspective will provide a new angle on the patterns observed in Chapter 7. This might also enable us to explain variance in implementation and achievements between the various countries and sectors.

Analytically, domestic pollution policies can be seen as a function of societal demands for environmental policy and governmental supply of policies to protect the environment. Here we must bear in mind that this point of departure serves as an organizing analytical concept only, since realities may look different. However, this perspective does take into account that domestic implementation processes cannot be fully understood either solely from the 'top', or from the 'bottom'. In essence, we need an integrated state/society approach in the study of downstream implementation processes. The societal dimension is here linked to the 'strength' of societal demands in general. The supply side will take us to vertical and horizontal distribution of competence between ministries and regulatory agencies as well as the specific policy tools applied to achieve higher-order goals. In contrast to the 'convergence' hypothesis, which suggests that different institutional arrangements operating within different national circumstances will lead to similar outcomes, I expect that different institutional arrangements will produce different outcomes. Some institutional arrangements will be more 'effective' in changing behaviour than others.

The first section of this chapter is concerned with the 'demand' side while the second and third sections focus on the 'supply' of pollution control. The demand side has a more general character than the supply side, since the latter will take us towards sector level. The fourth section discusses the problematic distinction between environmental institutions and regulatory styles rooted in history and tradition.

Change in social demands and channelling agents

Change in social demands may shed light on any direct relationship between change and variance in public opinion and the making and implementation of joint international commitments. Did the breakthrough at the 1987 London Conference occur as a result of a significant increase in 'green' values and attitudes prior to the conference? Can degree of mismatch between governmental ambitions and actual behavioural change be traced back to fluctuations in public attitudes?

Public opinion, environmental organizations and political parties

Several public opinion surveys have included questions about threats to the environment and attitudes towards environmental protection since the 1970s. From these surveys, we can draw the following conclusions with some certainty:[1]

- 'Green' attitudes increased significantly in the late 1980s in all three countries.
- The gap in attitudes between the Netherlands and the UK since the 1970s was reduced towards the beginning of the 1990s.
- In Norway, 'green' attitudes dropped significantly between 1989 and 1993.
- In the Netherlands, 'green' attitudes have remained quite stable since 1990.
- In the UK, 'green' attitudes have probably dropped since 1990, but how much is uncertain.

The green movement and 'green' political parties are important actors in translating public support for environmental protection into political power. They serve as agents for the attentive public by articulating and aggregating environmental concerns. Of course, other political parties than the 'greens' may be at least as important in articulating environmental concerns through national Parliaments. Thus, we will look at the responsiveness of political parties in general, not just concerning the 'green' parties. Let us start with the ENGOs. Here, I will focus on policy and pollution oriented ENGOs (in contrast to those involved in nature conservation) that have been actively involved in water and marine issues, and large national ENGOs that tend to focus on a broader spectrum of environmental issues. We should note that much of the growth in the green movement has taken place among the pollution-oriented ENGOs. Time-series data on membership and income patterns show the following patterns:[2]

- The ENGOs in all three countries increased in terms of membership and income from 1980 to 1993.
- The growth of the ENGOs has been most significant in the latter part of the 1980s.
- In this period, the growth of British ENGOs has been most significant.
- The Dutch ENGOs continued to grow until 1995.
- The British ENGOs have either stabilised, or levelled off somewhat in the 1990s.
- The largest Norwegian ENGO shows a steady decline in the 1990s in terms of income and membership, probably a general tendency among Norwegian ENGOs.

There seems to be a quite strong relationship between change in public attitudes towards environmental values and development in the green movement. Attitudes in the Netherlands stabilized at a high level in the 1990s and the ENGOs have continued to grow somewhat. In Norway, public attitudes dropped significantly in the early 1990s and the largest Norwegian ENGO levelled off as well. In the UK, change in public opinion was more uncertain, but we assumed that it had dropped somewhat in the early 1990s. Patterns for British ENGOs from 1989 are also mixed. Now let us turn to political parties and see whether the same tendencies appear here.

The success of the green parties in articulating environmental concerns in parliaments depends first and foremost on a certain level of environmental concern in society – but this is by no means a sufficient condition to ensure representation. Electoral systems, level of internal discord and other political parties' sensitivity to social demands are all important factors in this respect. From various sources, we see that there exist some distinct differences and similarities concerning the role and importance of green parties and party politics as mediators of environmental concerns in the three countries:[3]

- Political parties paid more attention to environmental problems in the latter part of the 1980s in all three countries.
- In the UK, the 'green' party and other political parties do not appear to be the most important agents for channelling social demands.
- In the Netherlands, both the green parties and other political parties are important agents in channelling demands.
- In Norway, there is no 'green' party, but other political parties have filled this niche and most parties have served as channelling agents for social demands, even when public attitudes towards environmental issues dropped.

Public opinion in all three countries changed significantly towards environmental attitudes especially in the late 1980s. Then, in the early 1990s, environmental concern dropped significantly in Norway, probably dropped somewhat in the UK and stabilized at a high level in the Netherlands. Change in societal demands for environmental protection has been channelled through both the political parties and the green movement in all three countries, though there are some striking differences. In the UK, the political parties appear as least significant while the green movement is probably most significant. Thus, changes in social demands in the UK are to a large extent channelled outside the traditional political system. One important reason for this is the majoritarian electoral Westminister system which makes it virtually impossible for new groups to break into British party politics as a result of the dominance of the two main political parties (Bohemer Christiansen and Skea 1991: 75). This means that the UK Green Party will be unable to develop a stable electoral base without proportional representation as in Norway and the Netherlands. In the Netherlands, both channels have been important. Green parties, other parties and the ENGOs have all been significant agents. The situation in Norway deviates from that in the Netherlands in one particular respect: 'other' political parties and ENGOs have been most important, as there is no separate 'green' party in Norway.

Interestingly, the significant change in public attitudes in the latter part of the 1980s occurred mainly after the 1987 North Sea Conference where the ambitious international commitments were originally adopted (Table 8.1). Thus, change in public opinion would not seem to have been a necessary condition for the change in the stringency of joint commitments. However, there is a relationship between national adoption of international commitments and change in public opinion. The national implementation plans presented at the 1990 Hague Conference were developed in a context of significant increase in societal demands for environmental protection in all three countries. On the other hand, we can see no linkage between developments in public opinion after 1990 and Level II implementation. The most significant mismatch between national goals and actual results can be found in the Netherlands, where 'green' attitudes have remained high and stable since 1990. Conversely, a relatively close match between national ambitions and actual results is seen in Norway, although public attitudes dropped significantly in the early 1990s. Thus, change in societal demands are clearly insufficient to explain Level II implementation as well as the adoption of more stringent international commitments. Accordingly, we expect to find the most important explanatory factors at the supply side.

Table 8.1 *Country pattern of the importance of environmental protection, 1976–91**

	1976	*1978*	*1983*	*1987*	*1989*	*1991*
Netherlands	67	70	53	61	83	73
UK	48	48	48	53	75	78
EC average	63	57	56	61	78	75

* Percentage 'very important'
Source: Hofrichter (1991).

Distribution of competence

Distribution of competence within the state apparatus takes us from the demand for pollution protection to governmental supply and actual ability to penetrate the policy levels and sectors relevant for implementing measures to achieve national and international goals. Whenever implementation of environmental policies affects different regulatory agencies (internally), other policy sectors (externally), and/or different levels of government, there is a risk of horizontal and vertical disintegration of pollution policies within the state apparatus. The core of this argument centers on the distribution of competence and different roles played by different governmental agencies. In short, P_6 (see p. 58) states that horizontal and vertical fragmentation within the state apparatus itself or within various levels of government tend to increase disintegration between national goals and the adoption of measures needed to implement relevant goals. According to this proposition, implementation 'success' or 'failure' does not depend on change in societal demands, nor does it depend on the use of specific policy tools. It depends on ability to integrate and coordinate policies among affected governmental agencies and sectors.

The Netherlands: struggling with complexity

Since 1980, there have been about 30 different authorities with responsibility for the administration of water pollution. This has been perceived as a problem in the Netherlands: officially dubbed the problem of 'compartmentalization'. In the view of the water authorities, compartmentalization describes the tendency of the different government bodies to be so preoccupied with their own objectives that they are unable to understand the viewpoints of their colleges in other ministries and sub-ordinated agencies.[4] In view of the complexity of the Dutch water pollution control system, we would generally assume that fragmentation has created problems for implementation.

There are actually three ministries involved in water-quality issues in the Netherlands. In addition to the Ministry of Housing, Physical Planning and the Environment (VROM), the Ministry of Transport and the Ministry of Agriculture have also played an important role. These three ministries and their subordinated agencies were assigned the key role in implementing the 1990 Dutch North Sea Action Plan. While VROM has the main responsibility for Dutch national environmental plans and programmes, water and marine pollution fall under the competence of the Ministry of Transport and Public Works. This ministry has traditionally been very influential and able to control the resources necessary to carry out its responsibilities. The water administration has a tradition of financial autonomy and economic ministries do not interfere in this sector. The 1993 Environmental Management Act (EMA) was adopted in order to cope with the remaining fragmentation of Dutch environmental law as well as responsible authorities. Until 1993, a company would frequently need up to four different licenses administered by four different authorities. The central idea of the EMA is for one and the same body to have responsibility for both licensing and enforcement. The only piece of legislation which was not integrated here was the Pollution of Surface Water Act. Separate licensing in accordance with this act is still needed.

Let us start by outlining a few facts that can help us to understand the importance and complexities of water management in the Netherlands.[5] The desire to keep one's feet dry has been first priority since water regulation commenced in the early Middle Ages. Water has a special meaning in the Netherlands, since one-third of the country lies below sea level, and another third faces flooding if dikes and channels are not carefully maintained. The complicated interplay between tide, surface waters and ground-water level, and the need for water irrigation requires complex management of water quantity. Adding to this are the thousands of canals used both for traffic and irrigation purposes. Moreover, the Netherlands depends on surface water for drinking water. Approximately one-third of the piped water delivered by the waterworks comes from the two largest rivers, the Rhine and the Meuse. An enormous water bureaucracy has developed to deal with flood protection, water supply, and ground-water protection, as well as surface water quality management.

The Transport Ministry's powerful Directorate General for Public Works – the Rijkswaterstaat – deals with both water quantity, and quality and is responsible for implementing the PSWA with regard to state waters. The agency has about 10,000 employees working in the central directorate in The Hague as well as 13 regional executive directorates. The Rijkswaterstaat is staffed with technocrats. It has traditionally relied on a technocratic working style and a more 'command and control' oriented approach as compared to the VROM. A certain reluctance about environmental management has been maintained in Rijkswaterstaat, and there is some tension between water quantity and water quality staff. According to the organization, the technocrats have not always found it easy to accept environmental concerns.[6] On the other hand, the agency has been regarded as equally professional concerning pollution control as in the fields of water quantity. Moreover, the Ministry of Transport and the Rijkswaterstaat have a profile that commands more respect than the Ministry of the Environment, especially in the eyes of target groups (Andersen 1994). As we shall see, the agricultural sector fears an increasing role of the PSWA in controlling agricultural pollution.

Primary responsibility for those surface waters which are not the responsibility of the state, the so-called non-state waters, lies with the 12 provincial authorities. Coordination problems are viewed as minor at provincial level, due the existence of one integrated decision-making body in each province dealing with water management. The municipalities have not been assigned any important role in water pollution control after the adoption of the PSWA. Approximately 3,000 firms considered to be serious polluters are under the responsibility of the provinces (Tak 1994). However, the provinces have the right to delegate responsibility for surface waters to water boards (WBs), and the most provinces have actually done so. Provinces have general tasks of supervising some of the policies of water boards, but how they actually perform this varies widely (Bressers, Huitema and Kuks 1994: 37). The provincial authorities have the right to overturn any Water Board decisions considered to be in conflict with the law or general interests. Central government – the Ministry of Transport – in turn oversees the provinces.

The task of the Rijkswaterstaat includes planning of management, granting of permits, imposing and collecting levies, inspecting water quality, and granting subsidies to reduce pollution from discharges into state waters. The authorities responsible for regional waters have the same functions, with two exceptions: they cannot grant subsidies, and they are responsible for building and operating waste water treatment plants. The Rijkswaterstaat has a decentralized structure consisting of regional directorates, so the regional water authorities of a province often interact with a regional directorate covering the same territory.

This complex constellation of governmental authorities at various levels calls for strong coordination. The 1973 Committee on the Implementation of the Pollution of Surface Waters Act (CUWVO) plays a central role in coordinating water policies. The CUWVO is composed of representatives of all the above mentioned authorities: two members from the Union of Water Boards; two members from the Interprovincial Consultation; one member on the behalf of the association of Dutch Municipalities; one member of the Directorate General of VROM; two members from the Rijkswaterstaat. The CUWVO has responsibility for coordinating policy among governmental agencies, studying aspects of water management as well as advising the state with regard to national water management based on sectoral studies, serving as a basis for permits. The participating agencies are equally authorized; they operate on the basis of consensus rules. The CUWVO is further separated into various permanent and *ad hoc* study groups, of which study group VI (emissions) is most relevant for industry. As we shall see below, the high number of authorities involved in implementing water pollution control has led to implementation problems, particularly in industry.

Industry The industrial sector represents the most important source with regard to most of the hazardous substances. The Netherlands falls short of compliance with regard to nine hazardous substances – four heavy metals and five organic substances. All discharges of waste, polluting and harmful substances into surface waters are in principle forbidden without prior authorisation. For indirect discharges (e.g. into a sewerage system) prior authorisation is necessary for most types of plants. However, in the late 1980s, it was revealed that more than one-third of the approximately 8,000 activities requiring a licence for discharge into state waters, i.e. the most serious polluters under the Pollution of Surface Waters Act, were actually operating without one (OECD 1995: 54). A similar problem was evident at the regional level. Clearly, then, a large proportion of polluting activities remained uncontrolled.

Lack of administrative capacity is cited as the main 'official' reason for this situation. Due to the high number of staff and the financial strength of the water administration, lack of capacity is probably more closely related to fragmentation and the need for coordination, than to lack of human and financial resources *per se*. More specifically, lack of capacity appears closely related to protracted decision-making and implementation within the CUWVO, due to the large number of agencies involved required to reach an agreement. Although licences may be granted on a case by case basis in the absence of sectoral studies, such studies make licensing much easier and efficient, since complex industrial sectors may be treated similarly: the CUWVO guidelines help determine what conditions should be attached to licences. In order to speed up licensing, two Royal Decrees have been issued in 1983 and 1989 in which international commitments were included. Still, study group VI had not finished its task of completing sectoral studies as of 1994.[7] A second, but related, reason concerns the attitudes in the Ministry of Transport and the Rijkswaterstaat. In the 1995 Annual Report of the Rijkswaterstaat, changing attitudes towards environmental concerns are identified as one major change in the Rijkswaterstaat in recent years. All in all, then, the distribution of competence between agencies with different roles and attitudes within the Dutch water quality sector has hampered the government's ability to adopt measures within the industrial sector.

Some industrial sectors are covered by PARCOM recommendations and decisions, and Dutch implementation here may give an indication of the extent to which measures are implemented compared to Norway and the UK. Approximately 70 measures are identified as having relevance for Dutch industrial sectors. Of these, 61 are reported implemented, although some uncertainty attends to measures in the iron and steel sector due to the form of the implementation report. Two refineries have not been made subject to two of the measures required, and some measures have not been implemented in the electroplating industry and the iron and steel industry. These results indicate that negative consequences linked to regulatory fragmentation has been increasingly counterbalanced – at least when it comes to implementation of PARCOM commitments.[8]

Municipal waste water Although water boards work together with central government and the provincial and municipal authorities, they are highly autonomous bodies concerned solely with the water management of a given area. In this sense, the construction and financing of treatment plants as well as purification of waste water are surrounded by a less fragmented regulatory system as compared to industry. As noted in Chapter 7, the Netherlands has one of the highest coverage of population served by advanced waste water treatment plants in the OECD. This high level of coverage has been related to the autonomous position of the WBs and the financing system for waste water treatment. The construction of treatment works is in the hands of WBs, which finance nearly 100 per cent of expenditures through effluent charges. Although this has the potential to create a negative feedback since the system relies on the polluters' willingness to pay, this negative mechanism is seen as much weaker than the system based on municipal competence, which existed until the adoption of the PSWA: 'Dutch practice has shown that municipalities invest too little in their sewerage systems, and instead invest in visible projects like luxury swimming pools' (Bressers, Huitema and Kuks 1994: 39).

Despite the high degree of coverage, only a small proportion of the sewage treatment works was equipped with a phosphorus-removal facility in 1985. In 1987, the government presented to the national assembly a plan for phosphorus reduction, and a phosphorus reduction programme was developed during 1988 by the CUWVO. The objective of the programme was to achieve 75 per cent removal efficiency by 1995. An agreement on this objective between the central government and the water authorities was signed in 1989; this goal has been reached. By contrast, nitrogen removal lags far behind targets. Average nitrogen efficiency in 1985 was 46 per cent. In 1988, the CUWVO started to develop a national programme for increased nitrogen removal at sewage treatment works. However, implementation of these obligations has been delayed and new targets have been extended up to the year 2005.

As noted in Chapter 7, the Dutch Union of Water Boards has successfully convinced the central authorities that the timing should be postponed due to opposition among the public as a result of rising water charges. These authorities may have been convinced easily. For example, the Rijkswaterstaat explicitly asks whether further increases in water charges are acceptable, and then leaves the question unanswered.[9] However, the WBs appear less sensitive to public preferences compared to e.g. municipalities, since they cannot be regarded as truly democratic organizations. The governing bodies of the water boards are not selected by general election as are the municipalities and provinces. The organization of the water boards is based on the Water Authorities Act, which sets out which groups of interested parties may propose candidates for the governing body.[10] Representatives from industry, farmers and households elect their representatives directly. Representatives from the public – households – are generally chosen by the municipalities. Thus, households represent one of three main groups; the Dutch experience indicates that this way of balancing interests has proved quite efficient for the general quality and coverage of waste water treatment.

In addition to local opposition, there are two other factors that shed light on the postponed nitrogen programme, and these have virtually nothing to do with the institutionalization of waste water treatment. First, there have been technical problems in constructing nitrogen removal works. Second, scarcity of space is a general problem in the Netherlands and an obstacle concerning any new construction. Moreover, the procedure for obtaining a site licence is very complicated and, if followed all the way, may take five years or more (Huitema 1993). Thus, we may conclude that the Dutch system of sewage treatment has generally proven effective, with sewage treatment coverage ranking among the highest in the OECD and with full compliance concerning phosphorus reduction. The nitrogen removal programme has been postponed but not cancelled, due to local opposition, technical problems, and scarcity of space.

Agriculture The Dutch policy system has generally strong neo-corporatist qualities. A deliberate target-group approach has developed in environmental policy aiming at close cooperation between target groups and authorities. VROM's cooperative approach was developed in the 'Indicative Multi-Years programmes' (IMP) for the Environment, commencing in 1984. However, the IMPs did not aim at integrating environmental concerns into the broad range of public policy. The breakthrough in this respect came with the 1989 National Environmental Policy Plan, which was signed by the Ministry of Agriculture. According to Weale (1992b), the planning team within VROM was unwilling to reorganize the state administration, for fear of distracting attention from substance to procedures. In addition, they sought to maintain authority over certain elements of environmental policy affecting other sectors. Since interministerial cooperation involves sharing responsibility, they were afraid that targets and priorities would be weakened by other ministries. Hence, VROM retained competence concerning goals, but was prepared to bargain on all other aspects of the plan. The 1994 NEPP 2 is also regarded as coherent with various plans in other policy sectors, and environmental objectives are increasingly taken into consideration by the agricultural sector (OECD 1995: 120). Vertically, the agricultural authorities are based on six administrative regions operating quite independently of the 12 provincial authorities. Control and enforcement are the exclusively purview of central authorities.

Dutch nutrient inputs are estimated to account for 15–20 per cent of eutrophication problems in the coastal areas of the eastern North Sea (Vertegaal 1993). Agricultural inputs of nutrients in the form of manure and inorganic fertilizer into Dutch surface waters accounted for 70 per cent of nitrogen and 27 per cent of phosphorus in 1990. In addition, agriculture causes significant inputs of some heavy metals and pesticides. However, the estimated result in 1995 was nil reduction compared to 1985 levels, and we would thus expect environmental concerns to have penetrated the agricultural sector only to a minor extent. However, since the late 1980s, environmental concerns have been included in the agricultural sector, which is headed by the Ministry of Agriculture, Nature Management and Fisheries (Ministerie van Landbouw, Natuurbeheer en Visserij). Among the EC countries, the Netherlands is actually considered to have the most advanced environmental regulations in agriculture (Conrad 1993).

The Ministry of Agriculture was established in 1935 in order to improve the market conditions for agricultural production. A culture of close consultation developed between the ministry and agricultural interests in both the development and the implementation of policy (Hegeman *et al.* 1992). In the mid-1980s, a Department of Nature Conservation was established within the ministry, followed by the Department of Environmental Quality and Public Health, which has main responsibility for nutrients. Taken together, approximately 120 staff of the about 1500 staff working at the ministry in The Hague are currently working on environment-related issues. Although the ministry still is regarded as an advocate of agricultural interests, agricultural and environmental concerns have become more balanced within the ministry itself the last decade. A second important change concerns the relationship between the farmers' organization and the Ministry. The consultation culture has gradually changed towards a more 'arm length' approach. Previously, the Agricultural University represented a common educational background for both the farmers' organizations and the Ministry. Today, other professions, such as the law, have gained increased access to the Ministry. Moreover, the relative economic importance of the agricultural sector has declined. These changes have formed the basis for a seemingly ambitious policy on agricultural pollution.

Besides the excessive use of artificial fertilizer, over-fertilization is mainly caused by extensive use of animal manure in the Netherlands. The high level of cattle production is made possible through imported foodstuff. Dutch fertilizer legislation was adopted in 1986, followed by a Policy Document on Manure and Ammonia that takes a three-phase approach to tackling the nutrient problem. The main objective of the first phase (1987–90) was to stabilize manure production; the second phase (1991–94) aimed at tightened quotas gradually; while the third phase (1995–2000) was to lead to a state of balanced fertilisation. The third phase has now been extended to the year 2010. Nevertheless, the original goal was reflected in NEPPs, thus indicating a joint effort between the Ministry of Agriculture and VROM. Relations between these ministries are described as good by both the OECD (1995) and by the department of agriculture within the Ministry of Agriculture. On the other hand, relations between the Ministry of Agriculture and the Ministry of Transport and Public Works are widely regarded as poor. Since regulation of agricultural pollution has been based on other legal instruments than the Pollution of Surface Waters Act, these ministries have cooperated only to a minor extent. However, the Ministry of Transport and Public Works has sought to expand the scope of the PSWA to include agricultural pollution, particularly a levy on nutrients. Due to the position and approach of the Ministry of Transport and Public Works, the Ministry of Agriculture has feared that increased involvement of the Transport Ministry may destroy what they term the 'sustainable level of cooperation' between the agricultural authorities and the agricultural organizations.[11]

An indication of the extent to which specific measures have been implemented may be found in the Dutch progress report to the Paris Commission on the implementation of national action plans to reduce inputs of nutrients from 1993.[12] Of a total of 40 measures, the Dutch authorities have considered 25 to be 'very practical' or 'practical' to implement in the Netherlands. These are measures that have actually been implemented by some sort of policy tool. Hence, lack of measures does not appear as the main cause concerning the grave mismatch between goals and results in the Dutch agricultural sector.

However, one important reason lies in the late adoption of measures. For example, if manuring were to stop tomorrow, accumulated phosphates would continue to leach out for years to come (Vertegaal 1993). Regulations in the agricultural sector were initiated about 15 years after industry and municipal waste water since the PSWA had not originally included diffuse sources. Moreover, there was a delayed response from the Department of Agriculture despite early signals from researchers in the 1970s about environmental problems in the sector (Hegeman *et al.* 1992). A second problem concerns the content and stringency of the measures. We noted in Chapter 7 that the farmers' organizations had successfully watered down specific requirements included in the general measures. As to the content, it has been held that too little emphasis has been put on nitrogen v. phosphorus substances and on artificial fertilizer v. animal manure. Thus, we can conclude that the main reason why farmers have not changed their behaviour is not due to lacking measures *per se*. The main problems are related to the late response by the Department of Agriculture and the content and stringency of measures. In the next section, we shall focus on the choice and consequences of policy tools to see whether the measures adopted have actually been implemented at the level of farmers.

On the whole, the Dutch system for water quality management is complex, especially horizontally, with two ministries and their subordinate agencies involved in water and marine related issues. In addition, implementing national goals related to the North Sea commitments affects other policy sectors, such as agriculture. However, our data only partly support the assumption that this has led to disintegration between national goals and the adoption of measures through the administrative system. In the industrial sector, nearly 3000 activities requiring a licence were in fact operating without one. This situation is linked to the complex constellation of regulatory agencies, but the scope of licensing has probably improved in recent years. Concerning waste water treatment, general coverage is among the highest in the OECD, due largely to the special way in which the water boards are organized. Delayed response to new requirements concerning nitrogen removal can be traced back to local opposition, technical problems, and a complex licensing system. The problems experienced in the agricultural sector seem related not so much to current lack of measures, as to late response to environmental problems and the content and stringency of measures. Dutch authorities have partly been able to counterbalance fragmentation with effective coordination. Deliberate coordination within the water sector commenced with the CUWVO in 1973, in the general environmental sector by the theme focus of the Multi-Years Programmes in 1984 and in other policy sectors with the NEPP in 1989. Thus, our data indicate that only part of the mismatch between goals and results is related to fragmentation within the state apparatus itself.

Norway: simplicity not so simple

Norway's pollution control system is marked by its simplicity in terms of legal basis and governmental agencies. There is a single authority, the State Pollution Control Agency, and one principal pollution law, the 1981 Pollution Control Act covering land, air and water pollution. The Ministry of the Environment has primary responsibility for this law. This system has also had responsibility for the industrial sector until 1993, when regulation of smaller industrial plants was delegated to the county level. Hence, there would seem to be scant risk of vertical and horizontal disintegration within the state apparatus in this sector. On the other hand, competence in the agricultural and municipal sectors is distributed vertically to counties and municipalities, which may mean more problems concerning the adoption of measures here.

Norway established its Ministry of the Environment (ME) in 1972. Several surveys have shown that recruitment patterns for the ME have differed significantly from those for other ministries. While the general ministerial tradition can be described as 'legal', many ME employees were found to have a natural science background. Moreover, they were younger, more inclined to support the environmental movement and less 'faithful' to political signals from above (Lægreid 1983; Reitan 1996). The State Pollution Control Authority was established in 1974. From 1981, it has been responsible for the administration of the Pollution Control Act, as well as for implementation of the Product Control Act. Today, the number of employees in the SPCA almost parallels those of the ME. The relationship between the SPCA and different types of interests have changed after the adoption of the PCA. From 1974 to the mid-1980s the SPCA generally gave priority to economic considerations of target groups in its licensing policy. Since the mid-1980s the SPCA is held to have given increasing priority to environmental protection at the expense of more purely economic considerations (Gjerde 1992).

Industry Direct discharges from industry have traditionally been the main source of hazardous substances. Due to significant reductions in the last two decades, more attention is now directed towards products. According to the Pollution Control Act, anyone intending to initiate anything entailing risk of pollution must apply for a permit. All such permits are issued by the State Pollution Control Authority. Approximately 1,500 industrial units – divided into four categories according to level of pollution risk – currently hold permits. In general, Norway has over-complied regarding the hazardous substances included here, and the permit system is generally given credit for the substantial achievements. For industry, discharge permits based on integrated pollution control have been a major advantage in terms of cost-efficiency compared to other countries where there are separate control authorities for water, air, and land pollution matters.

As in the Netherlands, industrial sectors covered by PARCOM Recommendations and Decisions may give an indication of the extent to which specific measures adopted at international level are implemented.[13] Considerable uncertainty exists as to implementation in the electroplating industry due to the form of the national report. Two measures have not been implemented in the iron and steel sector. The remaining requirements seem to have been implemented.

Municipal waste water and agriculture In 1982, an environmental division was set up at each of the 18 County Governor's Offices. These divisions have responsibility for the enforcement of the Pollution Control Act with regard to municipal waste water treatment, municipal waste, and agriculture; they also serve as the formal bodies for appeals concerning decision at municipal level. The environmental divisions at the County Governor's offices are part of a hierarchical structure of state authority and serve as instruments by which central authorities in Oslo seek to implement national environmental policies throughout the country (Jansen and Osland 1996). The county level is important for the implementation of national environmental policy in general, and national targets linked to the North Sea Commitments in particular.

Municipalities have also traditionally been responsible for several issue-areas with relevance for environmental policy. Of particular importance here is a law from 1974 that permits municipalities to finance all investments in waste water treatment through local taxes, leaving them significant discretion. As a follow-up to the 1987 Report of the World Commission on Environment and Development, *Our Common Future*, separate units with responsibility for environmental issues were set up in 1987 and entasked with preparing comprehensive environmental plans. The relationship between the municipalities and the state is very complex in both practical and legal terms, as well as varying according to issue areas from ‘command and control’ to ‘partnership’. When state initiatives are based on the Control of Pollution Act, the state may overrule the priorities of the municipalities. On the other hand, the state is cautious about using this authority in practice, due to the principle of local autonomy.

Local conditions and competence were taken seriously into account when the State Pollution Control Authority developed its plan on how to achieve the 50 per cent goals on nutrients, particularly concerning the agricultural and municipal sectors.[14] Two alternative sets of measures were analysed, both of which would fulfil North Sea requirements. The cheaper alternative did not take account of local water quality. Thus, the SPCA recommended the other alternative, which was somewhat more expensive, but would both meet the North Sea requirements and help to improve local water quality conditions. This approach was approved by the government. However, the municipalities were of a different opinion.

The municipal sector accounts for about 47 per cent of the inputs of nitrogen and about 67 per cent of the inputs of phosphorus substances discharged to the ‘sensitive area’. In addition, municipal waste water contains some hazardous substances. In 1990, the 1,387 municipal waste-water treatment plants served about 57 per cent of the population (2.4 million people), a slightly lower proportion than the OECD average (OECD 1993: 51). Many municipalities have lagged far behind the needs as defined by central government, which has specified that activity should be speeded up considerably by:[15]

- upgrading existing sewage treatment plants;

- constructing treatment plants including a phase of secondary treatment (chemical purification);
- including a phase of nitrogen removal at existing and new sewage treatment plants;
- renovation of the sewerage network.

Municipalities are responsible for necessary purification according to the Pollution Control Act and the principle of 'sector responsibility' (see below). The state, in the capacity of the County Governor, lays down specific requirements concerning drainage and purification in the permits granted. However, great expectations in Oslo have been dashed at municipal level. All affected municipalities submitted appeals to the Ministry of the Environment concerning the obligations for nitrogen removal issued by the county governor offices. Eventually, fierce opposition at local level contributed significantly to the cancellation of planned investments at 24 plants. Here, we should also bear in mind that the entire political climate concerning environmental measures had changed in the 1990s and the Minister of the Environment was repeatedly attacked in the Parliament due to the need of increasing local taxes. In other words, ambitious targets had been adopted when the environment was 'up', whereas implementation took place when public attitudes dropped.

The 'sector responsibility' approach was introduced in a White Paper to Parliament on the follow-up to the World Commission on Sustainable Development.[16] The aim was to integrate environmental concerns into other sectors, such as agriculture. In slight contrast to the Dutch approach, sector responsibility in Norway gave all relevant ministries responsibility for carrying out a 'sustainable' policy within their respective sectors. Moreover, the ME was reorganized in 1989 to make it better able to perform a more integrative role in relation to other ministries. Special sections were established to match the responsibilities of other ministries. Several other steps were also taken including integrated planning and the establishment of inter-ministerial committees. However, relations between the ME and other ministries have not been without problems. According to the OECD the 'sector responsibility' approach does not function as well as it should in practice (OECD 1993: 80).

As in the Netherlands, the relationship between the Ministry of the Environment and the Ministry of Agriculture is important with regard to national goals for fulfilling the North Sea commitments. The principle of 'sector responsibility', gives to the Ministry of Agriculture and subsidiary departments the main responsibility for agricultural pollution matters. However, the main legislation concerning agricultural pollution is the Pollution Control Act (PCA), which is administered by the environmental authorities. The Ministry of Agriculture started to pay serious attention to environmental issues in 1985; since then, environmental awareness has developed gradually. According to the Ministry of Agriculture, the North Sea Declarations place strong obligations on agriculture, and the Ministry places significant emphasis on following up the international commitments.[17]

As the ME deviates from the mainstream ministries in terms of natural scientific recruitment, so does the Ministry of Agriculture deviate in terms of agro-related background. More than half of the employees in central administration hold university degrees in land-use related subjects. At the local level, the corresponding figure is an impressive 72 per cent (Mydske and Steen 1994). Meetings on agricultural policy have been held twice a year between MA and ME since 1987. In recent years, this contact has been further formalized and meetings are now held more frequently. In 1989, the ME was for the first time included in the national committee conducting agricultural support negotiations. Since 1993, preparatory documents for these negotiations have been worked out jointly by both ministries, and cooperation has improved significantly. There has been a similar development at the county and local levels. In 1990, the Ministry of Agriculture appointed a committee to evaluate necessary reforms, partly because of the need for improving coordination between environmental and agricultural concerns at the county level. Cooperation between the environmental departments and agricultural offices has increased significantly in recent years.

The agricultural sector is one of the most important sources of inputs of nutrients to the North Sea. In order to fulfil national goals in this sector, inputs had to be reduced by 40 per cent for phosphorus and 44 per cent for nitrogenous substances between 1985 and 1995. However, the actual result in 1994–95 was 19 per cent reduction of nitrogen and 27 per cent reduction of phosphorus substances. A number of regulations based on PCA apply especially to agricultural pollution. We may distinguish between three phases in Norwegian attempts to combat agricultural pollution (Mydske and

Steen 1994). The first phase (1976–84) focused on run-off from fertilizer depots and silos. In the second phase (1985–88) implications of agricultural pollution became manifestly clear and attention was increasingly directed towards soil erosion and more diffuse run-off. The final phase, which commenced in 1988, involves several changes in operational practice. New regulations were introduced in 1988 on spreading of manure, and a tax was introduced on commercial fertilizer and plant sprays.

Concerning the implementation of PARCOM requirements, Norwegian authorities considered 30 measures out of 40 to be 'very practical' or 'practical'.[18] A total of 26 measures have been implemented. A combination of new measures and the stepping up of old ones was proposed in 1992, and most of these were actually implemented (see next section). Thus, we can say that Norwegian efforts to curb nutrient input from agriculture have been 'partly successful' in terms of national goals. In contrast to the Netherlands, Norway's agriculture has been regulated almost as long as industry and municipal waste water. Even though all measures, that were considered 'useful' have not been implemented, the main reason why national goals have not been met would not seem to lie in the lack of measures as such.

In summary, then, the Norwegian pollution control system appears very simple at first glance. Concerning the industrial sector, it is in fact very simple, both horizontally and vertically, and we have not found any indications that measures have been lacking, as was the case in the Netherlands. Our proposition is also supported regarding municipal waste water treatment. The decentralization of significant competence to the local level seems to be partly and directly related to Norway's failure to reach goals, especially concerning nitrogen. It is, however, agricultural pollution that stands out as the most complex, both vertically and horizontally. Significant differences in educational background also lead us to suspect that governmental actors within these sectors tend to bring in highly differing perspectives and decision criteria when faced with similar problems. However, our data also indicate that potential coordination problems have been increasingly dealt with at all levels of government through deliberate reorganization, and some significant reductions have been achieved, although results still lag behind targets. This may be related to late integration, since actual cooperation between environmental and agricultural authorities at all levels of government did not really materialize until the early 1990s. New measures may have been implemented too late to have had an effect that was visible in 1995. Another possibility is lack of implementation at target-group level, a point I will return to in the next section on policy tools.

The UK: reorganization problems

In Britain, pollution control concerning land-based water pollution has developed from a decentralized and complex system towards a more integrated one, culminating in the establishment of the Environmental Agency for England and Wales in 1996. This means that the risk of disintegration within the state apparatus may have decreased in the last decade. On the other hand, this process of developing a new institutional basis has taken place simultaneously with the adoption and implementation of the most important North Sea targets. Thus, institutional change may have created problems for the adoption of measures. Concerning dumping at sea, the licensing of waste is exclusively in the hands of the Ministry of Agriculture Fisheries and Food. Agricultural pollution will not, as mentioned, be included here, since the UK government has claimed that there are no 'sensitive areas' around the British coast.

Since 1970, environmental protection has primarily been the responsibility of the Department of the Environment. In 1993–94 the DoE employed nearly 7,700 people, of whom about only 10 per cent were actually involved with environmental protection, planning, rural affairs, and water (OECD 1994). Not only does the name seem misleading, it is also generally held that few Environmental Secretaries have shown any particular interest in the environment (McCormick 1991; 1994). However, this situation may be changing. According to Rawcliffe (1995: 20), civil servants now view a job position at the Environmental Protection Division as a promising career move rather than a sidelining. The 1990 White Paper on the environment aimed at integrating environmental concerns into other policy areas. Several committees and planning and reporting routines have been established to improve interministerial cooperation, although they have so far had limited practical effect (OECD 1994).

Up to the second half of the 1980s, the British government's approach to pollution control was marked by close cooperation between regulators and the regulated, as well as tight restrictions on the ability of non-target group constituencies to participate in the regulatory process (Vogel 1986). Significant institutional changes took place in the latter part of the 1980s, bringing easier access to ENGOs and a more 'arm's length approach to target groups. Her Majesty's Inspectorate for Pollution (HMIP) was established in 1987, but existed as an amalgam of existing inspectorates until the adoption of the 1990 Environmental Protection Act, which introduced the system of Integrated Pollution Control. The HMIP has responsibility for regulating releases to air, water, and land from cross-media polluting industrial processes. All polluting releases to water fall under the purview of the National Rivers Authority, whereas local authorities have competence for releases to air and land. Thus, while local authorities have generally a wide range of environmental protection responsibilities, water pollution is mainly in the hands of central agencies. The NRA replaced the system of regional water authorities and introduced a consent system for discharges into water. The Office of Water Services is involved in ensuring that the private water companies have financial means to carry out their task. Thus, while the water-pollution control system has become more simple both vertically and horizontally, significant complexities remained until 1996. The OECD (1994: 106) has opined that there is a lack of integration of decisions within general environmental policies.

The struggle for competence between NRA and HMIP was directly influenced by, and had consequences for, the INSC process and the implementation of the INSC Declarations. HMIP, established in April 1987, was appointed to serve as a regulatory authority for sewage effluent discharges, and to bring some consistency into water authorities' effluent sampling practices. Three months later the government proposed transferring these functions to the NRA, leaving HMIP with no clear role in water pollution control. The HMIP had been given overall responsibility for developing the application of the 'best practicable environmental option' and it pressed hard to retain control over sewage effluent discharges and major industrial discharges of hazardous substances.[19] The announcement by the UK government directly linked to the November 1987 Conference, that it intended to develop a new approach based on technology standards and a 'red list' of substances, reinforced HMIP's hand. The water authorities and their successor the NRA focused on, and had competence in, quality objectives in the receiving water. A shift in policy in the direction of technology standards would significantly strengthen the role of HMIP in water regulation.

The dispute between the NRA and the HMIP was not resolved until the UK issued its 1988 Guidance Note on the implementation of the 1987 Declaration. This note was criticized for being vague on concrete action especially with regard to inputs of hazardous substances.[20] Originally, the DoE had intended to produce a comprehensive White Paper on the water environment in response to both the 1987 Conference and a critical report on river pollution by the House of Commons' Environment Committee. However, this plan was cancelled due to the wrangle about whether the NRA or the HMIP should have control of discharges of hazardous substances to surface waters and into sewers. In addition, the Guidance Note did not specify which body would have main responsibility for coordinating implementation. For example, it was not clear whether the national plan would be a mere compilation of water authorities' plans, or whether DoE or the HMIP would coordinate these to produce an overall UK plan. The resolution to the conflict was announced in February 1989, after a consultation paper issued in the summer of 1988 by DoE on the introduction of IPC had explicitly raised the question of HMIP/NRA competences. The HMIP was given the authority to take the final decision in authorising discharges from those industrial processes containing specified hazardous substances, in consultation with the NRA. This implies granting to both agencies competence in those cases where Integrated Pollution Control (IPC) permits covers water in addition to land and air. Although the HMIP focuses on industrial processes, while the NRA is occupied with water quality, the cooperation between the two agencies has been described as 'fairly good'.[21]

Municipal waste water and industry One of the most important anthropogenic sources of pollution to inland surface and coastal waters in the UK is the discharge of sewage and sewerage works effluent. A significant proportion of hazardous substances end up in the sewerage system when not controlled at source. Sewage also accounts for about 75 per cent of phosphates flowing into surface waters (OECD 1994). About 74 per cent of the population in England, Wales and Scotland is connected to secondary or tertiary treatment at the 6,500 facilities in operation – a level among the highest in the OECD countries. The major problem has thus not been the degree of coverage, but the quality and performance of facilities. Opinions vary as to whether privatization has improved this situation. The authorities claim that significant improvements in environmental quality have occurred since capital investments have increased significantly;[22] others, however, hold that the water companies have failed to plough their increased revenues back into the network, with the result that the services they provide have deteriorated (Scofield and Shaoul 1997). Britains failure to adopt statutory Environmental Quality Objectives supports the latter view in the area of sewage treatment.

Although a quality classification system for rivers has existed in Britain since the 1970s, it had no statutory basis until the 1991 Water Resources Act. In 1978, a formal classification scheme was developed whereby stretches of rivers were classified as being of good, fair, poor, or bad quality. Previously, goals aimed at improving stretches of rivers had not been binding and thus not mandatorily included in permits covering the relevant stretches. When quality targets become mandatory, this leads to more stringent permits. This is why the introduction of statutory environmental quality objectives has been seen as a major instrument to cope with water pollution in general, one which has been included as a central measure in the UK North Sea Action Plan.

As noted in Chapter 7, there was a conflict between the NRA and OFWAT. This conflict resulted in two scenarios, 'progress maintained' and 'pure and green'. Arguing that poorer consumers already face problems in paying their water bills, the OFWAT rejected the 'pure and green' scenario, which included the introduction of statutory environmental quality objectives. The NRA argued that these costs would not result from new 'pure and green' targets, but would arise from the need to correct the policy failures and deterioration in water quality of the 1980s. Against this backdrop, the DoE suggested that the NRA should delay the introduction of statutory environmental quality objectives in 1992; since then, no schedule for their adoption has been announced (OECD 1994: 60). Lack of implementation may largely be traced back to the disagreement between the NRA and OFWAT on the quality goals to form the basis of the new system. Since the new act was proposed by the government and adopted in the Parliament, we would assume that there was political willingness to implement the new instruments. Moreover, the new system has the support of both the ENGOs and the Confederation of British Industry.

Implementation has also been delayed in the case of Integrated Pollution Control by HMIP concerning larger industries (Jordan 1993). The first set of IPC authorizations were rejected *en masse* by HMIP because they did not adequately define the process to be operated or the proposed abatement equipment. Delays have also resulted from conflicts over rising costs in administrative charges that HMIP has made for processing IPC authorisations, disputes concerning commercial confidentiality and the derivation of standards. Concerning the latter, some companies have challenged the basis and interpretation of standards by appealing to the Secretary of State. However, initial problems have largely been overcome. Since 1 April 1991, a total of 1,897 applications for authorization to operate a prescribed process under IPC have been submitted to the HMIP. Of these, 1,775 had been authorized by the end of March 1995.[23]

Implementation problems related to the new pollution control system are also reflected in the implementation of PARCOM commitments.[24] None of the required measures have been implemented, or information is lacking. In addition, the UK has filed reservations concerning two sectors. For iron and steel, implementation is in progress, in the sense that Process Guidance Notes are being prepared. New legislation is needed to implement a decision on the aluminium industry. The Oslo and Paris Commissions 1994 agreed that, for recommendations and decisions which include a deadline, implementation reports should be submitted the first year following the deadline in the recommendations and decisions. Belgium was the only country to reserve its position concerning this joint decision. However, the UK has not submitted all the implementation reports required.

Dumping at sea Dumping and incineration at sea have been regulated by licensing based on the Dumping at Sea Act of 1974, which was replaced by the Food and Environmental Protection Act of 1985 (Part II). This legislation formally implements the Oslo Convention. There is a wide range of specific requirements to be met before a licence is issued, e.g. the existence of alternative methods of disposing of the waste. This licensing procedure is well developed, and illegal dumping without authorization is rare due to the visibility of dumping operations. Traditionally, the Ministry of Agriculture, Fisheries and Food has been more closely linked to target groups (mainly fisheries and farmers) and more preoccupied with protecting their interests as compared to the DoE. Nevertheless, there are clear indications that norms concerning dumping at sea have changed within the MAFF itself. The head of the licensing section for disposal at sea underlined that the sea could no longer be used as a 'trash can', adding that he found it increasingly difficult to license what he termed 'nasty substances'.[25] This was also emphasized by the head of MAFF's laboratory, who stressed that dumping should be the 'last option', while also underlining that 'no scientific studies have ever shown any negative impact from dumping'.[26] The change in attitudes towards dumping is most clearly visible in the field of legislation. A major change introduced by 1985 Act was that dumping should be considered the 'last option' in the sense that the licensing authority was to take into account any alternative disposal method before issuing a license.[27] Interestingly, this change occurred before the 1987 North Sea Conference and the significant change in public opinion and growth in the green movement. This indicates that changes in UK dumping policy cannot solely be traced back to internal (see Table 8.2) and external pressure directed against the British government.

Table 8.2 *Questions asked in the British Parliament concerning dumping at sea, 1988–95*

	1988	*1989*	*1990*	*1991*	*1992*	*1993*	*1994*	*1995*
Sewage	2	3	13	4	2	1	2	–
Industrial	–	8	3	–	–	2	–	–
Incineration	1	1	1	–	–	–	–	–
Other dumping	6	7	16	5	7	5	3	6
North Sea general	4	3	12	2	4	–	–	1
Total	13	22	45	11	13	8	5	7

Source: Ministry of Agriculture, Fisheries and Food Archive.[28]

In summary, then, the establishment of new regulatory agencies has clearly given rise to a wide range of competence problems that have affected the implementation of measures. The struggle for competence between the NRA and the HMIP directly affected the

UK's North Sea Action Plan, particularly concerning hazardous substances. The conflict between the NRA and OFWAT has delayed the introduction of statutory Environmental Quality Objectives, while the HMIP itself has experienced problems in implementing IPC. This is also reflected in the implementation of PARCOM measures. The pot-pourri of legislation and agencies operating in the field of water quality has hampered the ability to get the new institutional procedures up and running. This has also been perceived as a problem since the government decided to merge the NRA and the HMIP into one Environmental Agency. On the other hand, institutional changes have clearly had a positive impact and can be expected to yield positive results in the future. Although the introduction of IPC encountered initial problems, most authorizations are now in place. Dumping at sea has been the responsibility of one ministry, and there are no indications that lack of implementation of measures has created problems here. However, we can note clear indications that the norms concerning dumping at sea have changed within the MAFF itself.

Consequences of distribution of competence: brief analysis

The 'municipal' sectors in the three countries under study are very difficult to compare in terms of fragmentation, due to the significant differences in organization – from municipal competence in Norway, to the peculiar water boards in the Netherlands, to the privatized water companies in the UK. Moreover, it is fair to say that all three arrangements at least work in the same direction concerning waste water treatment. Hence, at a general level, the significantly different systems in the three countries support the 'convergence' hypothesis. On the other hand, the clearest example of problems following *vertical distribution* of competence can be found in the municipal sector. Norway is the only country where municipalities have considerable competence in sewage treatment correlating with the lowest degree of coverage. Moreover, the municipalities have used their competence to postpone the introduction of nitrogen removal and to try to get the programme cancelled, even though the SPCA had developed measures taking local conditions into account. A comprehensive study of environmental politics and attitudes at the local level indicates that local opposition to state initiatives may be part of a general trend (Hovik and Harsheim 1996). Although increased decentralization and competence on environmental issues may have increased environmental awareness at local level, local politicians tend to defend local interests rather than serve as a link to national environmental politics. Moreover, most local politicians are generally sceptical to state environmental initiatives. If you sit at local level, you tend to oppose national initiatives whenever they are perceived to contradict local interests. If local opposition goes hand in hand with decentralization of competence in the relevant sector, there is a risk of defection from national and international goals.

While the 'municipal' sectors lend some support to the 'convergence' hypothesis, the industrial and agricultural sectors suggest that a high level of regulatory complexity leads to disintegration between goals and measures across countries (see Table 8.3). We see that our proposition is roughly supported in the sense that the cases that scored low have not experienced any problems in adopting measures, while those scoring medium and high have experienced such problems to varying degrees. With regard to *industry*, dumping in the UK and the regulatory system in Norway represent the only cases where only one central regulatory agency has been involved. In the Netherlands, a great number of agencies have been involved both vertically as well as horizontally. This has led to problems with issuing permits, at least partly due to protracted decision-making in the co-ordination committee to implement the Pollution of Surface Water Act where all affected agencies and ministries participate. The industrial sector in the UK scores 'medium' in terms of fragmentation since different agencies participate only at central level. This has clearly led to significant implementation problems, like the failure of adopting statutory quality objectives. Implemen-

Table 8.3 *Regulatory fragmentation and consequences in selected sectors, 1985–95*

	Sectors	*Regulatory complexity*	*Disintegration between goals and measures*
Netherlands	Industry	High	Medium
	Agriculture	High	Medium
Norway	Industry	Low	Low
	Agriculture	High	Low/medium
UK	Industry	Medium	Medium/high
	Dumping	Low	Low

tation problems have been reinforced by the reorganization of the system during the past decade. Regulation of the *agricultural* sectors in Norway and the Netherlands includes different ministries horizontally as well as regional agencies vertically. The main problem here is not lack of measures *per se*, but late introduction and the content of the measures adopted. In both countries, industry and municipal waste water were regulated before agriculture, while Norway regulated agriculture before the Netherlands.

While fragmentation has created problems for implementation, such problems have been increasingly dealt with through deliberate coordination and integration of environmental concerns into other sectors. In the Netherlands, coordination by the CUWVO and the Indicative Multi-Years programmes seems largely to have counterbalanced adverse consequences in the water sector. Agriculture has increasingly been included in national environmental policy commencing with the NEPP. In Norway, the agricultural sector has been increasingly integrated at all levels of government and a wide range of measures has actually been adopted. The problems experienced in the UK coincided with the transformation of the pollution control system into a simpler institutional structure. Here, it should be noted that in Britain the establishment of one integrated Environmental Agency based on Integrated Pollution Control occurred 14 years after the Norwegian system based on the same principles.

The proposition to be examined here rested on the assumption that distribution of competence does matter, since different ministries and agencies involved will bring in different decision criteria to bear on similar problems, due to different roles and positions in society. This assumption appears highly relevant. Different ministries and agencies show both distinct similarities and differences within and across countries. For example, the late response of the agricultural authorities to environmental challenges is probably related to the high share of civil servants with agro-related education, while a certain reluctance towards environmental management within the Transport Ministry in the Netherlands has been seen as linked to a 'technocratic culture'. In the UK, the NRA has been occupied with water quality, while OFWAT has given privilege to consumers facing increases in water charges. Also striking is the change in norms and attitudes within regulatory agencies. The water boards in the Netherlands have developed from 'peasants' clubs' to highly effective instruments in waste water treatment, while the norms in MAFF's disposal at sea unit have changed towards viewing dumping at sea as the 'last option'.

Thus, we may conclude that there seems to be a relationship between high level of regulatory complexity and disintegration between goals and measures. On the other hand, this conclusion should be modified according to at least two points: first, different institutional arrangements – such as the arrangements for waste water treatment – sometimes work in the same direction within different contexts. Second, the problems following from fragmentation have increasingly been dealt with through deliberate integration and coordination.

Policy tools

Once measures have been identified and adopted, they have to be implemented at target-group level by some sort of policy tool. The basic assumption underlying this section is that target groups have dual utility functions. Thus, our proposition (P_7, see p. 59) states that a combination of policy tools affecting both cost/benefit incentives and norms of environmentally friendly behaviour is likely to be most effective.

The former category comprises 'command and control' and economic tools, while the latter includes information/advice and voluntary agreements. Although the main focus here is on the consequences of different policy tools, it may also be interesting to see why different tools are applied across countries. Given that countries face similar problems and similar target group sectors across countries share some basic similarities, we would expect essentially the same set of tools to be applied if behavioural 'effectiveness' serves as the main motivating factor. Conversely, if standard operating procedures rooted in history and tradition determine choice of tools, we would expect different sets of tools to be applied when countries face essentially similar problems and target groups.

The Netherlands: when 'gentlemen' fail to comply with agreements

Water pollution in the Netherlands is mainly regulated by a combination of command in the form of permits and general regulations, economic tools, and different types of voluntary agreements. Control and enforcement has been acknowledged as the weakest link in the chain of Dutch pollution control. In 1993, the Dutch Minister of Justice pinpointed that lack of enforcement still represented a significant problem in the environmental policy chain in the Netherlands. The VROM has also acknowledged that study after study has shown that, despite increased environmental awareness in industry, strict law enforcement by the authorities is a company's biggest motivating factor when it comes to taking environmental measures.[29] Due to the reliance on commonly agreed goals between the authorities and affected actors, relatively little attention has been paid to the use of policy tools in the Netherlands.[30]

Licensing in the form of permits constitutes an important element of the Pollution of Surface Water Act. In addition to the problem of issuing the required licences, inspection of compliance and reaction to violations have traditionally been poor and weak. A recent CUWVO report on enforcement is quite illustrative concerning the latter. The report, a guide on how to proceed from an observed offence, states that the essence is to proceed through bargaining. Very few paths lead to actual sanctions, and the text contains many warnings about the difficulties to be expected in following the legal path (Bressers, Huitema and Kuks 1994). However, in the late 1980s a new approach was adopted, aimed at increasing the enforceability of permits, intensifying inspections and stepping up reactions. According to the OECD (1995), in those cases where penalty sanctions are used, they have proven sufficient to stop the offending discharges.

Most measures in the industrial sectors covered by PARCOM commitments are implemented by administrative tools, mainly in the form CUWVO guidelines that are not strictly legally binding and thus not legally enforceable. Hence, it could be argued that they are essentially voluntary, even though Dutch authorities hold that any deviations should be well motivated. In addition, the strategy of target-group policy has led to some 100 covenants covering all major industrial sectors. The status of these covenants is unclear. Some are formulated as 'gentlemen's agreements', which means that they are not enforceable by law. Others have a more binding character, but enforcement is still problematic: the agreements are often signed between the authorities and branch organizations implying that individual firms are not legally bound. Experience with voluntary agreements in the Netherlands is generally ambiguous, especially when it comes to actual implementation (Liefferink and Mol 1997).

The PSWA also introduced a system of levies to finance water pollution control regardless of what polluters discharge into. The most important criterion included in the levy is related to oxygen-binding substances; it has primarily affected certain manufacturing industries which discharge organic substances, such as food processing and pulp and paper. Various studies show that the levy has had significant impact on organic substances (Andersen 1994: 154). It has now been decided to include phosphorus and nitrogen in the basis for the levy, but until recently the core of the levy has not covered the most important substances included in the Dutch North Sea Action Plan. On the other hand, the levy has been used to finance sewage treatment plants and to subsidise industries, and may thus have had a general and indirect effect on the relevant substances.

In addition to information and a Manure Fund, a complex set of direct regulations provides the most important tools to achieve goals in the agricultural sector (Hegeman *et al.* 1992: 31). As pointed out in Chapter 7, farmers do frequently not see keeping the rules as being in their interest. Moreover, enforcement is weak and costly due to the high number of targets – about 124,000 farms in the Netherlands. Achieving environmental policy goals in the agricultural sector still relies mainly on the 'good faith' of farmers, though independent monitoring and enforcement are progressing. There are various reasons for lack of progress in reducing inputs of nutrients in the Dutch agricultural sector, but the choice of policy tools appears particularly important. There is no reason to expect that Dutch farmers should be more sensitive to tools aimed at stimulating norms of environmentally friendly behaviour, than to means for making desired behaviour less costly or undesired behaviour more costly. This is also underlined by the importance of the sector. The total gross value added in Dutch agriculture in 1993 was about 4 per cent of GDP; the intensive production methods used have enabled the Netherlands to rank consistently among the world's top four exporters of agricultural products (OECD 1995). Thus, Dutch farmers probably have greater faith in production growth and competitiveness than in environmental protection. Several studies – including a report from the Scientific Council to the Government – have concluded that direct regulations are less suitable as an instrument in the Dutch agricultural sector compared to economic instruments, in particular regulatory levies. However, the farmers and the Department of Agriculture as well as the Agricultural Board all oppose the introduction of economic instruments, fearing this will mean a reduction in competitive ability (Hegeman *et al.* 1992).

We may conclude that each sector in the Netherlands is made subject to both main categories of tools, but in different ways and to different extents. However, the Netherlands has paid relatively little attention to the use of policy tools in environmental policy. Agriculture relies mainly on a complex set of direct regulations. Striking in this sector is the absence of control and enforcement. In the industrial and municipal sectors, permits, guidelines and voluntary agreements are most widely used to curb discharges. The major problem here has also been lack of monitoring and enforcement, but such efforts have been intensified, and the OECD holds that penalty sanctions have a significant effect. Economic instruments have also been important, but such tools have not been directly linked to the main substances covered by North Sea commitments, beyond the financing of sewage treatment plants.

Norway: regulatory 'sticks' and economic 'carrots'

Norway's pollution control system relies heavily on command and control, and on economic tools. With the exception of information and advice, consensus tools are not considered important. There is general scepticism towards the use of voluntary agreements. Moreover, extensive reports on various aspects of the use of policy tools in environmental policy have been prepared by investigative commissions. Licensing discharges in the form of permits based on the Pollution Control Act is the main instrument concerning industry.

In contrast to practice in the Netherlands, administrative tools concerning industry are not optional guidelines, but enforceable permits based on the Pollution Control Act. The State Pollution Control Authority monitors compliance in the industrial sector through reports from companies, inspections, auditing, and source testing. The inspection work is financed by the companies through fees based on inspection needed. Norway is renowned for its deep and expensive controls of larger firms in particular. About 1,500 companies have been granted emission permits and the SPCA carries out 300 to 350 inspections and some 50 audits annually. In clear cases of violation, companies are prosecuted and fined, and any profits made by defection may by confiscated. From 1989 to 1990, the SPCA fined lack of compliance in 52 cases; in 48 of these, the companies took action within the time-limits set. In 1995, 395 firms were controlled and a total of 69 violations and irregularities were detected, of which 43 were followed up administratively, 9 were prosecuted and 17 were made subject to fines.[31] As noted in Chapter 7, Norwegian ENGOs helped in getting stricter enforcement concerning industry in the late 1980s.

The municipal sector is regulated by a combination of permits and economic measures. State subsidies to municipalities have been the most important economic tool, covering about 20 per cent of investment costs throughout the country up to 1993. Municipalities with emissions to 'sensitive areas' were granted between 25 per cent and 35 per cent, whereas total subsidies dropped significantly from NOK600 million in 1992 to NOK142 million in 1994.[32] Subsidies were increasing earmarked for national and international goals, however, subsidies to municipalities obliged to install nitrogen removal actually doubled. Thus, while total subsidies decreased significantly from 1993, those affecting the national goals linked to North Sea Declarations actually increased. Permits are granted on the basis of the CPA and are thus in principle enforceable along the same lines as those covering the industrial sector. County Governors process permits for municipal emissions. In practice, inspections are less frequent and reactions to violations more lenient compared to the industrial sector. Moreover, the control 'culture' varies from county to county. In 1992, a new directive was issued on 'internal control', aimed at strengthening the control authority of the environmental divisions at the County Governor offices. A study conducted in 1994 reveals widespread failure in implementing this directive at local level. Only 5 per cent of 381 municipalities had actually fully implemented 'internal control' for waste water and waste, and 45 municipalities had not even started to implement the directive.[33]

Some background information is needed for understanding the use of policy tools in Norway's agricultural sector. The approximately 90,000 Norwegian farms are heavily subsidized. On average, each person-year in agriculture is subsidized by NOK100,000 and these subsidies have nothing to do with environmental protection. Such subsidies are mainly intended to promote employment, security of food supply, and income parity between agriculture and industry. In addition, the so-called 'channelling policy' was introduced under regional policy by fixing artificial prices for different agricultural products. This has resulted in different production in different areas. Production of mainly wheat and to a certain extent cattle and pork has been 'channelled' to the south-east areas – 'sensitive areas' – which are best suited to agriculture. Production of milk and cattle for meat has been 'channelled' to less suitable areas in more rural districts of both the northern and southern Norway (Mydske and Steen 1994). These tools have most significantly affected the behaviour of farmers and thus, indirectly, the environment. The 'channelling' policy has actually caused artificial fertilizer and soil erosion to be more important for nutrient emissions than manure surplus in 'sensitive areas'.

One set of tools introduced from 1987 has aimed at cancelling earmarked subsidies that have encouraged actions which are more or less directly environmentally harmful. Another set of tools has been directly motivated to combat pollution problems. Such instruments are predominantly based on direct regulations set out in the PCA. From 1976 to 1988, these measures were aimed at run-off from fertilizer depots, silos, diffuse run-offs and soil erosion. From 1988, regulations have been increasingly directed towards run-off and erosion as well as operational practice in the form of change in soil tillage techniques and use of fertilizer. In addition, a tax was introduced in 1988 on commercial fertilizer and plant spray.

In contrast to the Netherlands, old measures were intensified and some new measures were introduced in the Norwegian plan on implementation of North Sea Declarations. These measures were mainly implemented by direct regulations and/or subsidies. Regulations are based on the PCA and inspections are carried out by the County Governor offices. Lack of compliance may result in penalties and prosecutions, but inspections and actual enforcement share more similarities with the municipal sector than with industry. The size of the fertilizer tax has received significant attention. The Environmental Tax Commission indicated that the tax level – administered by the Department of Agriculture – was motivated by a desire to increase state revenues, not environmental concerns. The committee concluded that it was uncertain whether the tax had affected fertilizer use.[34] Other evaluative committees have reached the same conclusion. However, the Norwegian Farmers' Union strongly opposes taxes on input factors in agriculture in general, and taxes on fertilizers in particular; as yet there has been no increase in the tax.

The Norwegian case would thus not appear to support the proposition that a combination of different types of tools is most effective. The patterns we have seen are actually the opposite. Industry has experienced significant achievements even though the sector is regulated almost exclusively by command and control. Particularly agriculture, but also municipal treatment, has been subjected to a wide range of tools, but both sectors have fallen short on goals. However, a different picture emerges if we look into the realities behind types of tools. Permits in the industrial sector are actually well monitored and companies are fined or prosecuted in clear cases of violation. In the municipal and the agricultural sectors, control is in reality much weaker, and sanctions are rare. Thus, economic tools and information aimed at encouraging desired behaviour are what are really important. 'Sticks' and 'carrots' are rarely combined in practice in the agricultural and municipal sectors.

The UK: from negotiated consent to regulatory 'sticks'

The UK regulatory system is based almost entirely on general regulations and permits. However, such tools were to a large extent 'voluntary' until the late 1980s. Even though the government has stated its intention to employ economic measures in environmental protection, such use has remained limited to energy taxation.

A discharge consent system was introduced by the Control of Pollution Act in 1974, covering both municipal waste water and industry. However, standards were generally not legally binding, and there was a tradition in the UK that officials should be given discretion in achieving broadly defined objectives. Enforcement was uncommon, and fines were low (OECD 1994: 110). Thus, one may argue that the regulatory system was essentially 'voluntary' and based largely on negotiated consent between inspectors and target groups. This system changed significantly in the late 1980s with the adoption of the 1989 Water Act and 1991 Water Resource Act. In addition, the 1990 Environmental Protection Act introduced Integrated Pollution Control for large industrial sources. In general, if any activity fails to obtain a licence or if it breaches conditions, there is no upward limit to the fine that may be imposed. Regulatory agencies are now more likely to initiate proceedings, and fines imposed have exceeded £1 million. About half of HMIP's 400 employees and about one-third of the NRA's 1,600 employees are pollution control inspectors. The implementation of IPC has resulted in a significant increase in inspections: from 4,372 in 1991–92 to 8,009 in 1992–93 (OECD 1994: 110). Even though most inspections have been related to authorization under the new IPC system, the most serious types of enforcement action have increased somewhat.

The NRA's focus on legal enforcement started almost immediately. In the first 12 month of its existence, the NRA brought 334 successful prosecutions: 49 per cent of these against industry, 48 per cent against farmers and only 3 per cent against water companies. In the next 12 months, the total had risen to 908 prosecutions.[35] In 1993, the water companies dominated the prosecution league: four of the five worst water polluters were water companies, although British Coal was in the lead.[36] Both regulators and industry have underlined the preventive effect of prosecutions and fines.[37] They also emphasize that the size of the fine is subordinate to loss of reputation and discredit in the public eye. Importantly, enforcement actions taken by the HMIP or the NRA are made public in the national or the local press. Thus the main impact of fines seems to lie more in the power to embarrass, than in a narrow change in the economic cost/benefit calculus. Hence, there is reason to suspect a relationship between this change and improvement in water quality from the 1990s, and the positive trend in inputs of hazardous substances.

Dumping and incineration at sea have been regulated by licensing.[38] Charges for licensing have been phased in to reach full recoupment of costs. Enforcement officers have been appointed to ensure compliance with license conditions. Twenty-eight officers, mainly in the MAFF's fisheries inspectorate, hold authorizations to enforce the 1985 Act. Inspectors are empowered to enforce licensing conditions by visits to production units, storage sites and dumping vessels. In England and Wales, 63 inspections were carried out in 1986 and 1987, mainly related to industrial wastes disposal, for which approximately 500 and 300 sailings occurred in 1986 and 1987 respectively. Formal warning letters are issued if detected irregularities are minor. In more serious cases, the license may be revoked and/or a prosecution may be launched. Several irregularities have been investigated. In 1986, three applications were turned down for liquid industrial waste. In 1987, a successful prosecution was made and a fine of £ 1,000 imposed for dumping of waste outside an approved dump-site. Thus, the British licensing system appears to be an effective tool to control dumping. Moreover, it has proved effective in implementing international commitments and national goals aimed at phasing out dumping. With regard to industrial waste and incineration at sea, licences have been gradually reduced in number, whereas dumping and incineration operations have actually ceased altogether. Licensing for sewage sludge has also been reduced, and the UK government is confident that this practice will end in accordance with joint commitments.

The British system has changed from essentially voluntary tools towards legally binding standards increasingly backed up by monitoring and enforcement. According to both regulators and target groups, enforcement activities have a positive effect on performance. Thus, it is reasonable to assume that the introduction of 'sticks' has had some effect, together with other factors identified in the preceding sections. Licensing appears a sufficiently effective tool for implementing international commitments and domestic goals aimed at phasing out dumping of industrial waste and incineration at sea. This indicates that the *type* of activities regulated may be at least as important as a combination of policy tools. Central in this respect is the visibility of dumping operations, combined with the fact that dumping activities are generally easy to target.

Consequences of policy tools: brief analysis

At country level, we find both some distinct differences and similarities in the use of policy tools, which would indicate that a combination of behavioural 'effectiveness' and standard operating procedures plays a role in the *choice* of policy tools. The Netherlands stands out as an advocate of different types of voluntary agreements combined with traditionally scant attention paid to control and enforcement, though the latter is progressing. Norway stands out with its high reliance on command and control, and scant attention paid to voluntary agreements. The UK has developed a system that relies increasingly on command and control. It also deviates from Norway and the Netherlands in that economic tools play only a limited role. Overall, then, the Netherlands has the highest degree of combination of policy tools, followed by Norway and then the UK. According to this interpretation, there is little support for our proposition focusing on a positive relationship between a high degree of policy tool combination and behavioural change. Behavioural change has been generally more significant in Norway than in the Netherlands. This does on the contrary imply that choice of policy tools plays a limited role in changing behaviour. The most striking observation from all three cases is that stepping up monitoring and enforcement of legally binding standards has a positive impact on target group behaviour, in at least two ways. First, sanctions may in some cases be sufficiently high to directly change the cost/benefit calculus. Second, prosecutions and fines may lead to discredit in the public eye and consequently affect incentives more indirectly through a decrease in demands for relevant products.

A similar pattern is found at sector level. As in the case of measures, comparing the tools applied in the 'municipal' sectors is very difficult, due to the differences between sectors. In the *industrial sector*, the Netherlands stands out with the highest degree of combination due to its reliance on voluntary agreements combined with enforceable permits. It is followed by Norway, which for a long time has relied solely on enforceable permits, and then the UK, which has changed its system from largely voluntary regulations towards control and enforcement. Although we do not know the impact of voluntary agreements in this specific issue-area, we do know that the Dutch experience with voluntary agreements is mixed with regard to actual implementation. Moreover, the Netherlands has perceived control and enforcement as the weakest link in Dutch pollution control, and greater emphasis has been put on sanctions. According to the OECD, sanctions in the form of penalties have been sufficient to stop offending discharges. The Norwegian system has been seen as an effective tool in controlling industrial inputs, and sanctions appear to have had a similar effect as in the Netherlands. The turn from 'negotiated consent' in the UK towards legally binding standards, monitoring and enforcement has been perceived as effective in changing behaviour. Dumping and incineration at sea have also relied merely on enforceable permits which have proven sufficient for controlling and phasing out such activities once the political decision has been taken. In short, 'command and control' appears to have had a positive impact on behaviour in our three countries.

The use of policy tools in the *agricultural* sectors in Norway and the Netherlands reveals both similarities and differences. On the one hand, both countries rely heavily on general regulations supported by information and some economic tools. These patterns indicate that a similar set of tools has produced different results in different countries. On the other, Norway to a more significant extent than the Netherlands stepped up the number and stringency of measures as a result of the North Sea Declarations. The additional 'package' of measures introduced in Norway clearly had an effect. In addition, Norway seems to put more emphasis on enforcement and economic tools than the Netherlands. Together with differences in measures, differences in policy tools help us to understand why Norway has achieved significantly more in the agricultural sector compared to the Netherlands.

The similarities in the use of different policy tools in different sectors also show that differences in activities under regulation are of major importance. All three countries license industry, while pollution work in agriculture is mainly based on general regulations, subsidies, information, and advice, with relatively weak monitoring and enforcement. This means that policy tools suitable for 'solving' one problem are not necessarily suitable for 'solving' another problem. Tools adequate for regulating industrial point sources are not necessarily adequate for regulating diffuse agricultural run-off. One distinctive difference between these sectors is the number of targets causing the problem. While each significant industrial plant may be licensed and controlled separately, applying a similar system to all relevant farms would be too complex and expensive. Thus, due to characteristics of the sector itself, agriculture has to be regulated by a different set of tools than industry. Given that adequate measures are identified and adopted – as they partly appear to be – neither Norway nor the Netherlands has been able to apply sufficiently effective tools to affect the behaviour of farmers. In this respect, we should note the strong resistance to taxes on fertilizer with a clear incentive effect that has been shown by interest organizations and the agricultural authorities.

The upshot of the above discussion is not that we should consider the proposition falsified, but rather that there are some important qualifiers to be attached. First, policy tools with a clear incentive effect appear most fundamental. This is evident in the industrial sector; moreover, information and advice in the agricultural sector does not seem to have been able to counterbalance lack of enforcement. This is also consistent with the observation in Chapter 6 that cost/benefit calculations constitute an important behavioural mechanism among target groups. Thus, whenever cost/benefit calculations represent a crucial motivating factor for behaviour, governments have to affect incentives whenever they seek to get target groups to do things they would not otherwise do. This does not imply that tools aimed at encouraging environmentally friendly behaviour are unimportant. Such tools may encourage target groups to go further than strictly required. Traditional regulation may also have this effect over time. As noted, the industrial sector has been made subject to regulation for a much longer time than the agricultural sector, and this may have contributed to a different attitude towards environmental problems. Second, the choice of policy tools is sensitive to the characteristics of the sector under regulation. This means that it may be more difficult to achieve a combination of tools affecting incentives and norms in some sectors than in others. Information and advice is probably more important in the agricultural sector not because farmers are easier to persuade than industrial leaders, but because other tools like permits are more difficult to apply.

Disentangling procedures and rules from policy styles

The reasons *why* institutions differ and change are not under scrutiny here, since the focus is directed on their consequences. On the other hand, it is problematic to ignore this question entirely; in order to trace the effects of distribution of competence and policy tools, we have to be able to disentangle institutional effects from more general regulatory styles embedded in national history and tradition. The distinction between explicit procedures and rules on the one hand, and regulatory styles on the other can also indicate the scope for institutional design, or social engineering at national level. While interaction between institutional arrangements and context may affect the consequences of such arrangements, the link between regulatory styles and institutional arrangements may affect the scope for 'choosing' adequate institutional arrangements.

Distribution of competence

In the Netherlands, the high number of water authorities and the fact that surface water pollution control is mainly under the competence of the Ministry of Transport and Public Works and not VROM has historical roots. The Pollution of Surface Waters Act was proposed as early as 1964. However, the Act was not passed until 1969 because various governmental authorities – including central government agencies, provinces, water boards, and municipalities – lobbied to become the principal authority (Bressers, Huiteman and Kuks 1994: 36). According to Andersen (1994: 147): 'One can hardly understand the Dutch experience, however, without clarifying the role played by the traditional water authorities. Rooted in centuries of water regulation, the autonomous water boards, together with the national water authorities, provide an exceptional infrastructure for integrated water management.'

While the 1980s were characterized by integration of environmental Acts, the Pollution of Surface Waters Act remained under competence of the Ministry of Transport and Public Works, the Rikswaterstaadt and other water authorities. Thus, the Netherlands has no genuine Environmental Agency like the State Pollution Control Agency in Norway or the recently established Environment Agency in the UK. On the other hand, there has been a development towards integration of environmental policy into other policy sectors such as agriculture. The 1989 National Environmental Policy Plan was the first serious step in that direction. Significant changes have also occurred vertically. The Dutch tradition is generally seen as more centralist than the Scandinavian tradition. Still, environmental protection was largely in the hands of local government up to 1970; then the 1970 Pollution of Surface Water Act divided competence mainly between regional and central levels of government.

As to Norway, the 1974 Act providing competence to municipalities for waste water treatment is part of a decentralist tradition, compared to the Netherlands. There have also been changes from the late 1980s towards more decentralization (Naustdalslid 1994), primarily through a new project, Environmental Protection in the Municipalities. On the other hand, the responsibility for environmental issues has been moved back and forth between the county prefect's office (state) and the locally elected county governments since 1971 (Reitan 1996). Horizontal integration of environmental concerns into other policy sectors is a recent phenomenon in the wake of the follow-up of the 1987 World Commission.

In the UK, central government has played an increasingly important role in pollution control in the pos-twar period, while implementation of policy has been decentralized (Vogel 1986: 81). However, whereas local authorities deal with emissions to air and land, we have seen that competence in water pollution control has developed from a complex and decentralized system towards a more centralized and integrated one, culminating in the establishment of the Environmental Agency for England and Wales in 1996. In addition, the 1990 Environmental Protection Act introduced the system of Integrated Pollution Control for cross-media polluters. Thus, institutional *change* characterises the distribution of competence concerning the regulation of water pollution in the UK.

Policy tools

As previously pointed out, the use of policy tools across countries and sectors reveals both striking similarities and differences. This indicates that a combination of standard procedures rooted in national tradition and regulatory 'effectiveness' are important factors behind the set of tools used in each country. It is tempting to say that the Dutch reliance on voluntary agreements is part of a consensual tradition. However, the target group approach introduced in the early 1980s was a reaction to the more 'command and control' approach of the 1970s (Liefferink 1995). Moreover, Dutch water authorities again stepped up 'command and control' in the early 1990s. Likewise, the informality and flexibility of the British tradition has undergone significant changes since the late 1980s, and legal standards and enforcement have been stepped up considerably.

What may we conclude then? First, relevant institutions appear influenced by general national features and regulatory styles. The Dutch consensual tradition, Norwegian decentralization, and the distinctive British approach to pollution control still underlie the current way of dealing with pollution problems in these countries. Here there is a problem of disentangling explicit rules and procedures from other factors rooted in history and tradition. Second, relevant institutions are by no means determined by such factors. In all three countries we have noted change in rules and procedures over the two past decades. Especially the UK has shown that fundamental features of pollution control that have evolved over the course of the century may be significantly amended within a relatively short time span. Thus, in this particular sense there is a wide scope for institutional design at domestic level. Third, different branches of environmental and pollution policy frequently deviate from main country patterns. In the Netherlands it is the water sector that differs from other sectors, while in the UK, the local authorities have competence in implementation concerning air and land, but not water pollution. Thus, in order to comprehend 'national' approaches to regulation, we have to assess general national features as well as differences between various branches of environmental and pollution policies.

Conclusion

This chapter has assessed how domestic institutions have affected domestic implementation linked to North Sea Commitments. In contrast to the Rational Actor model's emphasis on problem-related costs and benefits, change and variance in implementation are here assumed to be linked to change and variance in domestic institutions relevant for water and marine pollution policy.

We began by making a distinction between societal demands for environmental policy and governmental supply of policies to protect the environment. Let us now sum up the main results from the demand dimension. The first findings were related to the possible link between change and variance in societal demands and international and domestic achievements. The original breakthrough at the 1987 North Sea Conference was found to have come prior to the most significant increase in social demands for environmental protection in the late 1980s. This strengthens the conclusion in Chapter 6 that change in international institutions had a significant effect on the stringency of joint commitments. Moreover, change and variance in public concerns are clearly insufficient to understand change and variance in Level I and II implementation. For example, Norway gained the highest score on Level II implementation, even though public attitudes towards the environment dropped significantly in the 1990s. Conversely, significant mismatch between national ambitions and Level II implementation came concurrently with high and stable public attitude level in the Netherlands.

We then turned to questions of governmental supply of environmental policies. While the demand side was linked to environmental and pollution policies in general, the supply side focused more specifically at sector level. Our first proposition stated that horizontal and vertical fragmentation within the state apparatus tend to increase disintegration between national goals and measures needed to fulfil such goals. This proposition was based on the assumption that different ministries and agencies played different roles, in the sense that they tend to apply different decision criteria for similar problems. This proposition was roughly supported in that those sectors subject to a simple system had not experienced such problems, while those subject to a higher level of complexity in terms of fragmentation had experienced implementation problems. On the other hand, the analysis showed that at least one important qualifier had to be added: over the past decade, the potential adverse consequences of fragmentation have increasingly been dealt with through deliberate integration of environmental concerns into other public policy sectors as well as improved coordination within pollution control. The clearest example of vertical disintegration of pollution policies can be found in the Norwegian municipal sector, as Norway is the only country where municipalities have considerable competence in sewage treatment. This competence was used to postpone the introduction of nitrogen removal and to attempt to get the programme cancelled. Other studies also indicate that local resistance to national injunctions derived from international obligations may be part of a general trend. Thus, if local opposition goes hand in hand with decentralisation of competence, there is a risk of defection from national goals linked to international commitments.

Our final proposition focused on the use of policy tools, representing the means by which measures are implemented. Studies have suggested that implementing agencies may behave completely in accordance with higher-order goals and adequate measures may be adopted, and yet measures may still fail to secure behavioural change if the policy tools applied do not 'hit' the critical mechanisms that actually cause change in behaviour. Our proposition was therefore based on the assumption that target groups have dual utility functions sensitive to both cost/benefit incentives and norms of environmentally friendly behaviour. A combination of tools affecting these functions was expected to be most effective in terms of changing behaviour. This proposition did only get partial support, and two important qualifiers were suggested. First, policy tools with a clear incentive effect appear to be fundamental in changing behaviour. However, voluntary agreements and information and advice can be added to incentive tools in order to encourage more behavioural change than strictly required. Second, policy tools suitable for solving one problem are not necessarily the best ones for solving another problem, due to differences in the sectors under regulation. Nevertheless, our assessment of policy tools proved fruitful for further understanding change and variance in implementation. For example, in the Netherlands, reliance on voluntary agreements combined with low attention paid to enforcement has so far been insufficient to achieve both national goals and international obligations, particularly in the industrial and agricultural sectors.

Thus, we can conclude that on the supply side institutions matter in at least two ways. First, horizontal and vertical distribution of competence appear important for governments' ability to adopt adequate measures. Simple systems involving few governmental actors would seem the most effective. Second, the policy tools applied are important for the actual implementation of measures. Tools affecting cost/benefit incentives appear as more effective than tools aimed at encouraging environmentally friendly behaviour.

In the next chapter, I return to the international level and international institutions' impact on state–society relationships. One aspect in focus will be how international institutions may affect domestic institutions.

Notes

1 For country patterns in the Netherlands and the UK between 1976 and 1991, see Hofrichter (1991)/Eurobarometer. For UK surveys between 1991 and 1995, see O'Riordan (1995), Rawcliffe (1995) and Upsall and Worcester (1995). Concerning the Netherlands, 39 different surveys have been analysed by Bartels (1995). Public opinion data in Norway are not directly comparable with Eurobarometer data. Still, various sources indicate that significant variations have occured over time. See Aardal and Valen (1995) and Skjåk and Bøyum (1996).

2 All information supplied by the following groups: Netherlands: Society for Nature and environment, Greenpeace, World Wide Fund for Nature (WWF). UK: Greenpeace, WWF, Friends of the Earth, Royal Society for the Protection of Birds. Norway: Norwegian Society for the Conservation of Nature. See Jansen and Osland (1996), Bergesen and Dahl (1998), McCormick (1991) and Rawcliffe (1995). Even though all iformation is supplied by the groups, different sources show significant differences concerning income patterns. On the other hand, fig-

ures on membership are identical across sources, and reliability correspondingly high.

3 See Doherty (1992), McCormick (1991), Evans (1993), Lucardie (1995), Tak (1994), Seippel and Lafferty (1996), Bergesen and Dahl (1998) and Aardal (1993).
4 Ministry of Transport, Public Works and Water Management. Directorate-General of Public Works and Water Management 1996:18.
5 This section is mainly based on Andersen (1994).
6 Ministry of Transport, Public Works and Water Management. Directorate-General of Public Works and Water Management (1996).
7 Commissie Integral Waterbeheer(1996).
8 *Summary Record* (1994).
9 Ministry of Transport, Public Works and Water Management. Directorate-General of Public Works and Water Management (1996: 16).
10 Water Boards (1995).
11 Interview with Harm Smith, Ministry of Agriculture, 9 December 1996.
12 Working Group on Nutrients (1993).
13 *Summary Record* (1994; 1995).
14 State Pollution Control Agency 1992.
15 Ministry of the Environment (1992).
16 Ministry of the Environment (1989).
17 Ministry of Agriculture (1992).
18 Working Group on Nutrients (1993).
19 *ENDS Report* (1987b: 11–12).
20 *ENDS Report* (1988: 11–13).
21 Interview with Martin Clarke, Environment Agency, 4 December 1996.
22 Environment Agency (1996: 121).
23 Her Majesty's Inspectorate of Pollution (1995).
24 Summary Record (1994; 1995).
25 Interview with Graham Boyes, MAFF/Environmental Protection Division, 6 December 1996.
26 Interview with John A. Campell, MAFF/Fisheries Laboratory, 5 December 1996.
27 See Food and Environmental Protection Act of 1985 (Part II) 8.(1) as compared to the Dumping at Sea Act of 1974.
28 The figures are based on Graham Boyes' files. Boyes is the head of the licensing disposal at sea section within the MAFF and the files cover the answers prepared by this section. According to Boyes, the files are not necessarily perfectly comprehensive, but sufficiently reliable to show the main trends.
29 *Environmental News from the Netherlands* (1993: 7–10).
30 For exampe, there is virtually no discussion of policy tools in the 1989

National Environmental Policy Plan.

31 State Pollution Control Agency (1996).

32 NOU (1995).

33 State Pollution Control Authority (1995).

34 NOU (1992).

35 *ENDS Report* (1991: 6).

36 *ENDS Report* (1994: 31–2).

37 Interview with Jim Spooner, DoE/Water Resource and Marine Division, 4 December 1996 and Amanda Bradely, Confederation of British Industry, 4 December 1996.

38 Data in this section are from Ministry of Agriculture, Fisheries and Food (1989a).

9

International institutions: domestic impact and dynamic features

The preceding chapters have shown how the various models applied to different levels of analysis have all had something to contribute towards understanding the making and implementation of joint commitments for cleaning up the North Sea. These models have been based on more or less specific assumptions in order to come to grips with complex empirical relationships. In turn, these assumptions have restricted our ability to understand other relationships.

This chapter seeks to combine the analysis of international institutions with domestic politics. The domestic impact of international institutions has achieved increased attention in recent years, but this topic is still a poorly understood phenomenon. While Chapter 6 was concerned with the functioning and consequences of international institutions on states conceived of as unitary actors, the focus here lies on the impact on state–society relationships. Furthermore, the dynamic 'macro' aspects of international institutional influences have largely been ignored so far. Macro aspects should be understood as the conception of the North Sea/North-East Atlantic cooperation as *one* institution: essentially one set of rules and principles developed and transformed to combat transfrontier marine pollution. And by dynamic, I mean that institutional arrangements established in early phases may shape opportunities and constrain challenges faced at a later stage. Institutionalized international cooperation may lead to path-dependent processes where earlier events affect subsequent events. Here it will be important to understand why and how the cooperation changed from one pathway to another.

We start by focusing on how international institutions may affect domestic politics. Second, the notion of path dependency and dynamic aspects of institutions will be examined, before some concluding remarks are offered.

Domestic impact of international institutions

As pointed out in Chapter 3, the relevant literature indicates at least three main pathways through which international institutions may affect domestic politics. These pathways are by no means mutually exclusive and may very well coexist. First, there is the *legal pathway* in which international rules and procedures become incorporated in national law; it has the capacity to affect the interactions between governmental and societal actors. Second, the *political pathway* directs our attention to how government officials and societal actors can invoke international political declarations to further their own specific interests in domestic policy debates. Finally, international institutional procedures may become enmeshed domestically through the standard operating procedures of bureaucratic agencies. This third pathway – the *administrative pathway* – points to how international institutional procedures may affect national institutional procedures. In all these cases, international institutions may affect implementation and compliance by affecting the relationship between governmental agencies, target groups and ENGOs. We would also expect the probability for such influences to be strongest in cases where international rules and procedures are developed prior to domestic rules and procedures, or where national rules and procedures are but weakly developed.

Incorporation in national law

The Paris Convention on land-based sources was adopted and ratified by the parties after national legislation and domestic clean-up programmes were in place in most North Sea states. Conversely, the Oslo Convention on dumping at sea was adopted prior to national legislation and abatement programmes. Anyone had been able to dump anything, without interference from national authorities or international bodies. The Oslo Convention was implemented domestically by the parties in the form of new legislation covering previously uncontrolled activities. Consequently we would expect that the Oslo Convention, to a more significant extent than the Paris Convention, empowered national governments to take action aimed at target groups. This difference is clearly reflected in the content of the two Conventions. The Paris Convention is first and foremost concerned with joint measures aimed at regulating and harmonizing *interstate* relationships. The Oslo Convention focuses more on *intrastate* relationships by empowering governments to license, monitor and punish domestic target groups.

Let us take the case of the UK after the Second World War. Land-based sources of pollution had been regulated and monitored in Britain for more than 20 years by the time the Paris Convention was signed in 1974. The Control of Pollution Act, which replaced the old system in 1974, requires all discharges to inland, coastal and estuarial waters to be granted a consent, which may be given subject to certain conditions. Thus, the consent system in the UK (as in most other countries) was originally introduced completely unrelated to international rules and procedures. Moreover, the CPA made it difficult to incorporate later international developments into the conditions set for consents, since the Act did not empower the central government to set emission standards, or statutory quality objectives to be applied by the ten water authorities (Haigh *et al.* 1986: 11). Thus, the link between the international and national levels was in this particular sense almost totally absent. As we have seen, later international developments significantly affected Britain's rules and procedures concerning land-based sources, but not to the same extent as with dumping. In the latter case, international rules and procedures determined the basic national approach to regulation to a significant extent. In the UK, there was no systematic control concerning dumping activities prior to the Oslo Convention: indeed, until the mid-1960s, there was no control whatsoever. However, a general duty developed from the mid-1960s to inform the authorities concerning dumping operations, and the authorities automatically gave their consent. This informal practice changed profoundly when the Oslo Convention was formally implemented through the Dumping at Sea Act of 1974.[1] This Act, first, reflects the general requirement of licensing included in the Oslo Convention. Second, the Act linked the issuing of permits to environmental concerns and the need for monitoring and verifying licenses. Third, the Act also makes possible penalties in line with the Oslo Convention. In 1983, a Protocol amending the Oslo Convention was adopted in order to bring incineration at sea within the scope of the Convention. The UK responded by replacing the 1974 Dumping at Sea Act with Part II of the Food and Environment

Protection Act of 1985, which includes a licensing requirement for incineration at sea in addition to dumping.[2]

The dumping and incineration Acts empowered the *authorities* – in this case the Ministry of Agriculture, Fisheries and Food – to issue licences, monitor behaviour and enforce legislation, as well as giving specific rights to target groups and ENGOs. Thus, they influenced the interaction between affected subnational actors. *Target groups* were provided with a procedure whereby an applicant may appeal against the authorities' decision to refuse or to change a licence. An applicant may also make representations against any condition of a licence. Thus, the target groups were empowered to appeal against the decisions of the authorities. The 1974 and the 1985 Acts also introduced general provisions for transparency concerning licences. Transparency increased from 1986, when, following a recommendation by the House of Lords Select Committee on the European Communities and a 1986 debate in the Lords, the government commenced publishing annual implementation reports on the licensing, enforcement and monitoring of sea disposal. These provisions empowered especially the ENGOs with a factual basis against which they could base their opposition to sea dumping. In short, the Oslo Convention to a significant extent determined the rules of regulation and the procedures governing the relationship between authorities, target groups and ENGOs.

The incorporation of the licensing procedures into national law meant that the authorities gained full control over regulated activities. Such control was achieved by a combination of scrutinizing applications for licences, monitoring of dumping sites, and enforcement. Although most applicants have been approved, some have been turned down for failing to meet the criteria. In 1987 for example, two applications for dumping of sewage sludge were refused due to high content of cadmium and of zinc respectively. In addition to scrutinizing licence applications, disposal sites are monitored. After a comprehensive review of inputs into Liverpool Bay, a licence for the disposal of sewage sludge into the bay was renewed, but on the condition that the trace amount of mercury allowed in the sludge was further reduced by 30 per cent.[3]

Thus, the UK case supports the assumption that international influences are most likely when national rules and procedures are absent, or weakly developed. Second, it shows how domestic regulation as well as the interaction between state and societal actors was affected by designating specific rights and opportunities to different actors. Third, the chief consequence of the legal pathway was the empowering of the government to control target groups. This process enabled the government to gain full control over dumping and incineration activities; the international commitments on the phasing out of such activities could be implemented by simply withholding permits.

Invoking political declarations in domestic environmental politics

The North Sea Declarations were not legally binding, and were thus never ratified and formally incorporated into national law. However, the commitments adopted at the 1987 and 1990 conferences did have significant influence on domestic environmental policies. Moreover, there are strong indications that the most significant impact occurred in sectors responsible for nutrient inputs. While inputs of hazardous substances from the industrial sectors had been controlled since the early 1970s, especially the agricultural sectors were weakly regulated prior to the INSCs. Inputs of nutrients from the agricultural sector in the Netherlands had remained largely uncontrolled until the mid-1980s. Norway had regulated agriculture since the 1970s, but the scope of regulations had been limited to technical measures aimed at point sources. In both countries, the 50 per cent reduction target was used by the environmental authorities to further their interests *vis-à-vis* the agricultural authorities and to legitimise action against the farmers.

The 50 per cent reduction target became the core of Dutch policies to cope with agricultural emissions of nutrients. According to the 1989 National Environmental Policy Plan: 'An emission reduction in 1995 of the order of 50 percent relative to 1985 in nutrients which enter the Rhine and North Sea is being striven after.'[4] Even though the relevant ministries disagreed on sensitive areas, the North Sea Declaration forced them to cooperate on the reduction target. In line with the Dutch North Sea Action Plan, the three ministries agreed through consultations that the 50 per cent target was the basic policy aim. In Norway, the 50 per cent reduction target was actively used by the environmental authorities to legitimize stringent action in the agricultural sector. This seems to have been accomplished by the following strategy: First, the agricultural interest organizations were not informed or consulted prior to the international negotiations, in contrast to both ENGOs and other target group organizations (Skjærseth 1999: 354). Subsequently, the authorities argued that the 50 per cent reduction target was not open to discussions since it had already been adopted internationally. The Ministry of the Environment emphasized that Norway was committed to fulfilling the 50 per cent reduction target even though the Declarations were not perceived as legally binding. Moreover, the ministry argued that also other states were committed to take action. In addition, even though the insignificance of Norway's contributions to the North Sea as a whole was emphasized internationally, the environmental consequences for arable areas were emphasised domestically. Local benefits in the form of improved environmental quality were cited as a central argument towards local agricultural authorities as well as farmers.

We may conclude that the political North Sea Declarations have empowered national actors in domestic environmental politics. As in the case of the legal pathway, we have strong indications that the most significant influences have occurred in the sectors that cause nutrient inputs, in cases where domestic regulation has been weakly developed. In Norway and the Netherlands, the nutrient commitments have particularly empowered environmental authorities *vis-à-vis* agricultural authorities and the farmers' organizations.

Consequences for standard operating procedures

One change in international institutional procedures clearly had consequences for how things were done at the domestic level. The change in level of representation internationally affected the link between those authorized to negotiate international commitments and those authorized to make policy decisions on domestic implementation. Prior to the INSC process and the introduction of ministerial meetings in OSPARCOM, national delegations were composed of fairly low-ranking civil servants. These representatives would first have to obtain a mandate from higher political or bureaucratic level concerning specific national positions. Second, they would have to negotiate joint commitments on the basis of strict domestic mandates. Third, on returning home, they would have to communicate the content of international obligations to a higher level, and it was this level that would make decision(s) on any follow-up actions. In turn, these decisions would have to be communicated to and implemented at lower levels vertically, or in other sectors horizontally. In some cases, governmental decision-makers would also have to advocate implementation plans in the national assembly. In essence, the chain of 'micro' decisions would be long, both vertically and horizontally.

This way of organizing international/domestic decision-making would have at least two distinct consequences. Representatives in international negotiations, constrained by domestic mandates, would be cautious about supporting any commitments that could exceed their mandates. This would stimulate lenient commitments. Second, they would subsequently have to convince higher-level officials of the need to take domestic action on the issue. Depending on the degree of match between unilateral preferences and joint obligations, there would always be a risk that higher-level officials could block any further initiatives, or at least receive them with little enthusiasm. In cases where other sectors were affected, this process would also involve other bureaucratic actors than environmental authorities. In practice, one would have to establish interdepartmental groups both prior to and after international negotiations. Having more interests involved would increase complexity at both the input and output sides of international negotiations. The long chain of 'micro' decisions would increase the risk of both vertical and horizontal disintegration.

When the Ministers of the Environment began to participate instead of sending low-ranking civil servants, this had important consequences for domestic/international relationships. Now, the same person would have the final say in domestic preparations, international negotiations, and in initiating implementation. As noted in Chapter 6, this way of organizing international/domestic decision-making would increase aggregation capacity and promote more stringent international commitments. There is also good reason to believe that this decision-making process would ensure a closer match between international commitments and domestic follow-up actions, as the same person would have the authority to support or oppose international commitments and to make any grand policy decisions on domestic implementation. This is probably one important reason why the non-legally binding North Sea Declarations triggered significantly more implementation activity at the domestic level as compared to decisions and recommendations adopted within OSPARCOM. The North Sea Declarations led to comprehensive domestic implementation programmes while OSPARCOM decisions and recommendations largely 'disappeared' in the national bureaucracies. Of course, the fact that the North Sea Declaration specifically required more action at domestic level was important as well. Nevertheless, we may conclude that the change in the level of representation affected domestic procedures by closing the gap between the formulation, negotiation, and implementation of international commitments. In short, the decision-making chain, from national positions via international negotiations to implementation, was simplified by higher level of representation. This change come to reduce the risk of disintegration of environmental policies and promote consistency between those authorized to develop national positions, negotiate international agreements, and make policy decisions on follow-up actions.

Institutional path dependency

How have international institutional arrangements originally established affected what happened later in the cooperative process? We had introduced three perspectives. First, institutionalized cooperation may gather momentum through a 'snowball' effect generating positive feedback, facilitating further steps. According to this perspective, we can expect joint commitments to become more stringent and governments more ambitious in implementing them over time. The second perspective is based on the economists' 'law of diminishing returns'. Here, the first steps are likely to be the 'easy ones' in which marginal benefits clearly exceed marginal costs. When attempts are made to extend the scope of the institution or to tighten up joint commitments, marginal abatement costs tend to increase and benefits in the form of environmental quality tend to decrease. This perspective would suggest that it would become increasingly difficult to step up joint commitments, and governments would become more reluctant in implementing them over time. The third perspective focuses on the persistence and stability of institutions. According to this perspective, institutionalised cooperation is hard to change, especially after collective norms, behavioural regularities, and convergent expectations have developed. This perspective would suggest that both joint commitments and governmental responses developed slowly and incrementally, or remained roughly constant and stable over time.

The first decade: persistent and static

The institution established in the first decade was based on the Oslo and Paris Conventions. It clearly had a potential to gather momentum by leading the Contracting Parties to choose increasingly ambitious commitments and follow-up actions. The official picture of the OSPARCOM cooperation presented by the parties was one of a dynamic and rolling programme based on four elements:

- identification and 'diagnosis' of problems;
- action in terms of joint decision-making and implementation;
- verification and monitoring of effectiveness of measures taken;
- reappraisal.

These functions were also backed up by specific institutional bodies. The first function was to be fulfilled by the joint monitoring programme, the second function was to be taken care of by the Commissions, while stages three and four were to be taken care of by both the monitoring group and the scientific/technical bodies. In practice, the system of decision-making did not function as intended. The monitoring programme was not able to 'diagnose' problems in any precise way. The Oslo and Paris Commissions were only to a limited extent able to adopt joint commitments, and the scientific/technical bodies were very inefficient in their efforts at evaluating and verifying any consequences. There were various reasons for this situation – spanning from the UES/EQO dispute, to the lack of scientific methodologies. Two important reasons were clearly related to the institution itself. These phenomena may be understood in the light of internal contradictions among the constituent elements of an institution (Young 1989a: 96). First, while the OSPARCOM institution was intended to be dynamic, other institutional elements worked in the opposite direction. Important factors here included the legally binding nature of the cooperation that proved quite resistant to rapid change, and the bureaucratic and administrative nature of the cooperation. In addition, a norm of diffuse reciprocity developed which led to a cooperation 'climate' promoting incremental change and low aggregation capacity. Second, the Conventions covered the entire North-East Atlantic, including countries with no borders to the North Sea and virtually no interest in adopting stringent clean-up measures.

The second decade: dynamic

After very slow and incremental progress in the first decade, the International North Sea Conference Process significantly changed the cooperating process in the second decade. The establishment of the INSC process shows that the parties were able to change the 'rules of the game' in a rather peculiar way. Due to the persistency of the original institution, a sub-set of the parties decided to establish a new institution instead of transforming the old one in order to change the course of path dependency. In turn, this new institution also affected the original OSPARCOM institution.

In contrast to OSPARCOM, the INSCs represented a truly dynamic instrument. The identification and 'diagnosis' stage was taken care of by *ad hoc* scientific bodies that produced Quality Status Reports on the North Sea. These reports were more comprehensive and became more independent as compared to previous efforts. Second, the North Sea Conferences were able to produce stringent joint commitments. Third, verification and monitoring compliance were given high priority, and comprehensive and detailed implementation reports were published. Fourth, these results were utilised to change the course of action when needed. For example, the 1990 assessment of progress of the 1987 Declaration on Nutrients revealed that most countries would face problems in reaching the 50 per cent reduction target. Against this backdrop, the Ministers decided to arrange a working group meeting at ministerial level in 1993, prior to the fourth INSC in 1995, in order to discuss implementation problems.[5] Other institutional elements pointed in the same dynamic direction. First, since the Declarations were based on 'soft law' they could take instant effect. Second, the organization of the North Sea Conferences restricted the parties' opportunities to postpone unresolved problems. Third, the INSCs introduced a significantly higher aggregation capacity due to their high political level of representation. These institutional features also contributed to a different norm of cooperation, based on specific reciprocity.

The dynamic structure of the INSCs also became the main engine for changing the original OSPARCOM cooperation. As previously noted, the INSCs affected both the joint commitments of OSPARCOM as well as the original cooperative procedures. This process led to the new 1992 Convention on the Protection of the North-East Atlantic, based on the rules and procedures developed within the INSC process. Eventually, the process of international implementation cemented the political declarations within a framework of international law.

Collective and individual behaviour in the wake of the INSCs conform well with the dynamic 'snowball' mode. Joint commitments became more stringent and governments became more ambitious in changing behaviour over time. This development is evident concerning joint commitments on hazardous substances. The 1984 Bremen Declaration obliged particularly the Paris Commission and the EC to take urgent action on 'black' and 'grey' list substances. The 1987 Declaration required 50 per cent reduction in hazardous substances. The 1990 Declaration specified a list of 36 substances and required 70 per cent reduction for some of them. The 1995 Declaration aims at zero emissions and losses of hazardous substances within 25 years.

The institutional modes of path dependency are based on 'endogenous' institutional conditions and qualities. However, the preceding chapters have shown that more or less 'exogenous' (to institutions) factors may also be important for subsequent action. Cases in point include the overall patterns of state interests, development in public opinion towards environmental attitudes, the state of scientific knowledge, and shocks and crises related to the problem.

The interlink with exogenous factors

International environmental institutions do not operate in a vacuum. They operate and change within a political, economic, and social context that may change as well. Thus, the pathways taken are not conditioned solely by institutional conditions and qualities. Let us now look at the changes and influence of the main contextual variables included in this analysis.

As noted in Chapter 5, the basic interests of the three countries studied here did not change significantly over time. These countries were selected partly because each represented different basic interests in the cooperation: one exporter, one importer and one characterized by balanced pollution exchange. The basic cost/benefit calculus would not suggest any significant change in national positions and joint commitments, because these dimensions did not change significantly. Related to this perspective is the notion of power, capabilities, and the actors' ability to further their interests.

Even though this perspective has been excluded from systematic analysis, it does not stand out as a probable explanation – at least not recast as power in general. There has never been any state within the cooperation that has possessed a predominant amount of relevant resources and has acted as a 'benevolent' or 'coercive' hegemon (Snidal 1985). The UK, as the least ambitious actor, actually possessed the largest issue-specific capabilities and controlled all events important to it (Skjærseth 1991).

The production of greater expertise on both damage and abatement was closely linked to the functioning of the institutions and may thus not be seen as truly exogenous to institutional dynamics. On the other hand, rapid and significant changes in the knowledge situation could have been exogenous to this specific cooperation, and could have taken the form of a major breakthrough in marine science, or abatement science. For example, the detection of the Antarctic 'ozone hole' in 1985 came as the first empirical indication that something was wrong with the ozone layer. Similar rapid and drastic changes in the knowledge situation did not occur in the North Sea cooperation. Uncertainty was reduced gradually over time; the breakthrough in the stringency of joint commitments commencing in 1987 cannot be traced back to a corresponding special breakthrough in the state of scientific knowledge. As noted in Chapter 6, the Quality Status Reports presented in 1984 and 1987 were quite similar, in the sense that both painted a picture of high uncertainty. On the other hand, the reduction of uncertainty subsequent to the 1987 Conference strengthened the basis for stringent joint and individual action. In particular, recognition that a certain level of uncertainty was likely to remain strengthened the basis for the principle of precautionary action.

The exceptional toxic algae blooms and epidemic deaths of seals that occurred in the North Sea cannot shed light on the 1987 breakthrough since these events occurred later, in 1988 to 1989. However, they may contribute to explain the outcomes of the 1990 INSC and the parties' willingness to implement the international commitments adopted. This point should, however, not be exaggerated. We have strong indications that the potential political effect of these visible events decreased rapidly. At least two arguments support this interpretation. First, inputs of nutrients were identified as the cause of the algae blooms: all the same, the 50 per cent reduction targets on nutrients adopted in 1987 were not significantly strengthened in the 1990 Declaration. Second, Norway was most significantly affected by the algae blooms, and yet it failed to achieve the 50 per cent reduction target on nitrogenous substances.

Public opinion towards environmental values and attitudes changed most significantly after 1987. This observation was evident not only in the UK, the Netherlands and Norway but throughout the EC countries (cf. Table 8.1). Thus, as in the case of shocks and crises, change in public opinion can hardly in itself explain the 1987 breakthrough. Although the change to ministerial representation within the INSC certainly took place before change in public opinion, it became very important when the changes in environmental attitudes occurred. Since Ministers are responsible to their domestic electorates, the 'green wave' in the late 1980s was channelled more effectively into the international negotiations as compared to the previous low-level civil servant representation. In this way, the impact of the change in level of representation became closely linked to the change in public opinion. Public opinion towards environmental questions has been on the wane in some central North Sea states since the early 1990s. However, the 1995 INSC and OSPARCOM continued to tighten up previous commitments concerning hazardous substances in particular. This development indicates that the dynamic impact of the institution has continued despite fluctuations in public opinion.

The essence of changing pathway

Given the constant nature of exogenous factors prior to the transformation, why did the international institutions change and how did the change from one pathway to another occur? These questions are important not only for deepening our understanding of regime dynamics: they also add to our ability to change institutions in a desired direction. Let us start with the first question. In the initial decade, there were no indications whatsoever that the problems which the institution had been established to solve did in fact change significantly in a positive direction. The gap between expectations and what was actually delivered in terms of joint commitments and domestic implementation increased. As a consequence, frustration developed concerning the functioning of existing conventions: 'some countries were dissatisfied with the lack of progress in the competent international organisations charged with protection of the marine environment'.[6] As noted, internal contradictions in the form of conflicts among the various elements of the institution itself were probably most important for this situation. These internal contradictions were of two main types that were mutually reinforcing. First, although the pressing ecological problems concerned the North Sea, the Conventions covered the entire North-East Atlantic, and included countries such as Spain and Portugal. Second, the parties sought to establish a dynamic regime, one which, however, proved quite static and hard to change in practice. Thus, the majority of the parties were not able to change the course of action towards more stringent commitments and domestic implementation.

In such situations, we can expect three possible outcomes. First, institutions can remain unchanged for some time until the gap between expectations and outcomes develops into some kind of crisis. Second, the institution may collapse and the cooperation simply wither. Third, institutions can be transformed, or replaced by new ones. The latter was what in fact happened – now the question is why. Given a certain level of frustration with the existing conventions, the establishment of the INSCs is probably best understood as an act of leadership. This observation conforms well with general propositions related to the formation of institutions (Young 1989a; 1989b; 1991). Germany fulfilled the role as a leader by organizing the first INSC in Bremen 1984. The literature on leadership distinguishes between different types, or modes of leadership. Without going into a systematic discussion of these types here, we may say that Germany's initiative would seem to be – at first glance – like the role of an instrumental or entrepreneurial leader. Such leaders contribute to the development of 'good' solutions or the establishment of institutions and procedures conducive to good solutions (Underdal 1991: 140). At second glance, however, Germany's initiative could also be understood in terms of an intellectual leader (Young 1991). In June 1980 the Council of Environmental Advisors, an independent body of experts appointed by the German government, presented its report on the environmental problems of the North Sea.[7] The Council concluded that:

- a successful environmental protection policy for the North Sea had to be based on 'Vorsorgeprinzip', i.e. the precautionary principle.

- protection of the North Sea was only possible through international cooperation.

Thus, it was Germany that introduced the precautionary principle which was to become crucial to the further development of the North Sea cooperation. Germany provided both the intellectual basis for institutional change as well as the negotiating skill needed to bring about the changes.

Germany faced, essentially, two alternative ways of transforming the cooperation from one track to another. One, a new convention on the North Sea could be established: in fact this option was proposed in the European Parliament in 1983. This alternative would have solved the first internal contradiction by excluding the wider North-East Atlantic and consequently states with no borders to the North Sea. However, a new convention could also easily lead to new static and time-consuming arrangements due to the legal nature of conventions. Moreover, it would require a dismantling of existing conventions that would be neither politically feasible – or at least not easy – nor necessarily 'effective' in terms of producing stringent commitments and stimulating domestic implementation. As pointed out in Chapter 6, the 'symbiotic' relationship between the INSCs and OSPARCOM has been crucial for actual achievements. The second option was to generate political impetus to existing conventions, by convening a North Sea Conference aimed at adopting joint commitments that could take immediate effect. This possibility would cope with both contradictions and obviate the need for dismantling existing cooperative frameworks. The Bremen Conference was initially envisaged as a one-off event, although it was to evolve into a more permanent institution over time.

Thus, the INSCs became a soft law 'sub-regime' that proved truly persistent and dynamic in practice. While the INSCs had certain general qualities hat promoted more stringent outcomes, the reasons for its survival and success were also conditioned by more specific circumstances. First, the timing for its establishment appears as close to perfect in retrospect. On the one hand, it could draw on the experience of the OSPARCOM cooperation. On the other, social demands for environmental protection changed significantly in the late 1980s. Second, the INSCs were able to deliver significant results within a very short time. Thus, the gap between expectations and outcomes was almost removed by the 1987 London Conference.

What do these observations amount to, in terms of the prospects for changing international institutions? Bernauer (1995: 4) takes a positive stance, claiming that institutions are essentially choice variables. Young (1989a) is more pessimistic, claiming that they are difficult to reform, and particularly difficult to reform if they are to yield intended results. Regime design is held to be 'tricky business' in which unforeseen and unintended consequences easily occur. Moreover, international institutions are often the result of bargaining where parties give and take. Thus, they may well end up as 'hybrid' arrangements. The North Sea experience lends some support to both views. The original conventions clearly led to unintended consequences. However, changes were initiated by means of intellectual and entrepreneurial leadership within a context of roughly constant exogenous factors. Moreover, the breakthrough in terms of outcomes actually occurred before the circumstances changed in any significant way. In short, skilful social engineering was crucial to effecting the change from an increasingly destructive to a more constructive pathway within the North Sea cooperation.

Beyond 1995: towards diminishing returns

According to the diminishing return mode, we would expect that it would become increasingly difficult to further strengthen and expand the cooperation, and that the participating governments would become increasingly reluctant. The main patterns of outcomes from the 1995 Conference support this view only partly. The 1995 Conference tightened up the commitments on hazardous substances and aimed at phasing out all emissions within 25 years (*Esbjerg Declaration* 1995: para. 17). However, the UK added a footnote stating that it shares the ideal of these aims, but does not accept that they are currently practicable. We can also note recent signs that paragraph 17 has created a snowball effect affecting other regions and institutions (Parmentier 1997). A few months after the fourth INSC, the main content of paragraph 17 was adopted by the United Nations Environment Programme's (UNEP's) Intergovernmental Conference of Marine Pollution from Land-Based Activities. In 1996, paragraph 17 was adopted in different forms by both the Declaration of Environment Ministers of the Baltic Sea region and in a new Protocol on Land-Based Sources within the framework of Barcelona Convention covering the Mediterranean Sea.

The Intermediate Ministerial Meeting in 1993 and the 1995

Declaration reaffirmed the 50 per cent reduction targets on nutrients. In addition, the parties agreed to aim at balanced fertilisation for nitrogen and phosphorus in agricultural production by the year 2000 or 2002 at the latest. This would require more than 50 per cent reduction in, for example, the Netherlands. The UK and France did, however, add a footnote stating that they could not accept this paragraph.

On the one hand, we may conclude that a dynamic mode of positive feedback continues to yield predictions largely in line with actual outcomes in terms of joint commitments. This finding strengthens the argument that endogenous institutional qualities appear to have had an effect independent of more or less exogenous factors. On the other, the footnotes added by the UK and France indicate that they have become increasingly reluctant. Nor can we exclude the possibility that more countries will become more reluctant due to increased abatement costs of implementing the measures necessary to reach the targets set for the next century. While the producing of joint commitments may be relatively easy, producing substantial results at domestic level may prove significantly more difficult. And finally, since the parties' points of departure were quite modest in terms of stringency and scope of commitments, we would not expect the mode of diminishing returns to apply immediately. Hence, the actual merits of this mode can be determined with sufficient certainty only in the future.

Conclusion

The first purpose of this chapter was to combine the analysis of international institutions with that of domestic environmental politics, focusing on how, when and with which consequences the international institution governing the North Sea cooperation has affected state–society relationships. Three main pathways were identified. First, the case of UK showed how international rules and procedures became institutionalized into a domestic process through a *legal pathway* in the case of dumping and incineration at sea. Compared to land-based sources, the UK case also showed that this happened in a previously uncontrolled area. The main consequence of the Oslo Convention in this respect was the authorization of the British government to licence, monitor and punish domestic target groups. Second, the political North Sea Declarations had been invoked by the authorities to further their own interests. In Norway and the Netherlands, the environmental authorities used the Declarations to support actions concerning both agricultural authorities and interest groups. The impact of the *political pathway* on domestic politics was most significant in sectors causing nutrient inputs, sectors previously weakly regulated. The last pathway identified focused on the impact of international procedures on domestic procedures. The *administrative pathway* affected the decision-making chain between national and international levels.

The second purpose of this chapter was to analyse institutional dynamics, asking how the international institutional arrangements which had been originally established affected what happened later in the process. Three modes of institutional path dependency were presented. The main conclusion is that different institutional qualities clearly affect later events in different phases of the cooperation. We saw that internal contradictions within the institution temporarily 'trapped' most of the parties in a situation of inertia. However, the North Sea experience also shows how the parties were able to change their path by transforming the institution itself. The establishment of the INSCs significantly changed the 'rules of the game' and influenced subsequent processes. Germany was instrumental in bringing about the changes by means of both intellectual and entrepreneurial leadership – by introducing the principle of precautionary action, and by creating new institutional arrangements.

The first decade of the cooperation supported the notion that initial institutional arrangements may be hard to change particularly in cases where specific norms of cooperation develop. We saw that the parties were not able to change the course of action towards more stringent commitments and behavioural change. The second decade supported the notion of a dynamic institution leading to a snowball effect by continuously expanding in scope and increasing in stringency. Moreover, the change from the first to the second decade witnessed was not marked by slow or incremental change. The commitments adopted in 1987 represented a watershed in the cooperation. We also found that this change could only to a limited extent be traced back to the context in which the institution operated. This finding supports the assumption that the main reason for this change involved changes in the institution itself. More specifically, the parties were able to cope with the internal contradictions that had hampered the cooperation. The validity of the mode of 'diminishing returns' lies largely in the future. This mode may become more relevant when the time comes for the parties to implement the stringent international obligations in the next century.

Notes

1 Dumping at Sea Act (1974).
2 Food and Environmental Protection Act (1985).
3 Ministry of Agriculture Fisheries and Food (1989: 11).
4 NEPP (1989: 138).
5 Statement of Conclusions from the Intermediate Ministerial Meeting (1993).
6 Ministeral Declarations (1995: 7).
7 Ministerial Declarations (1995: 7).

10
Conclusions

To what extent and in what ways have environmental institutions affected the making of joint commitments of the North Sea cooperation and domestic implementation in three countries: Norway, the Netherlands, and the UK? This has been the principal research question in this book. In order to improve the functioning of international and domestic environmental institutions, we have to deal with such questions and to learn from previous experience and practice. The North Sea cooperation is an ideal source of learning since it provides us with elements of both 'failure' and 'success' over time. Moreover, this cooperation includes countries that vary significantly on both achievements and institutional arrangements. In addition to asking focused questions, we also have to develop analytical tools and strategies which enable us to improve our knowledge of how institutions work. Thus, before summing up the main empirical findings and their implications for analysis and policy, I will briefly recapitulate the main theoretical approach and logic developed in Chapters 1–3.

The explanatory focus has been joint international commitments and domestic implementation. As a point of departure for understanding change and variance in commitments and implementation, I presented a hypothesis we sought to refute stating that joint commitments and domestic implementation would not be different in the absence of institutional change and variance. The alternative hypothesis was that joint commitments and domestic implementation would be different in the absence of institutional change and variance, at least in part due to the impact of institutions. In order to assess these hypotheses, two models were developed. Although complementary, these models lead our attention in different directions and point to different explanatory factors. The first model – the Rational Actor model – was designed to represent a situation virtually devoid of influences from change and variance in institutional factors. This model was concerned with actor qualities; any changes in joint commitments and variance in domestic implementation would be attributable to changes and variance in the actors' problem-related cost/benefit interests. The second model – the Institutional model – was developed to represent the alternative hypothesis. This model focused on institutional qualities and emphasized how – in what ways – institutions can affect joint commitments and domestic implementation. The Institutional model claims that institutions affect commitments and implementation through the development of norms as well as by affecting the actors' cost/benefit calculus. According to this model, changes and variance in achievements would be attributable to change and variance in institutions. This approach lead to a two-step strategy based on weakening the hypothesis we sought to refute and strengthening the alternative hypothesis by means of pattern-matching and explanation building.

The Rational Actor and the Institutional models were designed to match both international and domestic levels of analysis. The main advantage of using different levels of analysis lies in the possibility of understanding different aspects of what we seek to explain. Capturing different aspects of 'realities' may in turn yield a more comprehensive perspective on the phenomena under scrutiny. One disadvantage, or at least one complicating factor, is the need to change the explanatory focus in line with changes in the level of analysis. In order to cope with this challenge, I have distinguished between Level I and II implementation. Level I implementation, linking joint commitments to national policy, was introduced as the prime focus when operating at the international level. Level II implementation, linking national policy to the behaviour of subnational target groups, relates to the domestic level.

The approach outlined above rests on two fundamental arguments that recur throughout this book. First, one must include institutions and actors at both the national and international levels in order to understand the role and significance of institutions in the making and implementation of joint international commitments. Second, one must include both cost/benefit rationality and norms as fundamental behavioural mechanisms in order to understand the functioning and consequences of institutions. This is referred to as the dual utility function.

Empirical findings of the individual chapters

Chapter 4 aimed at assessing the development of the North Sea commitments as well as national implementation in Norway, the Netherlands and the UK. From the mid-1970s to the mid-1980s the commitments adopted within the framework of the Oslo and Paris Conventions and Commissions were lenient, and the parties were not obliged to change their behaviour significantly. This pattern of inertia changed significantly in the second decade. Following the first International North Sea Conference in 1984, the breakthrough came at the 1987 London Conference which, by means of 'soft-law' declarations, required the parties to halve discharges from land-based sources by 1995 using 1985 as the baseline. Moreover, the parties were obliged to reduce and phase out ocean-based pollution activities. These requirements were to varying degrees subsequently adopted by the Oslo and Paris Commissions and to some extent the EC. This process of international implementation meant that the INSC obligations were transformed into legally binding obligations. Thus, the North Sea Conference process speeded up the work within the framework of existing institutions and eventually led to comprehensive legally and politically binding commitments aimed at substantial behavioural change among the parties.

Domestic vulnerability due to national causes and sources was found to be the main motivating factor behind national water and marine policy in the first decade. The joint commitments adopted reflected the interests and preferences of the least ambitious actors, and had scant effect on the priorities and behaviour of the parties. Then, from the second INSC in 1987, international commitments increasingly influenced the ambitiousness of relevant policies in all three countries (Level 1 implementation). Still, we found significant variation in the ambition of national policy. The Netherlands had adopted the most ambitious national goals linked to the international commitments followed by Norway and the UK.

The next topic was far more complex: the extent to which the parties had achieved their goals, as measured in terms of changes in inputs of regulated substances. After noting several reservations concerning data reliability, we saw that, in all three countries, discharges of regulated substances were generally headed in the right direction according to baseline years. Second, changes in behaviour could only to a limited extent be traced back to factors unrelated to governmental intervention. The 'control' factors considered were purely domestic concerns, economic fluctuations, technological innovation, availability of alternative means of disposal, and other international commitments than those linked to the North Sea. Third, significant variation among countries and sectors was noted concerning Level II implementation. The Netherlands had achieved less than Norway despite its more ambitious targets. The UK achievements roughly paralleled the level of ambitions. Our fourth finding was related to the sector level across countries: in general, the industrial sector emerged as most 'successful' followed by the municipal and agricultural sectors.

Chapter 5 sought to evaluate the fruitfulness of the Unitary Rational Actor model in explaining the making of and compliance with joint commitments. Due to the requirement of unity, the possibility of domestic implementation 'failure' is here ruled out by this model. As applied to international environmental politics, the core of the URA model involves abatement costs, damage costs, and the balance of pollution exchange. Concerning the latter dimension, I argued that Norway, the Netherlands and the UK were roughly representative of the North Sea states since they represented net exporters, net importers and balanced exchange of marine pollution. The direction of the North Sea currents placed these states in chain-wise order with the UK at the top, the Netherlands in the middle, and Norway at the end (see Figure 5.1). Hence, an agreement between these states would in important ways represent an agreement between all North Sea states.

The empirical analysis showed that the URA model predicted the basic positions of the states prior to the 1987 INSC fairly well. However, the URA model was not able to account for the changes that occurred in the stringency of joint commitments, behaviour and variance in compliance. The core variables underlying the URA model did not change significantly. For example, compliance levels turned out differently from what we would have expected. Since the Netherlands to a significant extent suffered the consequences of own actions, incentives for compliance were high. Conversely, Norway would actually have incentives for advocating stringent joint commitments and then defecting, due to its position as a small net-importer, which did not affect other states. Norwegian defection would clearly not affect the cost/benefit calculus of other states that exported their waste to the Norwegian coast. In other words, a 'pusher' in international environmental politics will not necessarily have incentives for implementing stringent joint commitments. And yet, contrary to our expectations, the actual compliance record showed that Norway had achieved more than the Netherlands. The data appeared sufficiently robust to seriously weaken the first part of the hypothesis we sought to refute – that commitments and compliance would remain the same even if the states merely pursued their own material interests.

Chapter 6 aimed at assessing whether and how international environmental institutions had affected joint commitments and level of compliance. From the institutional model we would expect institutionalization of the cooperation to have changed significantly prior to the changes in dependent variables. This expectation gained empirical support. We found that changes in institutionalization affected three crucial functions: a) cooperative environments; b) aggregation and integration capacity; c) constraint and discretion placed on the parties. Moreover, these functions affected not only the cost/benefit calculus of the actors, but also the cooperative and individual norms of environmental behaviour. The first OSPARCOM decade led to a cooperation climate based on diffuse reciprocity that promoted mutual confidence, persistence and stability. The second INSC decade – commencing with the first International North Sea Conference in 1984 – led to specific reciprocity marked more by economic self-interest, instability and flexibility. The Oslo and Paris Commissions and INSC became institutional twins, providing mutually complementary functions in the same issue-area. The strongest indication that these institutional settings created different cooperative climates was perhaps the observation that similar problems were approached very differently by the same actors at the same time within OSPARCOM and within INSC.

Faced with collective problems characterised by significantly different interests and preferences, the single most important consequence of the INSCs was their contribution to bringing an end to the Uniform Emission Standard/Environmental Quality Objectives controversy, which had hampered cooperation ever since the early 1970s. A necessary condition for resolving the conflict was a change in position of the UK, which eventually – albeit reluctantly –

accepted the UES approach. As a consequence, the principle of precautionary action was adopted for the first time ever in any international text by the 1987 INSC Declaration.

The second important consequence was that the INSCs served to increase aggregation capacity – i.e. the capacity to cut through deadlock and adopt stringent commitments in line with the preferences of the majority. This was accomplished by de-coupling non-North Sea states from the cooperation, and by raising the level of participation from low-level civil servants to Ministers of the Environment. Conversely, OSPARCOM increased integration capacity – i.e. the capacity to influence and combine interests and preferences – in three ways: by means of procedures that could differentiate between North Sea and non-North Sea states, by identifying alternative solutions acceptable to all parties, and by increasing scientific reliability and reducing scientific uncertainty. The major effect of reduced scientific uncertainty was perhaps the evolution of a shared recognition that there could never be absolute certainty concerning the links between inputs, concentrations and effects in the marine environment.

The third consequence of institutional change was lower discretion provided by increase in specificity and improved verification. This led to a higher degree of transparency which generated political pressure that could be brought to bear on the 'laggards'. In addition, the transformation of 'soft-law' declarations to legally binding commitments within the framework of OSPARCOM further constrained the parties. Since possibilities for international enforcement remained constant and low over time, the latter observation is hard to understand within the framework of cost/benefit analysis. We have strong indications that it was partly the authoritativeness of legally binding obligations in itself that triggered behavioural response. Thus, we saw that the 'soft law' INSC institution and the 'hard law' OSPARCOM institution could each fulfil functions that the other could not provide. The impact of international institutions in the North Sea cooperation lies in their symbiotic character and combined effect.

In Chapter 7 the focus shifted from unitary actors and compliance at the international level to sub-national actors and implementation at the domestic level. While Chapter 5 could shed light on change in positions, joint commitments and general compliance levels, it could hardly explain variation in compliance between countries, since obligations and institutional arrangements were equal for the states included in the analysis. Moreover, the international institutional perspective could not explain variation between target-group sectors across countries due to the requirement of unity. Since target groups – i.e. those actors causing discharges – normally control the behaviour that has to be modified, governments must depend upon their cooperation, whether active or reluctant. Given that the target groups acted on the basis of cost/benefit calculus, we could expect different incentives, positions, and behaviour based on the size and distribution of costs and benefits. However, the analysis did not lend much support to these assumptions. Variance in implementation and compliance at the level of the individual states could only to a limited extent be traced back to variance in incentives at target group level: target groups showed more similarities than differences across states.

Second, actual positions and behaviour matched expectations only partly. Industry had incentives for opposing stringent regulations, but did in fact advocate ambitious positions and managed to deliver significant behavioural change in line with requirements. Agriculture had essentially the same incentives as industry, but had adopted an intermediate position and delivered the lowest degree of reductions. The municipal sector had incentives for being more ambitious, but in fact adopted a reluctant position followed by a medium level of behavioural change.

Variation in the mobilisation of counterbalancing forces in the form of environmental non-governmental organizations may shed light on differences in positions and behaviour between industry and agriculture. The ENGOs have mobilized to a significantly higher degree towards industry than agriculture, and we saw how ENGOs under certain conditions may have a direct effect on the behaviour of target groups. Thus, according to this perspective, we might say that environmental policy is formed and implemented in the area of tension between ENGO mobilization and distribution of costs and benefits among target groups. In addition, we found indications that industry, to a more significant extent than agriculture, had developed norms of environmental behaviour based on social responsibility.

Still, this perspective proved unsuccessful in explaining the positions and behaviour of the municipal sector. Moreover, ENGO mobilisation frequently aimed at raising the ambitions of governments, and governments' ability to 'deliver' pollution control is probably more important than the direct impact on target groups. Finally, variance in compliance among target groups across states cannot explain variance in compliance between the states. In short, the hypothesis we sought to refute was weakened at the domestic level as well.

Chapter 8 sought to examine domestic implementation from a different angle than outlined in Chapter 7. The focus on the functioning and consequences of domestic institutions could also help us to improve our understanding of differences in implementation between the relevant countries and sectors.

The first part focused on changes in societal demands for environmental protection in general. We saw that the values and attitudes of public opinion changed significantly towards environmental concerns in the latter part of the 1980s. The 'green wave' was channelled by both the green movement and political parties. This significant change occurred mainly after the 1987 INSC, and can thus not explain the original breakthrough in the North Sea cooperation. In addition, we could not see any clear linkage between developments in public opinion after 1990 and Level II implementation. The most significant mismatch between national goals and actual results could be found in the Netherlands, where 'green' attitudes had remained high and stable since 1990. Conversely, a relatively close match between national ambitions and actual results was seen in Norway, although public attitudes dropped significantly in the early 1990s. Thus, change in societal demands were clearly insufficient to explain Level II implementation as well as the adoption of more stringent international commitments. Accordingly, we expected to find the most important explanatory factors at the supply side.

The second part took us from demand for pollution protection to supply of pollution control. On the one hand, we could observe that horizontal and vertical fragmentation within the state apparatus had led to failure in the adoption of adequate pollution control measures. The proposition was roughly supported in the sense that those sector-cases which scored low on fragmentation had not experienced any problems with the adoption of measures, while those cases scoring medium and high had experienced such problems to varying degrees. On the other, fragmentation had increasingly been dealt with by means of sector integration and integrated pollution control the last decade. The Netherlands has a highly complex water pollution control system in terms of legal basis and governmental agencies. These features shed light on implementation problems concerning both the industrial sector as well as the late response by the agricultural sector to environmental challenges. The Norwegian system is characterized by horizontal simplicity and vertical fragmentation. The former feature partly explains Norway's successful record in limiting emissions of hazardous substances from the industrial sector. The latter feature can shed light on Norway's implementation problems in the municipal sector. If local opposition to governmental goals linked to international commitments goes hand in hand with decentralization of competence, there is a risk of defection from national and international goals. The UK case is marked by significant change towards a more integrated system concerning legal basis and regulatory agencies. The presence of different regulatory actors with competence in water pollution control led to implementation problems concerning land-based discharges of hazardous substances.

The next topic was the specific policy tools by which measures are implemented. Here we found little support for the proposition that the most 'effective' policy tools aimed at affecting both cost/benefit incentives and norms of environmentally friendly behaviour. On the basis of the empirical analysis, two qualifiers were attached. First, policy tools with a clear incentive effect appeared fundamental. Second, the choice of policy tools is sensitive to the characteristics of the sector under regulation, such as the distinction between diffuse and point sources. Still, the analysis of policy tools showed that an additional reason for the mismatch between Dutch goals and actual results may well lie in its reliance on voluntary agreements, while Norway relied more heavily on traditional command and control. The positive development witnessed in the UK concerning hazardous substances appears linked to stepping up command and control.

In Chapter 9, we returned to the international level focusing first on the domestic impact of international institutions. International institutions do not only affect positions, commitments and behaviour of states conceived of as unitary actors. In addition, international institutions can, under certain conditions, have a direct influence on the domestic procedures governing intrastate relationships between governments, target groups, and ENGOs. Three pathways were identified. First, international procedures were incorporated in national law. The Oslo Convention empowered the British government in the case of ocean-based activities. This is likely to occur when national rules and procedures are absent or weakly developed. Second, the non-binding North Sea Declarations were invoked in domestic environmental politics. For example, the INSC declarations legitimized stringent action in the agricultural sector in Norway and the Netherlands. Third, international procedures affected domestic standard operating procedures by changing the decision-making chain between national and international levels.

The second topic under scrutiny here was the notion of dynamic development and institutional path dependency. We could observe that the first decade of the cooperation corresponded to the expectation that international institutions may be hard to change even though they produce unsatisfactory outcomes. This situation may be traced back to internal contradictions within the regime itself. First, the North Sea regime covered the entire North-East Atlantic including states with no borders to the North Sea, even though the pressing ecological needs concerned the North Sea. Second, the parties sought to establish a dynamic regime, but various institutional factors like the legally binding character of the Conventions actually worked in the opposite direction. Internal contradictions led to a gap between expectations and collective results. In turn, frustration with the existing framework developed. Since other factors exogenous to the regime itself remained roughly constant, the change towards a more constructive pathway can largely be traced back to institutional change. The INSCs managed to coped with both internal contradictions and represented a truly dynamic instrument that generated a snowball effect in terms of steadily increasing the stringency of commitments. Germany was instrumental in bringing about this change in institutionalization, acting as both an intellectual and an entrepreneurial leader. While the parties had been occupied with negotiating lenient standards for a few hazardous substances in the first decade, the 1995 INSC Declaration aims at phasing out discharges of all human-made hazardous substances within 25 years. There are recent signs that the mode of 'diminishing returns' may represent an obstacle in transforming this joint obligation to actual domestic implementation, but here the proof lies largely in the future. Increasing abatement costs and decreasing benefits in the form of environmental quality may increasingly become a problem when the time comes for the parties to implement the stringent international obligations in the next century.

Analytical implications

Our first observation relates to the complementary nature of rationalistic and institutionalistic, or sociological approaches to the study of institutions. The assumption of rational actors operating within institutions which provide incentives and information can bring us closer towards an understanding of the making and implementation of the North Sea commitments. The way in which international institutions worked to aggregate and integrate actor interests and preferences and constrained behaviour by increasing transparency is fully compatible with the rationalistic approach. In the same category at the domestic level we found how social demands were articulated and aggregated as well as how policy tools affected the behaviour of target groups. The latter point is in fact better understood within the rationalistic perspective than by the notion of norm-guided behaviour.

On the other hand, the assumption of actors having dual utility functions makes possible other complementary consequences. Cases in point here are the indications that legally binding international obligations constrain behaviour simply because the actors perceive defection as 'wrong' in itself, and the consequences of different governmental ministries and agencies playing different roles in implementation. In addition, we have the notion of different regulatory styles rooted in history and tradition that affect, but certainly do not determine, national styles and approaches to regulation. The most significant changes in relevant procedures have taken place in the UK only since the mid-1980s. Yet, as the world's first industrial nation, Britain has the oldest pollution control system in the world dating back to 1860s.

An example may help to illustrate the value of combining norms and cost/benefit rationality. The UK changed its policy and phased out dumping, for various 'internal' and 'external' reasons. However, the UK government, supported by virtually all important domestic actors, consistently and vehemently argued that dumping at sea had no negative environmental consequences. Internally, the rising demands of public opinion in the late 1980s were organized and articulated by ENGOs targeting the Parliament, the government, and the target groups themselves. Conversely, the pressure brought to bear by other North Sea states within OSPARCOM and INSC was perhaps even more important. In combination, internal and external pressure increased the political costs of dumping. However, less visible changes were under way beneath the surface. The principle of dumping at sea as the 'last option' was actually included when relevant British legislation was amended in 1985 – i.e. *before* internal and external pressure intensified. The question then becomes: why should dumping at sea be considered as the 'last option' when such activities were commercially profitable for companies and economically beneficial for the state, and at the same time claimed not to harm the environment?

The first possibility is that the British government was responding to changing norms in society. In this case, the change in norms will have an impact, but not in an authentic sense since other actors would actually convey the norms. Thus, there would be political costs involved in not responding to societal demands. While this possibility cannot be excluded, it is not very likely, for two reasons. First, environmental concerns ranked low on the agenda prior to 1985. Second, the only domestic actors that actively worked for a change in dumping policy were the ENGOs in general and Greenpeace in particular. As late as in 1989, the environment secretary Nicholas Ridly referred to ENGOs as 'extremists' and 'pseudo-Marxists' (McCormick 1991: 57). Thus, giving in to the environmental groups would definitely not represent a preferred option for the Thatcher government.

The second possibility is that the government was playing some sort of 'two-level' game. This possibility bears some significance, but only some. At the international level, the government would try to satisfy the interests of domestic groups that supported dumping, while at the same time minimizing the national political costs of continuing dumping. The main problem with this line of thought is that international pressure on British dumping policy mainly occurred *after* 1985.

The third possibility is that the British government itself had internalized new norms since signing the Oslo Convention in 1972. This would represent a genuine form of norm-guided behaviour. There is little doubt that those responsible for licensing dumping within the Ministry of Agriculture, Fisheries and Food have changed their attitude towards dumping over time. Recognition has evolved around the idea that using the sea as a trash can is 'wrong' in itself. Thus, change in UK dumping policy and practice from the early 1970s to the mid-1990s is probably best understood within an institutional perspective that includes both norms and cost/benefit rationality. Moreover, the development witnessed can be fully understood only if one analyses international as well as domestic changes.

The latter point takes us over to the second observation concerning the need for relaxing the 'unity' assumption and focusing on actors and institutions at domestic level. It is tempting to say that it does not make much sense to analyse the consequences of international institutions without opening the 'black box' of domestic policy. If the aim of the analysis is to study change in behaviour (a necessary condition for intentional problem-solving) one has to focus on those actors who actually cause the problem as well as relevant institutions that influence the behaviour of target groups. We should note first of all that the stringency of joint commitments does not tell us much about behavioural change. The three countries selected in the analysis were subject to the same obligations, but their responses varied significantly. Second, the link between joint commitments and the ambition-level of relevant policy provides more insight, but is still unsatisfactory. The Netherlands had adopted a more ambitious policy than Norway, but achieved less in terms of behavioural change. Thus, the interesting question is not whether to focus on the domestic level or not, but the depth of domestic analysis required. It is difficult to provide general advice concerning this question since requirements may vary according to the types of commitments, issue-areas and actors involved. Nevertheless, this study has shown that both governmental policy and target-group interests differ significantly at sector level. In such cases, one has to distinguish between the relevant sectors affected by the commitments under scrutiny. The proof of the pudding lies in the link between joint commitments, governmental policy ambitions and the behaviour of target groups. On the other hand, opening up the black box also involves costs in terms of time and energy required.

Third, linkages between different international institutions may be crucial for explaining collective outcomes. While the link between OSPARCOM and the INSCs was analysed in detail, we could also observe a link between these institutions and the EC. The

EC Commission and several EC member-states participate in the North Sea cooperation, but the EC also includes potential 'laggard' states that are not parties in their own right as such. Since the Council of Ministers has to take the final decision in those cases where legally binding decisions are proposed by the Paris Commission, single member-states can in principle block proposals in the Council if unanimity is required. The lesson is that institutional linkages may lead to a deadlock whenever there is a mismatch in participation and unanimity is required. On the other hand, such linkages may also have positive consequences since one institution may 'learn' from the other. Moreover, when the EC acts on specific issues it does so with significant weight, due to its supranational qualities. Since the EC participates in a number of international environmental cooperations, this point also bear significance outside the North Sea cooperation.

Even though this study has brought us closer to an understanding of the significant changes that have occurred in the North Sea cooperation, there is still room for other explanatory perspectives and approaches. Particularly promising would be a distinct perspective based on social learning and diffusion of knowledge. Even though epistemic communities were absent, intellectual leadership was seen to be present. The precautionary principle developed and introduced by Germany, which took the initiative to the first INSC, may be understood within the frameworks of social learning and diffusion of ideas. The ramifications of this principle within the North Sea cooperation have only been touched upon. An in-depth analysis of this principle would probably force us to reinterpret such crucial concepts as abatement costs and damage costs. The diffusion approach would also lead us to focus on a broader range of consequences of the North Sea cooperation. As pointed out, Article 17 of the 1995 INSC Declaration on the phasing out of hazardous substances has already affected other regions and cooperations concerned with water and marine pollution.

Policy implications

So what? Why is it important to know and understand more about the functioning and consequences of environmental institutions? The underlying concern in this book has been a desire to learn how to affect the behaviour of actors who cause pollution. Comparing relative success in environmental policies in various countries is important to progress towards more advanced environmental policies. A better understanding of the functioning and consequences of institutions is a necessary, though not sufficient, condition for putting such knowledge to practical use. Even though we had a well-developed understanding of these phenomena within a given context, there would still be a long way from knowledge to practice. The main challenge involves the *generalizability* of lessons learned from the North Sea cooperation and national implementation efforts. There are good reasons for optimism concerning the potential for generalising to other cooperative efforts and countries at a general level confined with causal patterns linking behavioural mechanisms of actors to problems and institutions. Environmental institutions affect collective outcomes and actor behaviour through various institutional factors and behavioural mechanisms conditioned by problem characteristics. Conversely, there are good reasons for caution when we move from the general level to specific policy advice, due to the possible interplay between specific institutional arrangements and context. Significantly different institutional arrangements have previously been identified and assessed as working in the same direction within different historical, cultural, and political contexts (Lundqvist 1980; Vogel 1986). Thus, we can only offer *conditional* advice as to how well specific institutional arrangements work.

Lessons, generalization and context

At the international level, institutional changes were undertaken within a context of roughly constant exogenous factors. Moreover, such changes took place concerning 'hard' collective problems characterized by highly asymmetrical interests and preferences.

The most significant substantial lesson to be drawn from this book is the results of combining soft and hard law institutions in the same issue-area. These two ways of institutionalizing environmental cooperation did not lead to duplication of functions. On the contrary, they complemented each other by fulfilling functions the other form of institutionalization could not provide. The legally binding OSPARCOM cooperation provided a highly cooperative environment based on diffuse reciprocity, high integration capacity and constraint placed on the actors by means of bindingness. The non-legally binding INSCs provided specific reciprocity, high aggregation capacity and constraint placed on the parties by means of specificity and transparency. The notion of *international implementation* assessed in Chapter 4 shows how the parties were able to benefit from both types of institutions. The soft-law institution speeded up the work of the hard law institutions, which subsequently cemented previous achievements in international law. Moreover, their dynamic features initiated a snowball effect that has continued to yield increasingly stringent commitments despite of varying contextual circumstances such as the greening of public opinion.

While the consequences of combining hard and soft law are likely to bear significance in other cooperative issue-areas, a wide range of more specific conditions contributed to the results witnessed in the North Sea cooperation. Institutional changes took place within a specific cooperation with a unique history. In particular, the *timing* for change appears good in retrospect. On the one hand, the INSCs could build on ten years of experience within OSPARCOM. On the other, social demands for more stringent environmental protection were on their way 'up' even though the original institutional changes came prior to the significant change in public opinion. Moreover, the change was initiated by Germany acting both as an intellectual leader that advocated the precautionary principle and as an entrepreneurial leader that organized the first INSC. Thus, we may expect the combination of soft and hard law institutions to be likely to produce some generalizable consequences in other issue-areas. However, there is no guarantee that such reforms will be introduced and produce the same set of consequences in other cooperative efforts within a different context. For example, the likelihood of developing diffuse reciprocity based on common norms of cooperation is probably strongly conditioned by the number of actors. Whereas such norms developed within the framework of the regional Oslo Convention on dumping at sea, they have probably not developed within the framework of the global London (dumping) Convention, which was established at the same time as the Oslo Convention. This example also indicates that we can further improve our understanding of critical conditions by comparing international regimes dealing with essentially the same problems and deviating on one, or a few specific variables. The North Sea case provides us on the one hand with lessons that bear significance for institutional design outside this specific issue-area. On the other, it also provides us with experience concerning how favourable conditions may interact. Accordingly, there is clearly room for 'luck' in institutional design.

The lessons to be learned at the domestic level are less clear-cut. In spite of pressure from international institutions towards standardization of ambitious goals, highly integrated EU states still vary significantly in both their response to joint commitments as well as in their actual achievements. This phenomenon is largely due to differences in relevant state institutions and it implies that the strength of states in pollution control depends largely upon how domestic institutions are designed. On the other hand, there are also striking similarities between the countries.

Fragmentation of competence in pollution control has been a serious obstacle to implementation. In general, simple systems involving few governmental actors appear most 'effective' in adopting adequate measures. Concerning horizontal fragmentation in environmental policies, i.e. the number of governmental agencies involved at each level of government, all three states have – although to varying degrees – developed from sector Acts and sector agencies towards integrated pollution control with one chief pollution control agency and one pollution/environmental protection Act. We have strong indications that this development has proved effective for the adoption of adequate measures, for two main reasons. First, disagreement and rivalry between different regulatory agencies is likely to be reduced. Second, target groups can rely on stable and predictable regulatory environments, since discharges to water, air and soil are managed by the same authority. Moreover, monitoring behaviour and enforcement becomes easier in integrated systems. Thus, a certain level of integrated pollution control is a necessary condition for effective domestic implementation whenever international commitments affect different sources of environmental problems (e.g. point and diffuse sources) and/or different media (land, air and water).

External fragmentation concerning other policy sectors such as agriculture has also been increasingly handled by means of sector integration of environmental concerns. In this study, the agricultural sector has been most relevant, as this sector represents an important cause of substances covered by the North Sea commitments. Since the causes of most pollution problems stem from otherwise legitimate activities within society, such as production of food, integration of environmental concerns has the capacity to prevent pollution. Furthermore, whenever international commitments affect different policy sectors, sector integration through tight and formalized cooperation between ministries and agencies appears a necessary condition for effective implementation.

Vertical distribution of competence, i.e. the distribution of competence between different governmental levels, to local levels may have a wide range of positive consequences for local environmental awareness and needs. Yet, we have indications that vertical distribution of competence in pollution control may create serious obstacles to implementation whenever transnational problems are attacked by means of international cooperation. It may prove impossible to distribute joint gains at the international level to local gains for each and every municipality contributing to the problem. Norway stands out here since significant competence in waste water treatment is in the hands of the municipalities. The Norwegian case shows that defection can be expected when local opposition goes hand in hand with decentralisation of competence. In order to cope with this problem, the general advantages of local competence have to be weighed against the obstacles in implementing international commitments.

At a general level, policy tools aimed at affecting incentives of target groups clearly have a positive effect on behaviour. Traditional command and control in the form of licensing has proved effective in the case of point sources in all three countries. Of particular interest here are the positive results achieved in the UK by changing from an essentially discretionary and voluntary system towards legally binding standards. Still, tools such as voluntary agreement aimed at developing norms for environmentally friendly behaviour may stimulate behavioural change beyond legal obligations. However, the impact of voluntary agreements is likely to be positively interrelated with decision-making styles based on negotiation, compromise and consensus. Of the three countries in this study, the Netherlands stands out through extensive use of voluntary agreements and a decision-making style based on consensus and compromise-seeking with target groups. This implies first that even though voluntary agreements may prove effective in the Netherlands they need not work in other countries. Nor does this study suggest that the extensive use of voluntary agreements in the Netherlands has been particularly 'effective' in a comparative perspective. If this observation also carries weight in other parts of environmental policy than water and marine environment, the implication is that such tools may prove less effective in other countries than in the Netherlands, if contextual factors are less fortunate.

Diffuse sources are more difficult to control than point sources. The combination of information/advice and general regulation has proven insufficient for reaching the targets in the agricultural sector. As to general regulations, monitoring and enforcement have proven difficult in practice due to the large number of targets. Economic tools in the form of, for example, taxes may improve this situation, but agricultural interests oppose taxes on input factors such as commercial fertilizer. As noted in Chapter 7, this study indicates that the cost/benefit line of thought in agriculture is by no means inferior to, for example, industry, although governments largely base their tools on the 'good faith' of farmers.

If we are to come to grips with complex real-world problems, we have to learn from previous 'successes' and 'failures'. Systematic empirical studies of environmental institutions at both the international and domestic levels will take us in that direction. Indeed, we can offer lessons and advice that will contribute to improving the functioning of environmental institutions and thereby the quality of the environment.

References

Aardal, B. 1993. *Energi og miljø: Nye stridsspørmål i møte med gamle strukturer*. Oslo: Institute for Social Research, R.93: 15.

Aardal, B. and H. Valen 1995. *Konflikt og opinion*. Oslo: NKS-forlaget.

Agora, 1–2. 1990. Debate on Jon Elster's Publications in 1989: 354–89.

Allison, G.T. 1971. *Essence of Decision: Explaining the Cuban Missile Crisis*. Boston: Little, Brown.

Andersen, M.S. 1994. *Governance by Green Taxes. Making Pollution Prevention Pay*. Manchester: Manchester University Press.

Andresen, S. 1992. International Verification in Practice: A Brief Account of Experiences from Relevant International Cooperative Measures, in E. Lykke (ed.) *Achieving Environmental Goals: The Concept and Practice of Environmental Performance*. London: Belhaven Press.

Andresen, S. 1996. Effectiveness and Implementation within the 'North Sea/North East Atlantic Cooperation': Development, Status and Future Perspectives, in *The Effectiveness of Multilateral Environmental Agreements*. Nord: 18, Nordic Council of Ministers, Copenhagen.

Andresen, S., S. Boehmer-Christiansen, K. Hanf, S. Kux, R. Lewanski, F. Morata, J. Skea, D. Sprinz, A. Underdal, T. Vaahtoranta and J. Wettestad. 1996. *The Domestic Basis of International Environmental Agreements: Modelling National/International Linkages*. Final report to the European Commission, May. Rotterdam: EC Contract EVSV-CT92-0185.

Andresen, S., J.B. Skjærseth and J. Wettestad 1995. *Regime, the State and Society: Analyzing the Implementation of International Environmental Commitments*. Laxenburg: IIASA, WP-95–43.

Andresen, S. and J. Wettestad 1995. International Problem-solving Effectiveness: The Oslo Project So Far. *International Environmental Affairs*, Vol. 7, No. 2, Spring: 127–49.

Axelrod, A. and R.O. Keohane 1986. Achieving Cooperation under Anarchy: Strategies and Institutions, in K.A. Oye (ed.), *Cooperation under*

Anarchy. Princeton N.J.: Princeton University Press.

Bartels, G.C. 1995. *Main Results of Environmental Communication Studies*. The Hague: Ministry of Housing, Spatial Planning and the Environment.

Baylis, J. and S. Smith 1997. *The Globalization of World Politics: An Introduction to International Relations.* Oxford: Oxford Unuversity Press.

Bergesen, H.O. and A. Dahl 1998. *Who Runs the Environment.* Lysaker: The Fridtjof Nansen Institute.

Bernauer, T. 1995. The Effect of International Environmental Institutions: How We Might Learn More. *International Organization*, Vol. 49, No. 2, Spring: 351–77.

Biersteker, T.J. 1993. Constructing Historical Counterfactuals to Assess the Consequences of International Regimes: The Global Debt Regime and the Course of the Dept Crisis of the 1980s, in Rittberger, V. (ed. with P. Mayer) *Regime Theory and International Relations*. Oxford: Clarendon Press.

Boehmer-Christiansen, S. and J. Skea 1991. *Acid Politics.* London: Belhaven Press.

Bressers H.T.A, D. Huitema and S.M.M. Kuks 1994. Policy Networks in Dutch Water Policy. In H.T.A. Bressers, L.J. O'Toole Jr and J. Richardson (eds) *Networks for Water Policy: A Comparative Perspective*. Special Issue of *Environmental Politics*, Vol. 3, No. 4, Winter: 24–51.

Cameron, J. 1994. The Status of the Precautionary Principle in International Law, in T. O'Riordan and J. Cameron (eds) *Interpreting the Precautionary Principle*. London: Earthscan.

Caporaso, J.A. 1992. International Relations Theory and Mutilateralism: The Search for Foundations. *International Organization*, Vol. 46, No. 3, Summer: 599–632.

CEFIC 1996. *Responsible Care*. Brussels: CEFIC.

Chayes, A. and A.H. Chayes 1993. On Compliance. *International Organization*, Vol. 47, No. 2, Spring: 175–205.

CNIE 1995. *Environmental Policy in the Netherlands: The Role of Industry*. The Hague: CNIE.

Collier, U. 1997. Sustainability, Subsidiarity and Deregulation: New Directions in EU Environmental Policy. *Environmental Politics*, Vol. 6, No. 2, Summer: 1–23.

Commissie Integral Waterbeheer (CUWVO) 1996. *Taak samenstelling werkwijze*. Den Haag: CUWVO-Secretariat.

Confederation of British Industry 1995a. *Britain's Business Voice*. London: CBI.

Confederation of British Industry 1995b. CBI Comments on the Draft North Sea Conference Declaration Text, 24 March. London: CBI.

Conrad, J. 1993. Agriculture and the Environment in Western Europe.

International Environmental Affairs, Vol. 5, No. 2, Spring: 79–93.
Cortell, A.P. and J.W. Davis, Jr. 1996. How Do International Institutions Matter? The Domestic Impact of International Rules and Norms. *International Studies Quarterly*, Vol. 40: 451–78.
Department of the Environment 1988. *Second International Conference on the Protection of the North Sea*. UK Guidance Note on the Ministerial Declaration. London: DoE.
Department of the Environment 1990a. *Third International Conference on the Protection of the North Sea*. UK Guidance Note on the Ministerial Declaration. London: DoE.
Department of the Environment 1990b. *UK North Sea Action Plan 1985–1995*. London: DoE.
Dessler, D. 1992. The Causal Analysis of International Environmental Institutions. Mimeo, April 23. College of William and Mary, Williamsburg, VA.
Dinham, B. 1993. *The Pesticide Hazard. A Global Health and Environmental Audit*. London: Zed Books.
Doherty, B. 1992. The Autumn 1991 Conference of the UK Green Party. *Environmental Politics*, Vol. 1, No. 2: 292–7.
Downs, A. 1972. Up and Down with Ecology – The Issue Attention Cycle. *Public Interest*, Vol. 28, Summer: 38–50.
Ducrotoy, J.P. 1997. Scientific Management in Europe: The Case of the North Sea, in L. Anathea Brooks and S.D. VanDeveer (eds) *Saving the Seas: Values, Scientists, and International Governance*. Maryland: Maryland Sea Grant College.
Dumping at Sea Act 1974. London: HMSO.
Easton, D. 1965. *A Systems Analysis of Political Life*. New York: John Wiley and Sons.
Eckstein, H. 1975. Case study and Theory in Political Science, in F.I. Greenstein and N.W. Polsby (eds) *Strategies of Inquiry*, pp. 79–137. Reading, MA: Addison-Wesley.
Ehlers, P. 1990. The History of the International North Sea Conferences. In Freestone, D. and T. IJlstra (eds), *The North Sea: Perspectives on Regional Environmental Co-operation*. Special Issue of the *International Journal of Estuarine and Coastal Law*, pp. 3–15. London: Graham and Trotman.
Elster, J. 1978. *Logic and Society: Contradictions and Possible Worlds*. New York: John Wiley and Sons.
Elster, J. 1989a. *Nuts and Bolts for the Social Sciences*. Cambridge: Cambridge University Press.
Elster, J. 1989b. *The Cement of Society:A Study of Social Order*. Cambridge: Cambridge University Press.
ENDS Report 1987a. New Campaign Puts Waste Imports, Disposal at Sea

under Pressure. No. 151, August.

ENDS Report 1987b. Water Pollution Control after Privatization: An Unfinished Business. No. 152, September.

ENDS Report 1987c. Shakier Outlook for Ocean Incinerator. No. 153, October.

ENDS Report 1988. Implementing the North Sea Declaration: A Framework Emerges. No. 157, February.

ENDS Report 1990a. Chemical Industry Tops Pollution Control League. No. 180, January.

ENDS Report 1990b. The Ever-Widening Agenda for the North Sea Environment. No. 181, February.

ENDS Report 1991. Decline in River Quality Continues. No. 201, October.

ENDS Report 1992a. NRA Wins Fight with Greenpeace over Discharge Control Policy. No. 206, March.

ENDS Report 1992b. The Costs of Water Quality: The Regulator's Turf of War Continues. No. 211, August.

ENDS Report 1994. Water Industry still Dominates Pollution League. No. 230, March.

Ends Report Index 1990–95. London: Environmental Data Services.

Environment Agency 1996. *The Environment of England and Wales: A Snapshot*. Bristol: Environment Agency

Environmental News from the Netherlands 1993. Enforcement: A Balance between Cooperation and Deterrence. No. 2.

Esbjerg Declaration 1995. Ministerial Conference on the Protection of the North Sea. Esbjerg, Denmark, 8–9 June. Copenhagen: Ministry of Environment and Energy, Danish Environment Protection Agency.

Evans, G. 1993. Hard Times for the British Green Party. *Environmental Politics*, Vol. 2, No. 2: 327–32.

Evans, P.B, H.K. Jacobson and R.D. Putnam (eds) 1993. *Double-Edged Diplomacy: International Bargaining and Domestic Politics*. Berkeley: University of California Press.

Fearon, J.D. 1991. Counterfactuals and Hypothesis Testing in Political Science. *World Politics*, Vol. 43, No. 2, January: 169–95.

Føllesdal, D. 1982 The Status of Rationality Assumptions in Interpretation and in the Explanation of Action. *Dialectica*, Vol. 36, No. 4: 301–16.

Food and Environmental Protection Act 1985. London: HMSO.

Franck, T.M. 1990. *The Power of Legitimacy among Nations*. Oxford: Oxford University Press.

Gibson, J. and R.R. Churchill 1990. Problems of Implementation of the North Sea Declarations: A Case Study of the United Kingdom. In D. Freestone and T. IJlstra (eds) *The North Sea: Perspectives on Regional Environmental Co-operation*. Special Issue of the *International Journal of Estuarine and Coastal Law*. London: Graham and Trotman.

Gjerde, K. 1992. Norsk foruresningspolitikk – et uttrykk for en 'avveiningstankegang'. En studie av SFT's regulering av storforurensende industri. Hovedoppgave i Administrasjon og organisasjonsvitenskap. Universitetet i Bergen.

Gourevitch, P. 1978. The Second Image Reversed: The International Sources of Domestic Politics. *International Organization*, Vol. 32, No. 4, Autumn: 881–912.

Greenpeace International 1990. Submission to the OSCOM extraordinary meeting of the *ad hoc* working group on dumping. London, 14 February.

Grieco, J.M. 1988. Anarchy and the Limits of Cooperation: A Realist Critique of the Newest Liberal Institutionalism. *International Organization* Vol. 42, No. 3, Summer: 485–507.

Gundersen, F. 1991. Utviklingstrekk ved miljøbevegelsen i Norge. *Sosiologi i dag*, No. 2: 12–35.

Haas, P.M. 1989. Do Regimes Matter? Epistemic Communities and Mediterranean Pollution Control. *International Organization*, Vol. 43, No. 3, Summer: 377–403.

Haas, P.M. 1990. *Saving the Mediterranean. The Politics of International Environmental Cooperation*. New York: Columbia University Press.

Haas, P.M. (ed.) 1992. *Knowledge, Power and International Policy Coordination*. Special issue of *International Organization*, Vol. 46, No. 1, Winter.

Haas, P.M. 1993. Protecting the Baltic and North Seas from Pollution: Amplifying Domestic Concern, in Haas P.M., R.O. Keohane and M. Levy (eds) *Institutions for the Earth: Sources of Effective International Environmental Protection*. Cambridge, MA: MIT Press.

Haas, P.M, R.O. Keohane and M.A. Levy (eds) 1993. *Institutions for the Earth: Sources of Effective International Environmental Protection*. Cambridge, MA: MIT Press.

Hägerhäll, B. 1993. The Evolving Role of NGOs, in G. Sjöstedt (ed.) *International Environmental Negotiations: Process, Issues and Context*. Stockholm: Utenrikspolitiska Institutet.

Haggard, S. and B.A. Simmons 1987. Theories of International Regimes. *International Organization*, Vol. 41, No. 3, Summer: 491–517.

Haigh, N., with G. Bennett, P. Kromarek and T. Lavoux 1986. *Water and Waste in Four Countries. A Study of the Implementation of the EEC Directives in France, Germany, Netherlands and United Kingdom*. London: Graham and Trotman.

Hall, P.A. and R.C.R. Taylor 1994. Political Science and the Four New Institutionalism. Center for European Studies, Harvard University, Cambridge. Paper prepared for presentation to the Annual Meeting of the American Political Science Association, New York.

Harsheim, J. and S. Hovik 1996. *From Global to Local Perspective: A Study of Local Implementation of the North Sea Declarations*. Oslo: NIBR-report: 6.

Hegeman, J.H.F, L. Korver-Alzerda, J.J. Bouma, F.J. Duijnhower, R.W. Hommes, F. Huysman, C. Cornelius, W. Verstraete, P. Thonart 1992. *Pilot Case Study: Management of North Sea Eutrophication*. Rotterdam: Erasmus University.

Her Majesty's Inspectorate of Pollution 1995. *1994–95 Annual Report*. London: HMSO.

Hofrichter, J. 1991. *Evolution of Attitudes towards Environmental Issues 1974–1991*. Zentrum für Europäische Umfragenanalysen und Studien: Universität Mannheim.

Hovi, J. 1992. *Spillmodeller og internasjonalt samarbeid: oppgaver, mekanismer og institusjoner*. Oslo: Institutt for statsvitenskap, Universitetet i Oslo.

Hovik, S. and J. Harsheim 1996. *Environmental Policy in Local Politics*. Oslo: NIBR-Report 1996: 5.

Huitema, D. 1993. Any Objections? An Explorative Study of the Rules of the Game, and their Effects on Time and Costs of Permitting and Siting Wastewater Treatment Works in the Netherlands and Alabama. Masters thesis, University of Twente.

Hurrell, A. and B. Kingsbury 1992. *The International Politics of the Environment*. Oxford: Clarendon Press.

IJlstra, T. 1986. *Enforcement of International Environmental Instruments in the North Sea: The Missing Link*. Netherlands Institute for the Law of the Sea: University of Utrecht.

Implementation Report 1990. The implementation of the Ministerial Declaration of the Second International Conference on the Protection of the North Sea. The Hague: Ministry of Transport and Public Works.

Inglehart, R. 1971. The Silent Revolution in Europe: Intergenerational Change in Post-Industrial Societies. *The Americal Political Science Review*, Vol. 65: 991–1017.

Interim Report on the Quality Status of the North Sea 1990. The Hague: Ministry of Transport and Public Works.

Jänicke, M. 1992. Conditions for Environmental Policy Success: An International Comparison, in M. Jachtenfuchs and M.S. Strübel (eds) *Environmental Policy in Europe: Assessment, Challenges and Perspectives*. Baden-Baden: Nomos.

Jänicke, M. 1997. The Political System's Capacity for Environmental Policy, in M. Jänicke, and H. Weidner (eds. in collaboration with H. Jörgens) *National Environmental Policies: A Comparative Study of Capacity-Building*. Berlin: Springer.

Jamison, A., R. Eyerman and J. Cramer 1990. *The Making of the new Envi-*

ronmental Consciousness: A Comparative Study of the Environmental Movements in Sweden, Denmark and the Netherlands. Edinburgh: Edinburgh University Press.

Jansen, A.I. and O. Osland 1996. Norway, in *Governing the Environment: Politics, Policy, and Organization in the Nordic Countries*. Nord: 5. Copenhagen: Nordic Council of Ministers.

Jordan, A. 1993. Integrated Pollution Control and the Evolving Style and Structure of Environmental Regulation in the UK. *Environmental Politics*, Vol. 2, No. 3: 405–27.

Keohane, R.O. 1984. *After Hegemony: Cooperation and Discord in the World Political Economy*. Princeton NJ: Princeton University Press.

Keohane, R.O. 1986. Reciprocity in International Relations. *International Organization*, Vol. 40, No. 1, Winter: 1–27.

Keohane, R.O. 1988. International Institutions: Two Approaches. *International Studies Quarterly*, Vol. 32: 379–96.

Keohane, R.O. 1993. The Analysis of International Regimes. Towards a European-American Research programme, in V. Rittberger (ed. with P. Mayer), *Regime Theory and International Relations*. Oxford: Clarendon Press.

King, G., R.O. Keohane and S. Verba 1994. *Designing Social Inquiry: Scientific Inference in Qualitative Research*. Princeton NJ: Princeton University Press.

Kinnersley, D. 1994. *Coming Clean. The Politics of Water and the Environment*. London: Penguin Books.

Klausen, J.E. 1996. Miljøpolitikken og den segmenterte stat. In J.E. Klausen and H. Rommetvedt (eds) *Miljøpolitikk, organisasjonene, Stortinget og Forvaltningen*. Oslo: Tano Aschehoug.

Knoepfel, P., L. Lundqvist, R. Prud'homme and P. Wagener 1987. Comparing Environmental Policies: Different Styles, Similar Content, in M. Dierkes (ed.) *Comparative Policy Research*. Aldershot: Gower.

Krasner, S.D. 1983. Structural Causes and Regime Consequences: Regimes as Intervening Variables, in S.D. Krasner (ed.) *International Regimes*. Ithaca, NY and London: Cornell University Press.

Krasner, S.D. 1988. Sovereignty: An Institutional Perspective. *Comparative Political Studies*, Vol. 21 No. 1, April: 66–94.

Kratochwil, F. 1993. Contract and Regimes: Do Issue Specificity and Variation of Formality Matter? in V. Rittberger (ed. with P. Mayer), *Regime Theory and International Relations*. Oxford: Clarendon Press.

Lægreid, P. 1983. Miljøverndepartementet. Ny organizasjon i etablert miljø. *Nordisk Administrativt Tidsskrift*, No. 4: 365–83.

Levi, M. 1991. Are there Limits to Rationality? *Archives Europeennes De Sociologie*, Vol. 32, No. 32: 130–41.

Levy, M.A. 1993. European Acid Rain: The Power of Tote-Board Diplomacy, in P.M. Haas, R.O. Keohane and M.A. Levy (eds) 1993. *Institutions for the Earth: Sources of Effective International Environmental Protection*. Cambridge, MA: MIT Press.

Levy, M.A, O.R Young and M. Zürn. 1995. The Study of International Regimes. *European Journal of International Relations*, Vol. 1, No. 3: 267–330.

Lewin, L. 1991. *Self-Interest and Public Interest in Western Politics*. Oxford: Oxford University Press.

Liefferink, D. 1995. Environmental policy in the Netherlands: National Profile. Paper prepared for the workshop 'New Nordic Member States and the Impact on EC Environmental Policy', Sanbjerg, Denmark, 6–8 April. Wagening Agricultural University.

Liefferink, D. and A. Mol 1997. Voluntary Agreements as a Form of Deregulation? in U. Collier (ed.) *Deregulation in the European Union: Environmental Perspectives*. London: Routledge.

Lucardie, P.G. 1995. General Election in the Netherlands, May 1994: The Triumph of Grey Liberalism. *Environmental Politics*, Vol. 4, No. 1: 119–22.

Lundqvist, L.J. 1980. *The Hare and the Tortoise: Clean Air Policies in the United States and Sweden*. Ann Arbor, MI: University of Michigan Press.

MacGarvin, M. 1991. *Greenpeace The Seas of Europe: The North Sea*. (Norwegian edition) Oslo: Aschehoug.

Malnes, R. 1995. 'Leader' and 'Entrepreneur' in International Negotiations: A Conceptual Analysis. *European Journal of International Relations*, Vol. 1, No. 1: 87–112.

Maloney, W.A and Richardson, J. 1994. Water policy-making in England and Wales: Policy Communities under Pressure? *Environmental Politics*, Vol. 3, No. 4, Winter: 110–37.

March, J.G. and J.P. Olsen 1989. *Rediscovering Institutions:The Organizational Basis of Politics*. New York: The Free Press.

March, J.G. and J.P. Olsen 1994. Institutional Perspectives on Governance, H.U. Derlien, U. Gebhardt and F.W. Scharpf (eds) in *Systemrationalität und Partialinteresse: Festchrift für Rennate Mayntz/Hans Ulrich Derlien*, pp. 249–70. Baden-Baden: Nomos Verlagsgesellschaft.

March, J.G. and J.P. Olsen 1996. Institutional Perspectives on Political Institutions. *Governance: An International Journal of Policy and Administration*, Vol. 9,No. 3, July: 247–64.

McCormick, J. 1991. *British Politics and the Environment*. London: Earthscan.

McCormick, J. 1994. Environmental Politics, in P. Dunleavy, A. Gamble, I. Holliday and G. Peele (eds) *Developments in British Politics*. London: Macmillan Press.

Mearsheimers, J. 1995. The False Promise of International Institutions.

International Security, No. 19 (3): 5–49.

Mensbrugghe, Y. 1990. Legal Status of International North Sea Conference Declarations, in D. Freestone and T. IJlstra (eds) *The North Sea: Perspectives on Regional Environmental Co-operation*. Special Issue of the *International Journal of Estuarine and Coastal Law*. London: Graham and Trotman.

Miles, E. A. Underdal, S. Andresen, J. Wettestad, J.B. Skjærseth, E.Carlin and M.Solin. (forthcoming). *Explaining Regime Effectiveness: Confronting Theory with Evidence*.

Milner, H. 1991. International Theories of Cooperation among Nations. *World Politics*, No. 3: 466–96.

Ministerial Declarations 1995. International Conferences on the Protection of the North Sea. Bremen 1984, London 1987, The Hague 1990. Copenhagen: Ministry of Environment and Energy, Danish Environment Protection Agency.

Ministry of Agriculture 1992. State paper no. 8 (1992–1993). Oslo: Ministry of Agriculture.

Ministry of Agriculture, Fisheries and Food 1989. *Annual Report: Report on the Disposal of Waste Water at Sea 1986 and 1987*. London: HMSO.

Ministry of Agriculture, Fisheries and Food 1989b. Dumping Industrial Waste at Sea to be Phased Out. News release, 4 December.

Ministry of Agriculture, Fisheries and Food 1994. *Monitoring and Surveillance of Non-Radioactive Contaminants in the Aquatic Environment and Activities Regulating the Disposal of Wastes at Sea, 1992*. Lowestoft: Directorate of Fisheries Research.

Ministry of Agriculture, Fisheries and Food 1995. *Monitoring and Surveillance of Non-Radioactive Contaminants in the Aquatic Environment and Activities Regulating the Disposal of Wastes at Sea, 1993*. Lowestoft: Directorate of Fisheries Research.

Ministry of Foreign Affairs 1972. *Concerning Norway's Ratification of the Oslo Convention*. State paper no. 99 (1971–1972). Oslo: Ministry of Foreign Affairs. (Original title: *Om samtykke til ratifikasjon av overenskomst av 15. februar 1972 om bekjempelse av havforurensning ved dumping fra skip og fly*.)

Ministry of the Environment 1975. *On the National Plan for Utilization of Water Resources*. Report No. 107 to the Storting (1974–75). Oslo: ME. (Original title: *Om arbeidet med en landsplan for bruken av vannressursene*.)

Ministry of the Environment 1984. *Minutes of the North Sea Conference in Bremen, 31 October to 1 November 1984*. Oslo: ME.

Ministry of the Environment 1985. *On Measures against Water and Air Pollution and Municipal Waste*. Report No. 51 to the Storting (1984–85).

Oslo: ME. (Original title: *Om tiltak mot vann- og luftforuresninger og om kommunalt avfall.*)
Ministry of the Environment 1989. *Environment and Development: Programme for Norway's Follow up of the Report of the World Commission on Environment and Development*. Report No. 46 to the Storting (1988–89). Oslo: ME. (Original title: *Miljø og Utvikling. Norges oppfølging av Verdenskommisjonens rapport.*)
Ministry of the Environment 1992. *Concerning Norway's Implementation of the North Sea Declarations*. Report No. 64 to the Storting (1991–92). Oslo: ME. (In English.)
Ministry of Transport and Public Works 1980. *Water Action Programme 1980–1984 The Netherlands*. The Hague: Rijkswaterstaat.
Ministry of Transport and Public Works 1990. *North Sea Action Plan. Netherlands Implementation Document*. Third International Conference on the Protection of the North Sea (provisional text). The Hague: Ministry of Transport and Public Works.
Ministry of Transport, Public Works and Water Management. Directorate-General of Public Works and Water Management 1996. *Annual Report Rijkswaterstaat 1995*. The Hague: Ministry of Transport, Public Works and Water Management.
Mitchell, R.B. 1994a. *Intentional Oil Pollution at Sea. Environmental Treaty Compliance*. Cambridge, MA: MIT Press.
Mitchell, R.B. 1994b. Regime Design Matters: Intentional Oil Pollution and Treaty Compliance. *International Organization*, Vol. 48, No. 3, Summer: 425–58.
Moravcsik, A. 1993. Introduction: Integrating International and Domestic Theories of International Bargaining, in P.B. Evans, H.K. Jacobson and R.D. Putnam 1993 (eds) *Double-Edged Diplomacy: International Bargaining and Domestic Politics*. Berkeley: University of California Press.
Mumma, A. 1993. Use of Compliance Monitoring Data in Water Prosecutions. *Journal of Environmental Law*, Vol. 5, No. 2: 191–280.
Mydske, P.K. and A. Steen (in association with A. Taarud) 1994. Land-Use and Environmental Policy in Norway, in K. Eckberg, P.K. Mydske, A. Niemi-Iiahti and K.H. Pedersen (eds) *Comparing Nordic and Baltic Countries – Environmental Problems and Policies in Agriculture and Forestry*. TemaNord: 572, Copenhagen: Nordic Council of Ministers.
Næringslivets Hovedorganisasjon 1992. *Helse Miljø og Sikkerhet: Investeringer og driftdkostander i industrien*. Oslo: NHO.
Naustdalslid, J. 1994. Innleiing: Globale miløproblem-lokale løysingar, in J. Naustdalslid og S. Hovik (red.) *Lokalt miljøvern*. Oslo: TANO/Norsk Institutt for By og Regionsforskning.
NEPP 1989. *National Environmental Policy Plan: To Choose or to Lose*. The Hague: Ministry of Housing, Physical Planning and Environment,

Department for Information and International Relations.

Nollkaemper, A. 1993. *The Legal Regime for Transboundary Water Pollution: Between Discretion and Constraint*. London: Graham & Trotman.

Norges Bondelag 1980–90. Årsmelding Norges Bondelag. Oslo: Norges Bondelag.

North Sea Quality Status Report 1993. London: Oslo and Paris Commissions.

North Sea Task Force 1990. *North Sea Environment Report No. 3*. London: North Sea Task Force, Oslo and Paris Commissions and ICES.

NOU 1992. *Towards a more Cost-Efficient Environmental Policy in the 1990s*. (Original title: *Mot en mer kostnadseffektiv miljøpolitikk i 1990-årene*.) Oslo: Ministry of Finance.

NOU 1995. *On Instruments in Environmental Policy*. Oslo: ME. (Original title: *Virkemidler i miljøpolitikken*.)

O'Riordan, T. 1995. Frameworks for Choice: Core Beliefs and the Environment. *Environment*, Vol. 37, No. 8: 4–9, 24–9.

OECD 1993. *Environmental Performance Reviews: Norway*. Paris: OECD Publications

OECD 1994. *Environmental Performance Reviews: United Kingdom*. Paris: OECD Publications

OECD 1995. *Environmental Performance Reviews: Netherlands*. Paris: OECD Publications

OECD 1996. *Pollution Abatement and Control Expenditure in OECD Countries*. OECD/GS(96)50, Paris: OECD Publications.

Olson, M. 1965 (1982). *The Logic of Collective Action*. Cambridge, MA: Harvard University Press.

Oslo and Paris Commissions 1984. *The Oslo and Paris Commissions – the First Decade. International Co-operation in Protecting our Marine Environment*. London: Secretariat of the Oslo and Paris Commissions.

Oslo and Paris Commissions 1990. *Progress Report on the Activities of the Oslo and Paris Commissions, November 1987–March 1990*. London: Oslo and Paris Commissions.

Oslo and Paris Commissions 1992a. *Nutrients in the Convention Area*. London: Secretariat of the Oslo and Paris Commissions.

Oslo and Paris Commissions 1992b. *Industrial Sectors: Best Available Technology*. London: Oslo and Paris Commissions.

Oslo Commission 1988. *Twelfth Annual Report*. London: Oslo Commission.

Oslo Commission 1989. *Review of Sewage and Sludge Disposal at Sea*. London: Oslo Commission.

Oslo Commission 1990. *Dumping at Sea*. London: Secretariat of the Oslo and Paris Commissions.

Ostrom, E. 1986. An Agenda for the Study of Institutions. *Public Choice*,

Vol. 48: 3–25.

Ostrom, E. 1990. *Governing the Commons: The Evolution of Institutions for Collective Action*. Cambridge: Cambridge University Press.

Ostrom, E. 1991. Review of March and Olsen's 'Rediscovering Institutions: The Organizational Basis of Politics'. *Public Choice*, Vol. 72: 95–6.

Ostrom, E. 1995. New Horizons in Institutional Analysis. *American Political Science Review*, Vol. 89, No. 1, March: 174–8.

Pallemaerts, A. 1992. The North Sea Ministerial Declarations from Bremen to Hague: Does the Process Generate any Substance? *International Journal of Estuarine and Coastal Law*, Vol. 7, No. 1: 1–26.

Paris Commission 1984. *Sixth Annual Report*. London: Paris Commission.

Paris Commission 1987. *Ninth Annual Report*. London: Paris Commission.

Parmentier, R. 1997. Implementing Para.17. Tackling Toxics Once and for All? *North Sea Monitor*, June: 4–9

Porter, M.E. and C. Linde 1995. Green and Competitive. *Harvard Business Review*. September–October: 120–34.

Powell, W.W. and DiMaggio P.J. (eds) 1991. *The New Institutionalism in Organizational Analysis*. Chicago, and London: University of Chicago Press.

Prat, J.L. 1990. The Role and Activities of the European Communities in the Protection and the Preservation of the Marine Evironment of the North Sea, in D. Freestone and T. IJlstra (eds) *The North Sea: Perspectives on Regional Environmental Co-operation*. Special Issue of the *International Journal of Estuarine and Coastal Law*. London: Graham and Trotman.

Pressman, J.L. and A.Wildavsky 1973. *Implementation: How Great Expectations in Washington are Dashed in Oakland*. Berkeley:University of California Press.

Progress Report 1987. Implementation of the Bremen Declaration. Second International Conference on the Protection of the North Sea, London, 24–25 November. Conference papers for delegates. London: DoE.

Progress Report 1995. Fourth International Conference on the Protection of the North Sea. Esbjerg, Denmark, 8–9 June. Copenhagen: Ministry of Environment and Energy, Danish Environment Protection Agency.

Puchala, D.J. and R.F. Hopkins 1983, in S.D. Krasner, (ed.) *International Regimes*. Ithaca, NY and London: Cornell University Press.

Putnam, R.D. 1988. Diplomacy and Domestic Politics: The Logic of Two-Level Games. *International Organization*, Vol. 42,No. 3, Summer: 427–60.

Quality Status of the North Sea 1984. A report compiled from contributions by experts of the governments of the North Sea coastal states and the Commission of the European Communities, prepared for the International Conference on the Protection of the North Sea, Bremen, 31 October–1 November. Hamburg: *Deutsche Hydrographische Zeitsschift*, No. 16, 1986.

Quality Status of the North Sea 1987. (Summary.) Second International Conference on the Protection of the North Sea. Scientific and Technical Working Group. London: HMSO.

Rawcliffe, P. 1995. Making Inroads: Transport Policy and the British Environmental Movement. *Environment*, Vol. 37, No. 3: 16–20, 29–36.

Reid, C. 1990. The Work of the North Sea Task Force, in D. Freestone and T. IJlstra (eds) *The North Sea: Perspectives on Regional Environmental Co-operation*. Special Issue of the *International Journal of Estuarine and Coastal Law*. London: Graham and Trotman.

Reitan, M. 1996. *Norway: A Case of 'Splendid Isolation'*. Oslo: Department of Political Science, University of Oslo.

Richardson, J. 1994. EU Water Policy: Uncertain Agendas, Shifting Networks and Complex Coalitions. *Environmental Politics*, Vol. 3, No. 4, Winter: 139–67.

Rosenau, J.N. and E.O. Czempiel (eds) 1992. *Governance without Government: Order and Change in World Politics*. Cambridge: Cambridge University Press.

Rothstein, B. 1994. *Vad bör Staten göra? Om välfärdsstatens moralska och politiska logik*. Stockholm: SNS Förlag.

Ruggie, J.G. 1983. International Regimes, Transactions, and Change: Embedded Liberalism in the Postwar Economic Order, in Krasner, S.D. (ed.) *International Regimes*. Ithaca, NY and London: Cornell University Press.

Sabatier, P. 1986a. What Can We Learn from Implementation Research? in F.X. Kaufman, G. Majone, V. Ostrom (eds. with assistance of W. Wirth), *Guidance, Control and Evaluation in the Public Sector*. Berlin: Walter de Gruyter.

Sabatier, P. 1986b. Top-Down and Bottom-Up Approaches to Implementation Research: A Critical Analysis and Suggested Synthesis. *Journal of Public Policy*, Vol. 6, No. 1: 21–48.

Sadowski, S. 1996. The Oslo and Paris Commissions: Their work, the 1997 Ministerial Meeting, and the Role of NGOs. *North Sea Monitor*, December: 14–16.

Sætevik, S. 1988. *Environmental Cooperation between the North Sea States*. London: Belhaven Press.

Sand, P.H. 1991. Lessons Learned in Global Environmental Governance. *Environmental Affairs Law Review*, Vol. 18: 213–77.

Sandford, R. 1992. Secretariats and International Environmental Negotiations: Two New Models, in L.E. Susskind, E.J. Dolin and J.W. Breslin (eds) *International Environmental Treaty Making*. Cambridge, MA: Programme on Negotiation, Harward Law School.

Schneider, A. and H. Ingram 1990. Behavioural Assumptions of Policy Tools. *Journal of Politics*, Vol. 52, No. 2, May: 510–29.

Schofield, R. and J. Shaoul 1997. Regulating the Water Industry. Swimming Against the Tide or Going through the Motions? *Ecologist*, Vol. 27, No. 1: 6–13.

Sebenius, J.K. 1983. Negotiation Arithmetic: Adding and Subtracting Issues and Parties. *International Organization* Vol. 37, No. 3, Spring: 281–316.

Seippel, Ø. and Lafferty, W.M. 1996. Relgion, menneske eller økologi: Om natursyn og miljøpolitisk engasjement. *Norsk Statsvitenskapelig Tidsskrift*, Vol. 12, No. 2: 113–39.

Skjåk, K.K. and B. Bøyum 1996. *Haldningar til Offentlege Styringsmakter og Offentlig Verksemd*. Bergen: Norsk samfunnsvitenskapelig datatjeneste (NSD), Report No-. 108.

Skjærseth, J.B. 1991. *Effektivitet, problem-typer og løsningskapasitet: En studie av Oslo-samarbeidets takling av dumping i Nordsjøen og Nordøstatlanteren*. Lysaker: The Fridtjof Nansen Institute, R:009.

Skjærseth, J.B. 1992. Towards the End of Dumping in the North Sea: An Example of Effective Problem Solving? *Marine Policy*, Vol. 16, No. 2, March: 130–41.

Skjærseth, J.B. 1993. The 'Effectiveness' of the Mediterranean Action Plan. *International Environmental Affairs*, Vol. 5, No. 4, Fall: 313–35.

Skjærseth, J.B. 1994. *Institutional 'Effectiveness' in International versus Supranational Environmental Problem-Solving*. Lysaker: The Fridtjof Nansen Institute. EED Working Paper nr.4.

Skjærseth, J.B. 1995. The Fruitfulness of Various Models in the Study of International Environmental Politics. *Cooperation and Conflict*, Vol. 30, No. 2: 155–78.

Skjærseth, J.B. 1998. The Making and Implementation of North Sea Commitments: The Politics of Environmental Participation, in D. Victor, K. Raustiala and E.B. Skolnikoff (eds) *The Implementation and Effectiveness of International Environmental Commitments*. Cambridge, MA: MIT Press.

Skjærseth, J.B. 1999. *The Making and Implementation of North Sea Pollution Commitments: Institutions, Rationality and Norms*. Oslo: Department of Political Science University of Oslo and Akademika AS.

Skjærseth, J.B, S. Andresen and J. Wettestad 1992. *EF-Landene og Norden i Internasjonal Miljøpolitikk: Standpunkter, Bakgrunnsfaktorer og Allianseforhold*. Forskernotater til Europautredningen. Oslo: Europauredningen.

Skodvin, T. and A. Underdal (in cooperation with Andresen S. and J. Wettestad) 1994. The Science-Politics Interface: Transforming Knowledge into Decision Inputs for International Environmental Regimes. Paper prepared for the Annual Meeting of the International Studies Association, Washington, DC, 29 March.

Snidal, D. 1985. The Limits of Hegemonic Stability Theory. *International Organization* Vol. 39, No. 4, Autumn: 579–614.

Somers, E. 1990. The Role of Courts in the Enforcement of Environmental Rules: 193-201, in D. Freestone and T. IJlstra (eds) *The North Sea: Perspectives on Regional Environmental Co-operation.* Special Issue of the *International Journal of Estuarine and Coastal Law.* London: Graham and Trotman.

Sprinz, D. and T. Vaahtoranta 1994. The Interest-based Explanation of International Environmental Policy. *International Organization*, Vol. 48, No. 1, Winter: 77–105.

State Pollution Control Agency 1992. *Ministerial Declaration on the Protection of the North Sea. Analysis of Measures to Reduce Nutrient Inputs.* Report 92:34. Oslo.

State Pollution Control Agency 1995. *Kontrol-resultater 1994.* Report 95:08. Oslo.

State Pollution Control Agency 1996. *SFTs kontroll-resultater 1995.* Report 96:12. Oslo.

State Pollution Control Agency 1996. *State of the Environment in Norway.* Oslo: SPCA.

Statement of Conclusions from the Intermediate Ministerial Meeting 1993. Copenhagen, 7–8 December. Copenhagen: Ministry of Environment and Energy, Danish Environmental Protection Agency.

Stokke, O.S and D. Vidas 1996. Effectiveness and Legitimacy of International Regimes, in O.S. Stokk, and D. Vidas (eds) *Govering the Antarctic: The Effectiveness and Legitimacy of the Antarctic Treaty System.* Cambridge: Cambridge University Press.

Strange, S. 1983. *Cave! hic dragones*: A Critique of Regime Analysis, in S.D Krasner, (ed.) *International Regimes.* Ithaca, NY and London: Cornell University Press.

Suman, D. 1991. Regulation of Ocean Dumping by the European Economic Community. *Ecology Law Quarterly*, Vol. 18, No. 3: 559–618.

Summary Record 1984. Summary record of the International Conference on the Protection of the North Sea, Bremen, 31 October–1 November. Bonn: Bundesminister des Innern.

Summary Record 1985. Ad hoc working group to evaluate the EQO and UES approaches, London, 19–21 February. EQUS/9/1-E. London: Secretariat of the Oslo and Paris Commissions.

Summary Record 1987. Summary record of the Second International Conference on the Protection of the North Sea, London, 24–25 November. London: Department of the Environment.

Summary Record 1988. Second meeting of the ad hoc working group to evaluate the EQO and UES approaches, London, 22–23 November. EQUS/Info.1-E. London: Secretariat of the Oslo and Paris Commissions.

Summary Record 1988. Tenth meeting of the Paris Commission, Lisbon, 15–17 June. London: Paris Commission.

Summary Record 1994. First meeting of the Programmes and Measures Committee, Dresden, 21–25 March. London: Oslo and Paris Commissions.

Summary Record 1995. Second meeting of the Programmes and Measures Committee, Oviedo, 20–24 February. London: Oslo and Paris Commissions.

Tak, T. 1994. Shades of Green: Political Parties and Dutch Environmental Policy, in M. Wintle and R. Reeve (eds) *Rhetoric and Reality in Environmental Policy: The Case of the Netherlands in Comparison with Britain*. Aldershot: Avebury.

This Common Inheritance 1990. A summary of the White Paper on the Environment 1990. London: HMSO.

Tinker, P.B. 1989. Efficiency of Agricultural Industry in Relation to the Environment, in J.R. Park (ed.) *Environmental Management in Agriculture: European Perspectives*. London: Belhaven Press.

Tsebelis, G. 1990. *Nested Games: Rational Choice in Comparative Politics*. Berkeley: University of California Press.

Underdal, A. 1979. Issues Determine Politics Determine Policies: The Case for a 'Rationalistic' Approach to the Study of Foreign Policy Decision-Making. *Cooperation and Conflict*, Vol. 14: 1–9.

Underdal, A. 1980a. *The Politics of International Fisheries Management: The Case of the Northeast Atlantic*. Oslo: Universitetsforlaget.

Underdal. A. 1980b. *'Integrated' Marine Policy: What? Why? How?* Lysaker: The Fridtjof Nansen Institute, R:004.

Underdal, A. 1987. International Cooperation:Transforming 'Needs' into 'Deeds'. *Journal of Peace Research*, Vol. 24, No. 2: 167–83.

Underdal, A. 1990. Negotiating Effective Solutions: The Art and Science of 'Political Engineering'. Second Draft, Department of Political Science, University of Oslo.

Underdal, A. 1991. Solving Collective Problems: Notes on Three Modes of Leadership. In *Challenges of a Changing World*, Festschrift to Willy Østreng. Lysaker: The Fridtjof Nansen Institute.

Underdal, A. 1992. The Concept of Regime 'Effectiveness'. *Cooperation and Conflict*, Vol. 27, No. 3: 227–40.

Underdal, A. 1995. Implementing International Environmental Accords: Explaining 'Success' and 'Failure'. Paper prepared for presentation at the 36th Annual Convention of the International Studies Association,

21-25 February, Chicago. Oslo: Departement of Political Science, University of Oslo.

Underdal, A. 1997. Patterns of Effectiveness: Examining Evidence from 13 International Regimes. Departement of Political Science, University of Oslo. Paper prepared for presentation at the 38th Annual Convention of the International Studies Association, Toronto, 19-22 March.

Upsall, D. and R. Worcester 1995. You Can't Sink a Rainbow. Paper presented at Wapor Conference, 21 September The Hague.

Vertegaal, P. 1993. Nutrient Reductions in the North Sea. A Failing Policy: The Example of Dutch Agricultural Emissions. *North Sea Monitor*, June: 3–8.

Vogel, D. 1986. *National Syles of Regulation: Environmental Policy in Great Britain and the United States*. Ithaca, NY and London: Cornell University Press.

Vogel, D. 1995. *Trading Up: Consumer and Environmental Regulation in a Global Economy*. Cambridge: Harvard University Press.

Walton, R.E. and R.B. McKersie 1965. *A Behavioural Theory of Labor Negotiations*. New York: McGraw-Hill.

Waltz, K.N. 1979. *Theory of International Politics*. Reading, MA: Addison-Wesley.

Water Boards 1995. *Union of Water Boards*. The Hague: Water Boards.

Weale, A. 1992a. Implementation Failure: A Suitable Case for Review? In E. Lykke, (ed.) *Achieving Environmental Goals. The Concept and Practice of Environmental Performance Review*. London: Belhaven Press.

Weale, A. 1992b. *The New Politics of Pollution*. Manchester: Manchester University Press.

Wendt, A. 1992. Anarchy Is What States Make Out of It: The Social Construction of Power Politics. *International Organization* Vol. 46, No. 2, Spring: 391–425.

Wettestad, J. 1992. 'The 'Effectiveness' of the Paris Convention on Marine Pollution from Land-based Sources', *International Environmental Affairs*, Vol. 4, No. 2:101-121.

Wettestad, J. 1998. Combatting Land-Based Marine Pollution in the North-East Atlantic: The Paris Convention (PARCON) and The North Sea Conferences, in S. Andersen, T. Skodvin, A. Underdal and J. Wettestad. *Science and International Environmental Regimes*. Manchester: Manchester University Press.

Wettestad, J. and S. Andresen 1991. *The Effectiveness of International Resource Cooperation: Some Preliminary Findings*. Lysaker: The Fridtjof Nansen Institute, R:007.

Wilson, J.Q. 1973. *Political Organizations*. New York: Basic Books.

Working Group on Nutrients 1993. *Overview of Progress Reports on the Implementation of National Action Plans to Reduce Inputs of Nutrients and the Need for Further Action*. Eighth meeting of the Working Group on Nutrients, Gothenburg, 13–17 September. NUT 8/3/1-E. London: Secretariat of the Oslo and Paris Commissions.

World Commission on Environment and Development 1987. *Our Common Future*. Oxford: Oxford University Press.

Yin, R.K. 1989. *Case Study Research: Design and Methods*. London: Sage.

Young, O.R. 1979. *Compliance and Public Authority. A Theory with International Applications*. Baltimore, MD and London: Johns Hopkins University Press.

Young, O.R. 1986. International Regimes: Toward a New Theory of Institutions. *World Politics*, Vol. 39, No. 1, October:104–23.

Young, O.R. 1989a. *International Cooperation. Building Regimes for Natural Resources and the Environment*. Ithaca, NY: Cornell University Press.

Young, O.R. 1989b. The Politics of International Regime Formation: Managing Natural Resources and the Environment. *International Organization* Vol. 43, No. 3, Summer: 349–75.

Young, O.R. 1991. Political Leadership and Regime Formation: On the Development of Institutions in International Society. *International Organization*, Vol. 45, No. 3 Summer: 281–308.

Young, O.R. 1994. *International Governance: Protecting the Environment in a Stateless Society*. Ithaca, NY and London: Cornell University Press.

Young, O.R. and K. von Moltke 1994. The Consequences of International Environmental Regimes: Report from the Barcelona Workshop. *International Environmental Affairs*, Vol. 6 No. 4, Fall: 348–70.

Zürn, M. 1991. Consequences of Regime Definitions and Definitions of Regime Consequences: Proposals for a data Bank on International Regimes. Working Paper, presented at the workshop entitled 'Regimes Summit', Institute of Arctic Studies, Dartmouth College, Hanover, New Hampshire, October.

Zürn, M. 1993. Bringing the Second Image (Back) In: About the Domestic Sources of Regime Formation, in V. Rittberger, (ed. with P. Mayer). *Regime Theory and international Relations*. Oxford: Clarendon Press.

Zweip, K. 1990. The Wadden Sea: A Yardstick for a Clean North Sea, in D. Freestone and T. IJlstra (eds) *The North Sea: Perspectives on Regional Environmental Co-operation*. Special Issue of the *International Journal of Estuarine and Coastal Law*. London: Graham and Trotman.

Index